Breakthrough Agile

Workplace Culture – The culture can be defined as the ways people in the organization behave and the attitudes and beliefs that inform those behaviors (i.e., "the way we do things around here").

"Company Culture Is Everyone's Business," Denise Lee Yohn, *Harvard Business Review,* February 8, 2021.

Agile is being adopted within every type of organization across the world. It is no longer used by software development organizations. This book shows how anyone can adopt the systems of an Agile organization to change their culture and create customer-centric value that will sustain the business in the future. This book contains a blueprint on how to start a successful Agile transformation initiative.

Why another book on Agile? Organizations are facing unprecedented challenges and opportunities in today's business world – turbulent macroeconomic environments, soaring inflation, geopolitical tensions, rising protectionism, digital disruption, globalization, and changing business models. Leaders across every type of business are identifying that their current ways of working need to change to deal with this Volatile, Uncertain, Complex, and Ambiguous (VUCA) world. However, after decades of lack-luster transformation efforts across every industry, the idea of rebranding or launching a new transformation platform like Lean or Agile seems to leave leaders asking, "not again, is there another way?"

This book takes a different approach to a transformation deployment. The author, having spent the majority of his career working within organizations as a transformation champion, is sharing his experiences on the transformation journey and recommending a different way to start. This is a breakaway approach from most other implementation strategies on transformation. Starting with a principle-based approach, the author has discovered that there are specific processes that impact the culture more than the systems or tools of the transformation platform. The key to a successful transformation is to change how the company executes on these day-to-day processes, through a new set of principles that will change the culture to be more Agile and deliver value that is customer centric. Starting with a high-level overview of what companies are seeking to achieve with a transformation platform, this book illustrates what works and doesn't with the common strategies used in today's business world. This book then takes the reader on a learning journey that reveals common themes across all business that are described as cultural business processes.

Currently, there are three main transformation platforms practiced within the business world – Lean, Six-Sigma, and Agile. After a brief comparison showing the similarities and differences of these platforms, this book presents a blueprint for a successful Agile Transformation within any type of organization by focusing on five cultural business processes.

By starting the transformation with a commitment to change your decision making, conflict resolution, performance management, project management, and strategic planning processes, any transformation is on the path for breakthrough results. This book discusses each cultural business process and the real-life-limiting impact that these processes have on the ways of working in a traditional hierarchical organization.

The tour de force for this book is the theory that for any transformation to succeed, organizations need to change their working principles toward the execution of the cultural business processes. Regardless of the platform, a successful business transformations will only give the company the value they are seeking, when the working principles of the organization change. This means all employees, leaders and team members, need to change how they act, behave, and communicate throughout the organization. *Breakthrough Agile* provides a blueprint for the principles of each five cultural business processes.

Essentially, these five cultural processes influence peoples' behaviors and actions more than the application of any Agile system or tool. Everyone's day-to-day work is shaped by the cultural business processes that are discussed in this book and this is a breakthrough in transformation theory.

Breakthrough Agile
The Five Key Business Processes
for Cultural Transformation

Christian Cater

Routledge
Taylor & Francis Group

A PRODUCTIVITY PRESS BOOK

First published 2024
by Routledge
605 Third Avenue, New York, NY 10158

and by Routledge
4 Park Square, Milton Park, Abingdon, Oxon, OX14 4RN

Routledge is an imprint of the Taylor & Francis Group, an informa business

ISBN: 9781032371771 (hbk)
ISBN: 9781032371764 (pbk)
ISBN: 9781003335702 (ebk)

DOI: 10.4324/9781003335702

Typeset in ITC Garamond
by KnowledgeWorks Global Ltd.

Contents

Contents

Preface

The writing of this book has been 25 years in the making. That is the length of my career working in a modern organizational setting as a people leader and team member. During that time, I have been part of the automotive transformation to Lean in the 1990s, the post-economic 2008 market crash transformation, started a life as an expat, and experienced the challenges of leading an agile transformation on a global scale during the pandemic. I have met and discussed transformation with thousands of people from C Suite professionals, to senior leaders, to individual contributors. In my experience, I have been with top-tier, number one or two multinational organizations throughout my career, and have seen the complete supply chain – from raw materials to customer return (design, MFG, and commercial). The journey comes with peaks and valleys; with stories of success and failures. It is a learning journey, and this book contains the insights I gained on this journey. It has been a journey pinpointed with major business events, tens of thousands of hours of research, discussion, and implementation. My role has been from the problem-solving on the floor, to getting my hands dirty with creating visual boards and laying 5S lines in an area, to coaching teams through new and novel MVPs. As a change agent, I've coached hundreds of leaders at all levels, led and/or coached hundreds of teams, and conducted thousands of hours of training and capability seminars. I have seen processes from the simple to the complex within organizations. From a professional change agent point of view, I have seen the good, bad, and ugly with how people respond to the transition of going from the way things were to a new way of working. This book highlights one of the more foundational learnings of my career. In all of the efforts to make companies better at what they do, there are five foundational cultural business processes that define a company's culture. These five cultural business processes are more impactful to the shaping of the culture of an organization than the personalities, geography, or products of the company. This book discusses how to have a successful transformation by focusing first on these five processes.

This book is written in the spirit of being in the middle of the organization. At times, I find that current mainstream business books rely on the survey or interview approach a little too much. Authors of great books tend to start by saying they interviewed tens of thousands of managers to get to their conclusions. The ironic part is that conclusions seem common sense to me. For example, to build trust, it is important to develop relationships. To me, being from this middle of the organization, this is a given. I don't know if I needed the research of 10,000 business professions to comment on a survey to conclude that it is important to trust each other; I have seen it, lived it, both good and bad. Another aspect of this book that might be different from others similar books, is that it is told from someone who has worked in the middle of the organization, not the C suite or academic ivory tower. I can't state that I flew my fighter jet to work or made statements to Wall Street that affected the stock price, but I can say that I improved the quality of products that have reached millions of people by deploying a transformation framework. Granted, we all have a vicarious curiosity about the life and day-to-day activities of celebrity business professionals. In this book, you will read about my experience in touching and improving the products that went into customers' hands. Improving processes that resulted in better quality, creating more efficient operations that were safer for employees, reducing product cost, and growing a business from transformational efforts. For a transformation, I find that the stories about the impact of business transformation are best told from the middle. This perspective on a transformation and how leaders lead others generally gives one the flavor of what works and doesn't work when rolling out an organizational-wide transformation. With that said, this book is for everyone. I know that as a reader you will agree, disagree, and sometimes feel challenged by what I have written. Some readers are much smarter than I am, and others have done more in their careers. I am not competing on the level of whose experience or knowledge is more relevant or exacting. The information in this book will give a reader a good start on how to implement a large-scale transformation across a multinational organization. It will also provide a small organization a successful roadmap to use when seeking to improve and develop a culture of trust, accountability, and innovation.

I was once told by a well-known author that once he finished writing a book, he didn't read it again. He knew that at the time of publication what he had written was based on his current knowledge and that the day after it was published, he would gain a deeper understanding of the topics he wrote about. I feel the same way. I know that after the publication of this book, I will find out more about the topics I write about here, and become wiser in how they are deployed within an organization. I do know that most of the observations in this book are lasting and will serve as lessons for others for years to come. I hope you enjoy reading this book as much as I enjoyed writing it.

Finally, there are hundreds of people who are on my thank-you list. Throughout my career from being a military officer to the roles that I recently had, I had multiple colleagues who sharpened my understanding of the why, what, and how of leading a transformation. I am grateful for those who have engaged me in these conversations and hopeful that the time spent for them was valuable.

Sincerely,
Christian Cater,
Singapore,
March 2024

Acknowledgments

The work that went into this book is the result of thousands of hours of discussions, failed experiments, successful experiments, and knowledge gathered from others. Trying to single out a few people who have been exceptionally influential in this effort would minimize the impact that the collective group of people throughout my career have had on me. Without the support of my family, colleagues, and friends, this book would not have been written. That emotional support and encouragement is the foundation of being bold and courageous, which is what it takes to write a book. Working over the past two decades within all types of organizations, in a people leader capacity, as a team member and a change agent, this wealth of knowledge that has no name was created. Lastly, I want to acknowledge the reader, as without your participation in reading this book, my opportunity to share with others would not exist. Thanks to everyone who made this book possible.

About the Author

Over the past 25 years, Christian Cater has led transformational programs across the globe. Having started his career working for a Japanese automotive company to delivering results for the world's leading pharmaceutical companies, Christian has held roles that are pivotal to cultural and business transformations. With enough dirt under his fingernails, Christian has created a transformation deployment model that will enable organizations to move past the "flavor of the month" programs to those that unlock the breakthrough results of transformational methodologies. Christian's in-depth experience in gaining results through Lean, Six Sigma, and Agile provides a reader with a fresh look at what needs to happen first to start the transformation journey. With experience across all business functions, the keys to unlocking value start with a principle-based approach to key cultural business processes. From senior leaders to technicians, applying a principle-based approach to transformation will free the organization from the constraints of the traditional way of working. Having worked consistently in the United States and later taking international roles, the perspective Christian brings to the reader is unique and novel. Readers will at times align, support, and/or disagree with the insights discussed in this book.

During Christian's career, he has sharpened his ability to see the core issues that prevent transformation from succeeding. From walking the production floor of America's top selling vehicles to increasing the production rates of the world's leading cancer-treating drugs to developing digital technology solutions for China, Christian's background anchors the approach discussed in *Breakthrough Agile*. Having led first-hand thousands of improvement, problem-solving, and strategic workshops, understanding the key five business processes better will enable organizations to move past the predictable and achieve breakthrough. Christian lives and works in Singapore with his family. He continues to work with teams and individuals to bring higher value and fulfillment to their organizations.

Chapter 1

Foundations of Breakthrough Agile

Though nature grants vast periods of time for the work of natural selection, she does not grant an indefinite period; …, if one species does not become modified or improved in corresponding degree with its competitors, it will soon be exterminated.

Charles Darwin, Origin of Species

A look inside:

- Brief context on Agile as a transformation framework
- Discussion on a transformation team
- Overview of Breakthrough Agile
- Introduction of principle-based cultural business processes

Agile as a way to working is becoming the proverbial "lightning in a bottle" for businesses today. Either as a fast fix for short-term wins or for long-term cultural transformation, businesses are keen to try it out for size and see how it works. Agile comes across as an appealing new way of working that feels safe for an organization to experiment with. With its roots in the software industry, the Agile approach fosters a sense of belonging to a generation of professionals who are used to implementing technology into their day-to-day activities. Agile also finds champions with senior personnel in an organization who have come to the realization that the methods of management defined by Taylorism and, scientific management are too rigid

DOI: 10.4324/9781003335702-1

to meet the customer demands of a more knowledgeable customer in the 21st century. Agile systems are becoming that bridge between the old and new schools of leading, working, and meeting customers' needs and wants across the world. In its simplest form, most people view Agile as a project management methodology. However, since its early years of adoption in the 1990s, Agile has grown into a holistic transformation methodology with applications that go far beyond the idea of adopting Scrum to run projects and develop software products.

In a broad sense, Agile systems have grown in depth and breadth to service the entire scope of a business. Its terminology and systems are being used by organizations far from the software development space and reaching into pharmaceutical companies, manufacturers, and service-oriented industries. Companies such as Microsoft, Tesla, IGM, Apple, Kaiser Permanente, and Netflix are embedding the self-managed team-based approach to their organizations to tap into the innovative spirit of the "many" versus the traditional approach of a select few "experts" creating value for the organization. Organizations that have Agile has their transformation framework are changing how they work to foster a culture of innovation and self-management. Leaders recognize that within the Agile approach, there is an "energy" unlike the energy from other transformation methodologies. Tapping into this energy and shifting to an Agile mindset and behavior, companies will become more competitive through customer centricity and developing employees with a higher level of passion for their work. How this happens in an Agile organization is by focusing, the organization on identifying and delivering value based on what motivates the customer. This has led to novel products in today's world that have changed the way we live and work. The challenge to become an Agile organization, is designing a transformation strategy that will grow and develop this team-based energy. Breakthrough Agile dives deep into this discussion, and this book illustrates what it takes to transform an organization's culture to be more customer centric and team based.

As work demographics are ever changing, Agile grows as the best fit for an organization that introduces advanced technology to manage data, fosters open and transparent communications, and seeks to capture the best performance of its employees. Like other transformation platforms, Agile is developing a loyal following within all industries. Coaches, scrum masters, product owners, Lean experts, SAFe roles, and senior-level agile champions are all more visible in today's business world. Do a quick search on LinkedIn and hundreds of open positions for these roles are being sought after. In companies like financial services, healthcare, and manufacturers, as

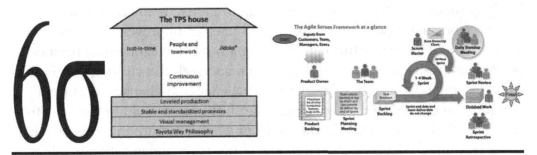

Figure 1.1   Today's most known transformation methodologies.

well as the traditional information technology companies, there is a shift for organizations to become more Agile. Agile has broken onto the main stage with other transformation methodologies such as Lean or Six Sigma with top-tier consulting firms such as BCG and McKinsey dedicating entire teams to the topic and creating deployment models for companies to adopt this new way of working (Figure 1.1).

As with its older transformation siblings, Agile has already delivered results for companies that follow its work systems and have successfully operationalized them in their day-to-day processes. With customer centricity and self-organizing teams being a focal point of an Agile culture, customers are realizing the benefits in terms of greater innovative products in the market. As employees embrace Agile ways of working and work together, they are becoming more passionate about the outcome of their work and its benefit to customers. The biggest names in business are on this list – Google, Amazon, Microsoft, Apple, etc. For organizations that still cling to a traditional, hierarchical culture and way of working, the risk that they will be out-performed by a competitor is realistic. Ironically, most businesses know they need to change their old ways of working in order to compete in the 21st century. Whether it's driven by more complex business processes due to integrated autonomous information technology, or the ability of customers to be more selective in their purchases, the business world feels the pressure to evolve and Agile is the current platform of choice. The search is on for the strategy that can integrate this new way of working and what transformation strategy will realize the potential of Agility and deliver more value to the organization while simultaneously creating a better culture.

The question for most when starting an agile transformation is "how far will the organization go" with changing the status quo. When it comes to changing the culture of an organization, there are some serious legacy and cultural pressures that need attention. The scope of a transformation will help shape the strategy. For some organizations, their strategy may only develop small sprint teams for limited internal improvements. For others, it could be restructuring, redefining job roles, creating new business models, and reshaping how 1–1 contact is made with the customer. In both situations, the new way of working will challenge and change the current culture of an organization. The greater the shift from the old to the new, the more benefit the organization will see from its new culture in terms of value to the customer. Whatever the strategy will be, every organization needs to decide how far they will change their current culture and at what pace.

For many leaders and employees, transforming to an Agile culture will create a sense of anxiety or even fear of the unknown. The what and how to change seems foggy to leaders, and making a strong commitment to leading the change shows up as a risky undertaking for a conservative leader in a traditional organization. For companies that are successful and hold a high level of market share, choosing the instability of a transformation over the stability of the status quo is a big leap of faith. When this is augmented by the lack of internal capabilities to work as coaches or guides, the motivation to choose "bolt-on" adoption over "breakthrough" transformation becomes more appealing. When these two polarities in thought converge, the need to change and the need to maintain stability, general thinking is to choose the one less risky and safe.

In practice, a transformation of any scale creates conflict in the organization. The conflict is between the old way of working and the new way of working. Employees at all levels experience this conflict as the organization moves forward with their efforts to become more competitive. This conflict can derail an organization's best efforts at making significant change to its culture since it implies that employees need to choose one way over the other. Unfortunately, most transformations end dubiously as a result of this conflict. In many cases, current business processes remain the same in an organization that initially spent millions on gearing up for a cultural transformation through Agile or Lean. Numerous polls by consulting firms will confirm this observation. As a result, the organization falls back on its old ways of working, missing the full benefits of the transformation methodology. Breakthrough Agile's approach provides insights into what needs to change for companies to make the full transition and how they can do it without falling into the trap of their Agile transformation being another "flavor of the month" program.

What the reader needs to understand, and this is true for any transformation platform, is that a friction point develops within the organization when starting a transformation. The friction point is the clash between the principles of the old way of working and the principles of the new way of working. If the traditional principles of the organization play through and are not retired during the transformation, then the organization will struggle to bring the new ways of working into the organization and change its culture. A common place within the organization to feel this conflict and friction point is its leadership mindset. A traditional principle of leadership is the belief that command and control is visible by retaining a hierarchical structure. This is a view created by an early industrialist by the name of Frederick Taylor. The Tayloristic view of leadership proscribes that the management principles of span of control, direct supervision, managerial oversight, disempowerment, and centralized decision making is superior to leading through an Agile Leadership Mindset. Unfortunately, the Tayloristic approach impedes change, limits innovation, minimizes employee development, and disempowers instead of empowers. Tayloristic organizations view people with limited job scopes that are focused primarily on a set of tasks that need to be completed under direct supervision of a manager. In this role, the manager, then uses his power over his team to motivate and lead them to a higher efficiency (Figure 1.2). The business process of performance management gives the manager the positional influence to tell the employee what to do and how to do their job that limits resistance or the freedom of the team member to question the direction of the manager.

Leaders are final decision makers in the traditional organization. The mental model of their role and the job of the team members is a zero-sum game. Whether the leader is more concerned about their image with peers and promotional opportunities or if they crave having authority over others, the team's function viewed by a traditional leader's mental model

Figure 1.2   Role of the traditional manager.

is that there are limited opportunities for innovation and growth. Reacting and protecting their work, reputation, business status, or some other aspect of the team is how they make decisions, prioritize work, resolve conflict, strategize, and reward team members. With this mental model, the leader is either winning or losing within the work environment and beyond. Their first reaction is either, fight, flee, or freeze when faced with a challenge or an event outside their comfort zone. Let's look at a case study.

Kodak is a classic example of an organization that held on to a conservative mental model at a time when change was banging at its door. One could say they froze when faced with an external challenge. The end result was disastrous for the company. With the innovation of digital camera technology arriving on the market in the late 1990s, Kodak, one of the world's leaders in personal cameras, stuck to the principles of its current ways of working and failed to innovate or experiment. It failed to meet the customers' needs and expectations and held on to its view that its current products were the best. Whether a result of their legacy products, processes, or capabilities, the organization froze when it needed to evolve. I worked closely with a person who witnessed this first hand at the C room level at Kodak. As a result (Figure 1.3), the company missed the change in consumer demand and fell from their market position.

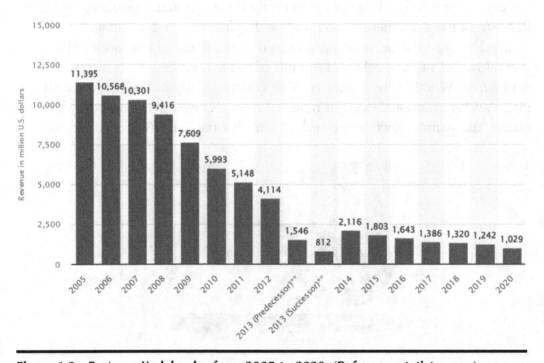

Figure 1.3   Eastman Kodak sales from 2005 to 2020. (Ref. www.statista.com.)

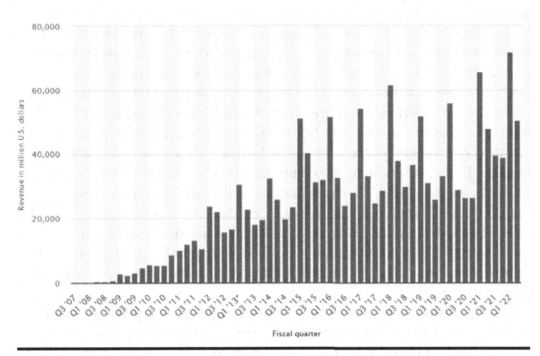

Figure 1.4   Apple iPhone revenues 2007–2022. (Ref. www.statista.com.)

At the same time, a new market leader came from an unlikely business segment that at the time Kodak didn't even register as a competitor. Because of their traditional approach to protecting its current business, Kodak experienced how an Agile company can shift customers' demand at a high cost to organizations that hold on to their legacy ways of working and cultural principles (Figure 1.4).

What could be different with the iPhone today had Kodak applied Agile principles to its decision making in 2005. Could Kodak have brought their experience and knowledge of cameras or understanding of photography to Apple? Could they have collaborated on a product together? Could we be walking around with a Kodak phone? It was an opportunity missed and Kodak inevitably lost its position as a market leader in personal cameras within a few years. Kodak's culture at that time, its principles in how it worked, effectively led to the loss of customers due to a better product in the market. Kodak missed the evolution in technology that changed the personal camera market faster than it could think and act.

Making the decision to change your company's culture is a perilous decision for most. One factor that creates fear and anxiety for these decision makers is the lack of internal capabilities to coach and guide the organization through the transformation. When starting a transformation, internal capabilities are minimal. Organizations with deep pockets will reach out to external consultants to help kick start the organization. Those with shallow pockets will spend time grooming internal employees and externally hiring others to build the capability to support the organization's efforts. In my experience working in the United States, I worked with many ex-Danaher employees in Lean transformations. They were hired into the organization for the purpose of bringing their experience with the Danaher Business System to the company. These individuals were hired to create the Lean culture. They provided the initial and sustaining push to change the organization. In these instances, the Lean transformation moved forward quickly and delivered sustainable value for the organization. It confirms the observation that the need to have internal capabilities to lead a transformation is a key to success for any organization that has a strategic interest to transform.

Whether through external consultants or another way, getting started is the key for any transformation. With external consultants, they provide appropriate and valuable training and direction to the organization. However, there is a fundamental value/cost proposition that plays a role with their engagement. To balance the fees and costs, the expectation is that consultants will deliver tons of information and experience to the organization, too much for the organization to absorb and operationalize in most cases. However, decision makers of this action see this trade-off as a win, since a mountain of material has been delivered to the newly anointed internal champions at the organization. This abundance of theory and tool knowledge will exceed most people's abilities to understand and implement at a sustainable pace. Usually, these consultants provide the view of a gold standard of an Agile organization at its fully matured state in the beginning. Granted, this is a good outcome and target for the transformation, but the internal capability building is non-existent. In most cases, external consultants take the organization from step 1 to 100 without walking with teams and people through the 98 steps in the middle. Struggling along the journey of a transformation is where true capability is built within the organization. The failures and successes of the multiple actions provide the learning and maturity that every organization needs to develop its internal capabilities. Many times, writers will talk about how Toyota has spent over 50 years building capabilities with its production system. For an organization to truly commit and people to feel within their hearts that the transformation will deliver better outcomes and value for the organization takes time and resources. When relying upon highly skilled experts from a top tier consulting firm to bring the organization to the same level as Toyota with Lean is wishful thinking. In reality, the external consultants are contracted to deliver a product that has been agreed upon through a negotiation. Usually, a part of the negotiation is someone getting more, or getting their way in the contract. At this junction, we see the traditional mindset of leadership playing a role in the start of the transformation. The principle that the time and expense of bringing in these experts, needs justified through a value/cost proposition influences the decision makers who are most likely are trying not to look "vulnerable" for hiring a third party consultant to lead the transformation.

With Breakthrough Agile, the starting point is to focus the organization on business process that everyone knows. By starting the transformation on these business processes, the transformation platform in the end will dramatically shape the culture of the organization. In Breakthrough Agile, we start with changing the principles of the organization and working with the company's employees on applying them to key *cultural business processes (CBP)*. This approach entrenches Agile in the core cultural business processes that are truly the foundation of the organization's culture. As individuals and teams practice with the new cultural business processes, then the way of working across the organization also changes. Through this change in business processes, the culture changes to one with a more Agile mindset. We will discuss this approach in much more detail in the later chapters of this book. A word of caution, there is no substitution for having internal capabilities that understand the transformational methodology on a deep level.

Having a cadre of strong internal coaches to support the transformation is fundamental to a successful effort. When starting with Breakthrough Agile, the organization needs to be deliberate and make it a strategic priority to build high caliber coaches to support the growth and scaling up of the transformation platform. A structure needs to be designed to give these coaches the opportunity to influence and connect across the organization and serve as a shepherd of the journey through the different maturity stages. Although many will understand this need, there are ways to undermine this need to build internal capabilities.

A common red flag than an organization is holding on to its old ways of working is to examine its transformation team. This is the team that is initially responsible for the change and represents the internal coaches for the organization. This team leads the organization into the transformation and guides people along its journey as it matures. If under-resourced, this team will be staffed with less experienced personnel who have limited knowledge of how to lead a transformation. When a transformation team lacks this credibility and capability, there is a recipe for a stalled or a fallback transformation. Add into the recipe, a mix of unrealistic expectations on the transformation team from the old school "core" leadership, then the proverbial final nail of the transformation coffin has been hammered. When expectations for success far exceed anything realistic in terms of time of a minimally staffed and capable transformation team, the principles of the old way of working have stifled the transformation. Showing short-term wins at the cost of building mindset, skills, and knowledge of the new way of working, will derail a transformation. After a few years of practice in this environment, the initial motivation and energy for the transformation will wane and decision makers at a high level make a decision to sideline the transformation efforts.

In my experience, most companies take this path after a few years – the organization bolts on a new function called operational excellence (OE) into the organizational chart in a way that reflects the organization's commitment to transformation. For example, in my career in OE, I have had reporting lines to finance, human resources, supply chain, manufacturing, and general management. From this list, you can tell what the intent for the OE team was by the functional leader for each organizational unit. In finance, OE will focus on cost cutting activities; In HR, the team focuses on building personnel skills; In supply chain, reducing inventory and lead times; In manufacturing, it is about efficiency and cost. These companies talk the talk but do not walk the walk when it comes to supporting the transformation at the cultural level. Their misunderstanding is overvaluing their current principles and undervaluing the new principles of the transformation. The transformation becomes an option for the organization and the culture business processes continued as before.

In an ecosystem where organizations seek to bring the best out of their employees, resources, and products an Agile transformational methodology is appealing. If doing and being Agile are driving organizations to breakthrough earnings at Apple, Google, Amazon, and Tesla, then most organizations can also benefit from this way of working. In my experience, when a traditional organization is given a new way of working based on the success of one of these companies, a common reaction is for people who fear loss of control and power is to react with statements such as, "it worked for Google, but we are not Google." "Or we are not an automotive company," when a Lean framework is being considered for a non-automotive company. If this is happening in your organization at the start of the transformation, then prepare for some battles between the new and old ways of working in the near future. And remember, for those who are champions of the old way of working, each battle is a zero-sum game – they either win or lose the battle for control.

At the start of its transformational journey, every organization needs to identify what truly needs to change in order to achieve breakthrough results. Organizations all have missions, visions, strategies, purposes, and value statements to guide their organization toward the future. Usually captured by slogans and visualized across the organization, these phrases help leaders articulate where they see their business in the future and help teams identify what they need to do to realize the future state. In many cases, underlying the vision is the unilateral theme is that the organization needs to change to stay competitive. The what and how of the change is encapsulated by a transformational methodology like Agile, Lean, or something else. Typically, a change management plan is developed on the deployment and communicated across the organization. Included in this communication is a description of the change, the outputs that management expects, and possible changes to organization structure. The transformation team is introduced in the communications. Slogans, posters, visual backgrounds, presentation templates, icons, tee shirts, etc. are created and deployed across the organization to indicate the change has started. In this communication plan, there are descriptions of the new way of working and how it will drive benefits across the organization for everyone. White paper type of documents with a clear why, what, and how of the transformation are cascaded throughout the organization and across leadership teams.

As the initial curiosity and enthusiasm fuels the desire to change, the transformation impacts people differently depending on their current social status as defined by the organizational chart. Senior leaders (C-room, business leaders, and divisional leaders/directors) generally see the transformation as something others in the organization need to do as they continue to appease stockholders and board members and manage the public image and finances of the company. As you move down into the organizational chart, employees start viewing the transformation with a lens of skepticism. They see the current way of working being role modeled by the behaviors and actions of peers and leaders. Across the organization, everyone sees the gap between what is stated in the communication plan to what is happening day-to-day. People see that leaders haven't changed their mindsets, and they justify resisting or being indifferent to the transformation based on what they are seeing and hearing in the organization. How people sense the transformation in the organization will be a significant indicator of progress on the cultural change front. What people see, hear, and experience in meetings, through town halls, in conversations, and all other interactions will influence the adoption of the new way of working principles. If people sense that nothing has changed, so why should they. If people throughout the organization sense that leaders at the top feel the transformation doesn't include them and the middle of the organization has actions of doubt and skepticism toward the transformation then it becomes an "rocky and bumping" journey for the transformation team. As those in influential positions continue to act and behave following the principles of the old way of working, it indicates to others that the change to a new mindset and set of behaviors needed for the transformation isn't important. In many instances, I have heard employees on all levels make statements like, "what made me successful is how I worked in the past," "why would I risk doing something different?," or "I am already working as an Agile leader or transformed leader, so I don't need to worry."

As this ambivalent transformation daze grows, people start to hear a different message from their leaders. The message that we need to change gets softer and the purpose of the transformation then takes on a more superficial tone. In these informal communications, the message about the transformation becomes one of choice – use the new way of working as needed or when it is less risky. In one of the conversations I had, a senior leader told me that as long as the team didn't have to work for the end result, then the transformation makes sense. It is another way to say change is optional and as long as it doesn't prevent you from hitting your traditional KPI or goals, then you decide its fit for purpose. In these cases, the middle of the organization decides how far to take the transformation into changing the culture of the organization. Individuals and teams in the middle decide what they want to use out of the transformation "toolbox." This demographic of the organization balances gaining favor with their seniors and upsetting employees as the measure of transformational success. This usually ends with actions that are well within the comfort zone of the current way of working. After all, stability and limiting disruption is a key principle within a traditional organization. The softer approach also minimizes negative feedback from employees toward the management team on creating too much change. As an output, the actions discredits the role of the transformation team in influencing change throughout the organization. At this point the transformation team loses its change compass and seeks to find acceptance within the organization.

The ability of the transformation team to influence and have access to teams is critical in the early stages of the transformation. As the change management program is rolled out, the transformation team becomes more visible. Usually starting out with a high degree of passion and enthusiastically, this group starts to train, retrain, and coach the employees on the systems and practices of the transformation platform such as Agile or Lean. These specialists are the toolbox guardians and design the space to practice the new way of working. At first, they will follow the road map as described by the change management plan. This is usually a unilateral roll out of basic training and awareness. The next step is followed up by high-profile activities that showcase the practices of the new way of working. These high-profile activities generally are promoted to show that the senior-level leaders are behind the transformation and the new way of working. At other times, these activities were pre-planned actions that are using the transformation platform as a good "cover" to enact. Restructuring a function or spinning off a business are some activities that might fall into this category of high-level activities.

As the momentum builds up in the first few years, the transformation team and the new ways of working find their first big obstacle to sustainability. The challenge comes from the annual financial planning event for organizations. With most companies, the budget process starts its cycle mid-year. In an Agile organization, this process is incorporated into a rhythmic the 90-day planning cycle. Inherently, the synergy between the transformation initiatives and this financial process are clearly linked and each can support the other. Since most transformation platforms deliver improvements in business systems or ways of working, then it will have a significant impact on how money is earned and spent by an organization. However, depending on the influence of the transformation team, any changes to the budget process is more of a relabeling of the old process with the nomenclature of the transformation platform. For example, a list of improvement projects might have been called a "bucket list" now becomes a "backlog." How it is managed and deployed stays the same. Top-line growth drives the need to work harder and longer for commercial employees. Headcount reduction or freezes drive a need to become more cost efficient in supply chain functions. In Lean organizations, kaizen events are planned and executed to meet these expectations. The short win or "low hanging fruit" cycle permeates the work during the annual budget planning exercise. There is little regard to long-term growth or impact for the organization's staff or business or customers. This short term focus gives everyone a sense that they did something in the transformation space, but in reality it was the same work as before under different slogans. Kaizens and Sprints are ran using a waterfall project management approach, just like the way they did before the introduction of the transformation. In these cases, the activities stay the same and the opportunity to innovate or create novel solutions isn't created.

In other instances, organizations simply relabel their old way with a new name. For instance, OKRs is a framework for getting results faster in an Agile organization. As stated earlier, a company going through an Agile transformation would start by relabeling their goals or KPIs as OKRs. An organization that is practicing Lean uses an X matrix or Hoshin Kanri to document the strategic initiatives to meet the future business needs. However, if not deployed properly, the PMO that manages the initiatives will opt out of the X matrix for an excel spreadsheet using a waterfall format as they feel the matrix is too complicated. In the end, the content and execution of the work follows the old way of working.

For OKRs, they become a set of annual goals based on business KPIs with infrequent reviews and less accountability for completion. The X matrix is replaced by a spreadsheet managed by a project management office that shows a multiyear waterfall approach to strategic initiatives. This merging of the old way and new way is how the organization copes with the knowledge gap naturally arising with the introduction of new tools and systems that replace the traditional methods during the transformation. In the end, since people are more familiar with their old way of working, and it is known better throughout the organization, the old principles and systems are continued by the organization at times with a new name.

Going into the second and third years, most transformations lose energy and enthusiasm to change. The shine of the transformation wears off. Cynical people start to ask where is the value that the transformation promised to deliver? They are quick to point out all the time, effort, and money that was spent on the rollout, training, and change management efforts. Even when successes are documented, the underlying communication is that the organization succeeded by working without changing to the new principles of the transformation methodology. The transformation team keeps hitting barriers of implementation within the organization due to the traditional way of working until they become exhausted. The "choose what works" or "fit for purpose" mantra continues to be the fallback for people. Ambitious and persevering organizations will continue to repeat this cycle every few years by rebranding the transformation and hiring in new talent to lead the transformation. As one can predict, then with each rebranding cycle, the cultural friction point repeats itself with fresh change agents facing off with the organization's entrenched mindset and culture.

The key point is that an Agile transformation platform has principles that differ greatly with the organization's current way of working. Organizations that commit to the new way of working need to adopt these Agile principles and retire the principles of the past. Executing on this idea is critical to the transformation efforts as it will create the right environment for the transformation to succeed. The letting goes or retiring of principles is also very challenging and hard for an organization. Some see the history and legacy of the organization and stubbornly hold onto the past. These people sense that protecting the past is a better business plan than embracing the future. This is especially true of organizations that are highly successful in their market. When the burning platform is absent, senior leaders do not sense the threat to their business. This creates a mindset that questions the purpose of the transformation with skepticism or rejection. The risk of losing, whether market share, key employees, reputation, or higher costs, will be a strong inhibitor to change.

By way of example, following the principle of customer centricity for Agile, the entire value chain for the organization will change. For example, the commercial end of the value chain moves from winning transactional agreements to creating experiences and services that match the customer's need, motivations, and their business vision. In a traditional organization, the mindset is one of give and take. The company has a product and the customer has the money for it and we trade, or transact one for the other. In an Agile organization, this is an output that we achieve, but it no longer represents the business relationship or outcome with the customer. Empathizing with the customer, enabling the customer to succeed at a higher level will lead to strategic actions taken by commercial teams that will change relationships and interaction with the customer. In return, the customer will seek to do more business with the company that is helping them to achieve their strategic goals. In another example, at the upstream end of the organization where the manufacturing of the product takes place, customer centricity will find its way into the organization through its vision and strategies. Manufacturers will move from efficiency and cost reduction to understanding the customer's demands. Building flexible manufacturing and support processes that can adjust to changing customer demand quickly and still retain a competitive lead time will drive a new way of working. Reducing safety stocks and allowing more readily available stock for consumers will be challenge for these organizations. How quickly a product reaches the market regardless of product style or model will shape new ways of working for the organization. Asset utilization no longer becomes the key metric but inventory turns, lead time, and replenishment time will drive how upstream operations are performed. Without question, all parts of the organization will benefit when a transformational effort is deployed that changes both the mindset and behaviors of all the people in the organization.

Measuring the success of a transformation effort requires the ability to see the changes in mindset and behaviors through the different actions taken to deliver exceptional results for the organization. What and how this is done becomes the core lesson from this book and underpins why transformations are challenging. In my experience, transformation efforts succeed at a higher level when the senior most leaders role model the principles of the transformation methodology. When a senior leader participates as a product owner or team member of a Scrum event, then this signals to the organization that the Agile system is part of the new way of working. This is the commitment it takes for a transformation to become successful. And this senior leader participation doesn't happen only once but becomes a standard practice for senior leaders' time and time again. It is a personal objective for the senior leader.

In Breakthrough Agile, we introduce *principle-based cultural business processes (CBPs)* that are the core of a company's culture. When starting a transformation, an organization needs to adopt the principles of the transformation platform first. Capabilities need to be developed to understand at a core level these principles before taking the next steps in the transformation journey. These new principles and how the organization executes its principle-based CBPs will define the new culture of the organization. After the organization is trained on the principles, then Breakthrough Agile introduces five key principle-based CBPs that make up the activities of the company's culture. After these first two steps, then the systems of Breakthrough Agile are introduced to the organization and teams leverage this model to identify and realize the value of breakthrough results. As the transformation journey starts, an organization needs to spend time and resources understanding how Breakthrough Agile's principles influence the five principle-based CBPs. To help understand this approach, let's take for example decision making, which is one of the five cultural business processes (5 CBPs).

Employees within the organization need to understand how decisions are made at every level. To get to this point of understanding, first the organization needs to understand their current decision-making model. Once the current way of making decisions is understood, then the organization applies the principles of Breakthrough Agile to the decision-making process. Through the lens of Breakthrough Agile's principles, the organization makes better and faster decisions. From these decisions new solutions are created that will identify and realize value that was previously unknown to the organization. If still adhering to the old way of working, then these new solutions would not have surfaced. The decisions that are influenced by Breakthrough Agile's principles shape the new culture of the organization while also delivering the business value to make the organization competitive.

In Breakthrough Agile, one of the principles for decision making is that leaders at all levels in the organization need to embrace letting go of control of the decision-making process. Decisions are made by those who are closest to the customer, problem, or activity. Having the person at the right level make the decision is key to Breakthrough Agile. If leaders do not let go of this control they will continue to limit empowerment, innovation and novel problem solving. The organization will continue to use past practices as it innovation actions. The transformation will be seen and experienced as a superficial attempt to change. Leaders will continue to hold onto control of making decisions for their teams by requiring employees to seek their endorsement or provide an escalation channel for decisions to the leader. Groups of leaders will continue to meet in committees or other layering types of decision-making bodies. These bodies will require that decisions on all projects need to be routed through this layer or committee for approval before taking action. In this example, when an employee escalates a decision to the manager or presents to a decision-making body/committee, then the organization is reinforcing the status quo and hierarchical organizational culture. It is also protecting its traditional mental model of a leadership behavior – one that reflects a difficulty of letting go control of the decision-making privilege or authority. Each of these examples would slow the pace of transformation and limit the impact that the transformation has on the business. In this book, we discuss each of the 5 CBPs and the key principles of Breakthrough Agile that need to be adopted by the organization.

Another common experience for transformation efforts is the ubiquitous "fit for purpose" model of deployment. As mentioned earlier, as a transformation methodology begins, especially in a brownfield organization, leaders will placate reluctant personnel by telling them the transformation changes are "fit for purpose." Use what works for you and don't worry about the bigger picture because we also want you to continue to work as "business as usual" for the most part. The end results of this approach are a number of independent efforts across the organization that have little impact on the cultural change of the organization. Usually, the independent efforts are led by leaders with a passion for change and a confidence to try something new. To their credit, these leaders also realize that having examples of transformation on their resume is a way to give themselves a competitive advantage when discussing their impact on the organization to influential decision makers during their performance review or career development. When a "fit for purpose" approach is taken, the number of variations to the standard of the transformation platform are overwhelming. Anyone and everyone gets to define their transformation as it is personalized in a "fit for purpose" approach.

The various implementation strategies across the organization all have varying degrees of application and success. Too many times, the systems of the transformation platform are watered down so they fit the current way of working. Anyone who has led the effort of transformation will have seen this happen. What used to be an extended meeting is now called a kaizen or sprint. A person used to be a project manager and now they are a product owner or kaizen leader. Lean standard work is a standard operating procedure (SOP). Design thinking turns into a nice way to say we are implementing a pre-determined solution. The list goes on and on as to the variation of this approach. Teams using the nomenclature of the transformation platform to fit their current way of working, implies that we are still doing things the same as before. Ironically, in the "fit for purpose" model, teams begin to use their "local" method which leads to different deployment strategies. In some organizations, transformation silos are created. One organizational area uses SAFe while another uses Business Agility, and then others just focus on mindsets and behaviors. The "fit for purpose" approach is a gentle way for leaders to say, the old way of working isn't going away because it has gotten us to where we are today. As the "fit for purpose" approach continues, the transformation platforms' new ways of working are seen as "bolt on" activities and additional work for the employees. Since most teams feel overwhelmed all the time, the additional work of following the standard of the transformation is not followed. In time, the transformation effort slows and fades into the shadows of the organization structure. As the "fit for purpose" approach includes a short-lived experience of learning and growth, it consistently ends with the transformation being a footnote in the history of the organization. The short-term gains made by the passionate leaders give them enough credibility to seek a better role and they move on. Succeeding leaders step in with rhetoric of rebranding or redirecting their predecessor's work because they were too focused on transformation or too eager to change the organization. Another red flag that organizations that are driven by personalities have a hard time at changing or deploying transformations. Across the organization, the effort subsides and becomes a reference point for future change initiatives.

Breakthrough Agile, as a transformation platform, requires support from within to be successful. It is short sighted to think being successful at this magnitude of change without providing the adequate resources, time, and commitment will occur naturally over time. Strong investment at the beginning of a transformation will support the success of the transformation and change the culture to benefit from the new way of working. To a seasoned practitioner, this investment is evidence that the organization is committed to transforming itself. The investment is usually seen as new visions, purpose statements, strategy canvases or maps, and at times even changes in leadership or additional roles. The new roles might be Chief Transformation Officer (CTO), the introduction of skilled personnel, or Agile coaches with a level of technical expertise and confidence to bring change to the organization. As the transformation momentum increases, and internal capabilities with Agile systems scale throughout the organization. People began to see the shift in culture and experience different realities than before. Stories of success change from winning, to one with elements of collaboration and mutual support. By using the principles of Breakthrough Agile, teams will develop new actions to realize their vision and fulfill their purpose. This different mindset and perspective as to what can be done will propel the organization ahead of its competition. As the Agile principles change, the outputs of the 5 CBPs, the transformation takes off and innovation actions emerge from teams that better serve the customer needs, wants, and motivations. Throughout this change, building internal capabilities continues on the transformation methodology. People hone their new skills and become subject matter experts in the new way of working for the CBPs and the Agile systems. Leaders take on different roles like facilitators, trainers, and coaches to their teams. At this point, the culture of the organization is changing and a shift is experienced where everyone feels the responsibility of shaping the culture through the new principles of Breakthrough Agile.

Transformational success comes with the benefit of leaders letting go of their old ways of working. Everyone needs to let go of the old principles, especially as they influenced the execution of any of the 5 CBPs. People need to understand the principles of Breakthrough Agile and apply them to the CBPs. In my experience, "letting go" is a large barrier for transformation progress. This is a challenge for organizations and at times, it is ultimately the undoing of the transformation. Leaders and people do not let go of the past. As a result of not letting go, a conflict develops between the principles of the old way of working and Breakthrough Agile principles. Both sets of principles are designed to influence the execution of the 5 CBPs. If there is a conflict, the stress from the conflict creates enough pressure that people just fall back to the old way of working. The solution to addressing this conflict is to make it transparent and resolve it by leaning into the principles of Breakthrough Agile.

To ensure that this conflict is minimized and resolved, actions need to be taken at the start of the transformation to change everyone's mindset and behaviors. In Breakthrough Agile, by redefining your principles to those of the transformation platform, it insures systematic change. How people engage and execute the 5 CBPs is the evidence of this cultural transformation. As more and more people adopt the principles, then the culture will reflect the change. Once the culture begins to adopt the new way of working, additional effort is required to sustain the momentum. The transformation team can support leaders through this stage, and help foster the adaption of the new principles. When sustainability is achieved, and the culture is self-perpetuating, breakthrough results will occur.

This is the key premise in this book. Organizations change by changing their principles as it relates to what they do and how they operate. Organizations will not change by simply applying the tools or systems of Agile. Organizations that see their future as being more customer centric, focusing on innovation and growth, and unleashing the potential of their employees will embrace this type of change. Organizations that remain in the traditional, command and control, slow decision making, bureaucratic, polarized culture will continue to see weak innovation, growth, and limited engagement from its employees. A Breakthrough Agile organization values the creativeness of its employees, enables teams to decide what initiatives to start and stop, empowers individuals to make decisions and be creative, and pushes teams to experiment on a broad scale. The challenge with this approach is that it is hard and when faced with a hard task, it is far too easy to fall back on the way things worked in the past.

Breakthrough Agile requires the organization to have a high degree of self-awareness within its leadership teams. It will find its strength to change when these teams recognize the potential of Breakthrough Agile. People within the organization need to know what and how the 5 CBPs operate and influence the way people work in its current state, so it has a clearer picture of what the future will look like. They need a clear focus on what is the gap between today and where they want to be in the future as it relates to the CBP. Then all employees become role models of the principles and how they work. Breakthrough Agile isn't achieved by a few handful of senior leaders directing a group of SMEs to find the "pots of gold" and mine them. Breakthrough Agile requires everyone from the newest and least experienced person to the tenured and most senior employee to work in a new way. This way of working is anchored by Breakthrough Agile's principles. The outcome is that this way of working will change how the 5 CBPs are enacted. By changing the mode of work for the 5 CBPs, then the culture is changed to reflect the way of working in these 5 CBPs. It is a journey that takes time. Once an organization reaches the moment in time when the energy to change exceeds the energy of resistance, then the business value and benefits of Agile flow into the organization. Let's take a look at these CBPs.

In this book, principle-based CBPs are fundamental processes that every organization uses day-to-day. They are the processes that everyone participates in at some point in time at work. Since they are so predominant and everyone is impacted by them, then they are the processes that create the organization's culture. In my experience, the 5 key CBPs are *decision making, conflict resolution, strategic planning, project management,* and *performance management.* One way of connecting the CBP to Breakthrough Agile's principles is to consider principles as the "rules of the game." In other words, how we think, act, connect, and relate to each other at work is governed by principles.

It is important to note that there are other CBPs that are left off this list. In my experience, these particular 5 CBPs are the key levers in influencing the culture of the organization. Breakthrough Agile is about reshaping these 5 CBPs through transformative principles. Once the journey started, then the actions and experiences of these 5 CBPs reshape the organization's culture. Continued application of Breakthrough Agile's principles will sustain the transformation over time. This would include changing how other CBPs are

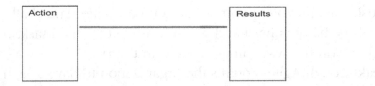

Figure 1.5 Causal relationship between action and results.

performed day-to-day after first reshaping the 5 key CBPs. In this book, we discuss the 5 CBPs in depth, the link between them and the principles of Breakthrough Agile, and how the actions from these processes deliver results for the organization.

Why start at the level of principles is a question you might ask? In most cases, when an organization commits to changing itself through a transformation platform, there is a tendency to put short-term gains ahead of changing the culture. Let's "grab the low hanging fruit," "get some quick wins," and "develop some success stories early." Sound familiar. It should and like many readers, I have lived through these experiences more than once. What you are experiencing when you hear these statements are the cultural principles of the organization shaping the transformation. To gain a better understanding of how the principle-based CBPs are so forceful in shaping the culture, let's review a simple model. Most people intuitively agree to the model (Figure 1.5).

Action leads to results. And within most organizations, we are rewarded and recognized for the results we achieve. Although a simple diagram, it can help us explain how the five principle-based CBPs work. For instance, recognition is a part of *performance management*. Deciding what action to take illustrates a *decision-making process* at work. Depending on the content of the action, it might have a significant impact on the future competitiveness of the organization. At some time before executing on the action, a team went through a *strategic planning* process and decided on the action. At this point, we already see three principle-based CBPs at work – performance management, decision making, and strategic planning. As an individual or team was completing the action, the action owner may have developed a *project plan* to complete and communicated it with their team. And finally, as the team was meeting and completing the action plan, *conflicts would have arisen*. These might be as simple as two people disagreeing on a course of action, or potentially, and more significantly, who would be the beneficiary of the results of the action. With these final two CBPs, project management and conflict resolution, we round out the five principle-based CBPs that make up Breakthrough Agile's transformation platform. With this simple model, one can see how these five business processes are the foundation of the organization's culture and shape the employee's ways of working.

The impact that the 5 CBPs has on an organization's way of working, how people relate to one another, and what the organization produces at the end of the day, is deeply embedded within the organization's culture. Using the DNA analogy, how a company makes decisions, resolves conflict, strategically plans, executes projects, and reward people is part of its DNA. Within this book, we will discuss how using Breakthrough Agile will work similar to CRISPR DNA, where we look to remove unwanted DNA of the past, and replace it with the DNA of the future. This change in DNA is evident when the organization changes its principles related to work. It is almost expected when an organization embarks on this transformation journey that it will recreate its vision, mission, and purpose. That it will keep and reshape the principles that are successful and align them with the agile transformation. The output of these steps will redefine the beliefs of the organization, and help it to change the actions it takes to meet and exceed customer's needs, wants and motivations.

A high-level overview of Breakthrough Agile is shown below. This graphic helps illustrate the influence that principles have on the CBP. It also provides us a view of a dynamic learning cycle. When deployed successfully, the results of the new actions reinforce the principles and new ways of working with the CBPs. Let's review the model (Figure 1.6).

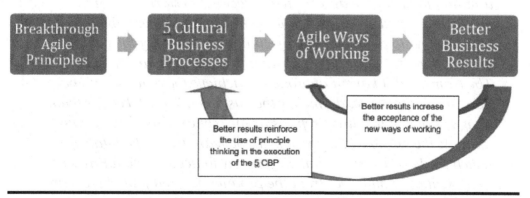

Figure 1.6   Breakthrough Agile's model of sustainment and self-improvement.

This simple diagram can serve as a roadmap for achieving Breakthrough Agile. In my career, I was able to live this experience firsthand on a number of occasions. Let's look at an example from an organization that deployed a successful principle-based approach using Lean transformation framework:

At this time in my career, I held the role of an OE practitioner in a midsize electronics company that was deploying a Lean Transformation. Their Lean framework was influenced by the Danaher Business System. Danaher in theory followed the Toyota Production System. Danaher and this electronics company strongly followed the principles of Lean in their ways of working across all of their business units and functions. One of the Lean principles for the company was "one piece flow" for every process. This principle influenced decisions on what strategic initiatives, prototype development, production planning and ordering, it shaped the measurement of what was good, and it was held as a performance measurement for the design and implementation of a Kanban or pull system. Embedded within their transformation framework, all business units used value stream mapping as a strategic planning system. Additionally, the Lean principles of eliminating waste, reducing lead time, meeting customer demand shaped these strategic planning processes.

A future state value stream map(VSM), will create an output of kaizen activities that move the organization closer toward its future state. In this case, creating 1pc flow in every process. As a team completed the VSM process, a team decision would prioritize what to focus on. In this example, I was working at a manufacturing site and the team decided to start with one production cell with its 1pcs flow approach. From here, the intent was to scale up across the site by changing the rest of the cells to the 1pc flow standard after learning from the first kaizen event. The team used a kaizen approach to achieve the outcome of 1pc flow and a shorter lead time for the customer. The VS Leader then assigned one of his direct reports as the owner of the future state plan. As the OE coach, my role with the team was to facilitate and coach the kaizen teams on their journey to achieve the future state organization. Employees from the production area joined the team as well as support staff. To manage the individual kaizen events, the project lead used an A3 process. To radically change the MFG cells, each event was a 5 day kaizen which the site performed at a rhythm of one every month.

As an output of the 1st kaizen, the team expected to realize a 1pcs flow, a safer work environment, balanced work loading, a reduction in footprint, reduced WIP, standard work, take time production monitoring board (Heijunka & hourly board), weekly performance board (SQDC), reduction in cycle time, and just in time inventory to the customer. During the event, the kaizen team identified how to improve the safety of the employees working in the cell, how much time the cell actually needed staffed, and improved efficiency in downtime and quality. At the end of the event, the team was recognized by the president of the division for its work, held a celebratory party afterward at an offsite location, the OE person gained an internal certification as an SME in Kaizen, and the VS leader and his team gained credibility within the organization. Let's see how this example relates to the CBP model (Figure 1.6).

Lean principles: One piece flow, eliminating waste, Care of the Worker, Transparency, and Customer focused.

Cultural Business Processes: Decision Making (Future State Project Plan), Strategic Planning (VSM), Project Management (Kaizen A3), Performance Management (Celebration and certification), Conflict Resolution (Self Organized Team).

Actions: Kaizen, production leveling, reduced footprint, reduced WIP.

Result: Safer work environment, better quality product, reduction in lead time, reduction in inventory, higher customer satisfaction due to on time and in full deliveries.

The example above illustrates how the CBP shape the actions of an organization, and the results it produces. The results of the kaizen are what delivers value to the customer and organization. This is what the customer sees, hears, and experiences with its interaction with the organization. The example demonstrates how the principles of the Lean transformation effort influenced the CBP as they were practiced using the Lean systems. Across this organization, every month, a kaizen event occurred at each manufacturing facility. The approach included all 8 manufacturing sites including international sites. It is important to note that CBP would impact the ways of working across and up and down all levels of the organization.

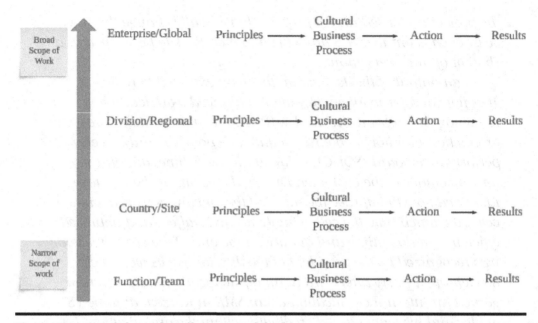

Figure 1.7 Breakthrough Agile's span of deployment across an organization.

Whether it is an organization of 100,000 people spread across the world or a small-sized business, each is capable of realizing the advantages of Breakthrough Agile to achieve superior business results. The model above (Figure 1.7) demonstrates how different levels are influenced by CBP.

With this model, the principles as well as the CBPs stay the same at each level. What would be different between the levels is the content of the work and actions. This will become clearer throughout this book.

Another point I want to address before getting deeper into understanding Breakthrough Agile is the topic of leadership. Over my career, being a people leader and watching other people leaders in action, I am absolutely convinced that leadership is one of the key elements to a successful transformation. I am also convinced that it is one of the hardest to change. When attempting to change your organization using Breakthrough Agile, how leaders show up will impact the speed of transformation overall.

In this book, I am offering you a different approach than to start with changing the mindset and behavior of the leaders first. The approach discussed in this book looks at the business processes that create the culture of the organization. These processes, the CBPs, influence the behavior and mindset of the leader. By redefining how these processes are practiced will change the mindset and behaviors of the leader.

An analogy might be that a carpenter has worked his whole life with a claw hammer. Then one day, he is introduced to a nail gun. As the carpenter continues to use the nail gun, he develops a different mindset on hammering. Their principles as to how long it might take to complete a specific job will change and with a more robust hammering process the quality of work will improve. Now, the creaking floors or flexing roofs go away because the consistency of the nail being driven is the same and possibly with better accuracy. By changing the system of work, going from a claw hammer to a pneumatic nail gun in this case, there is a change in mindset by the user, the carpenter.

Let's look at another example of how principles influence individuals. Take Amazon as a way to understand this. Amazon's cultural foundation is automation. Its business model is a website that can provide anyone with anything across the world and at most times within 24 hours. From their customer service to warehousing operations to customer complaints, the organization has an automated business system that promotes speed and accuracy. This belief in a principle, *automation*, influences how leaders make decisions on how to run their business. The resulting system of taking and receiving customer orders is then impacted by these decisions. The mindset and behaviors of Amazon's leaders see the value of the automated system and its value for customers and align their way of working to maximize the value of the principle. Can you imagine a manager or director at Amazon not believing that automation holds value for customers? As with any transformation, the need for a senior leader to champion the cause is highly desirable and with Amazon Jeff Bezos fulfills that role.

When we look at achieving Breakthrough Agile, if we practice the CBPs by leaning into the transformation's principles, then changing the mindset and behaviors of leaders will follow if not naturally, at least with less resistance. The final chapter of this book discusses the role of the leader in more detail. It is clear that a new way to lead is necessary to achieve the value derived from Breakthrough Agile.

Summary and Key Takeaways

For each chapter, I will introduce a sensing guide to help people to understand what an organization should be experiencing, seeing, and hearing as it transforms. As part of the sensing guide, I will also include what I call the anti-patterns. The sensing guide is a technique for individuals to measure the impact of a transformation on an organization as it moves through a transformation.

Here, we will define the different elements of a sensing guide for the reader.

- **Experiencing:** Statements about experiences should include those that people live through. An example of an experience would be people participating in a scrum event. Or people being told that they are the decision makers for a given topic. These events will help the organization sense if the principles of the transformation are taking hold with the employees of the organization.
- **Seeing:** Statements about seeing should include what an observer sees when they attend a meeting or observe interactions among employees in the organization. These observations are both interactions internally and externally. For example, a "seeing" statement might be that leaders asking more open-ended questions to teams and individuals. Individuals are speaking up and providing diverse opinions in meetings. Organization structures are being redefined to enable a more Agile organization.
- **Hearing:** Statements about "hearing" should include what is being said by leaders, employees, customers, and stakeholders that reflect the new ways of working. These observations are both internally and externally. For example, a "hearing" statement might be that customers are feeling more focus is given to their concerns. Employees are bringing "out of the box" ideas to meetings to solve problems. Leaders are using forward looking statements like "imagine if" or "how might we" to conversations to enable innovation. Leaders making statements that reflect empowerment of employees within the organization.
- **Anti-pattern:** Anti-patterns are the statements or actions that reflect a fall back to the old way of thinking and acting. For instance, as an organization begins to empower its employees, an anti-pattern to empowerment would be the establishment of "forums" or "committees" that are put in place to review or endorse a team's decision. Another typical anti-pattern that may be observed is relabeling current activities with the transformation's methodology language. For instance, calling target setting through KPIs an OKR process. Calling staff meetings sprints. Not preparing well enough as being Agile. Hearing people make statements like, "we are already doing this." Anti-patterns are a way for the organization to measure the resistance to the transformation and the fall back to old ways of working.

To operationalize a sensing guide, here is an example of how one would be created.

Leadership Sensing Guide				
Leadership Features of the Organization	Experiencing	Seeing	Hearing	Anti-Pattern
Servant Leadership	Employees are developed by their leaders through cross-functional job rotations.	Leaders are doing less talking and directing in team meetings.	Leaders are asking open-ended questions like "what" and "how".	Leaders judge employees' work and performance in front of others. Leaders create an environment of fear of failure.
Coaching	In 1-1 conversations, employees feel safe to discuss their weaknesses and faults. Leaders listen actively without judgment. Leaders support the career growth of all employees, whether on their team or not.	Leaders are not passive or distant from any team members. Leaders are genuinely showing concern for employees' work and performance. Leaders speak less and listen to understand.	Leaders are not providing solutions in discussions. Leaders openly state their role as a coach and do not take on the responsibility of the employee's work.	Leaders listen to respond. Leaders create the environment in which employees follow their guidance. Leaders show favoritism toward some and minimize others.
Transformation Champion	Leader commits time and resources from his team to learn and practice the new ways of working.	Leader takes personal time to understand and learn the different aspects of the transformation journey. Leaders will hold to the new way of working when challenged by peers.	Leader will speak up and support the new principles over the old way of working.	Leader delegates his transformation responsibilities to someone on his team. Leader prioritizes routine work over transformation activities. Leader uses phrases like "we are doing it now" or "this doesn't work".

Chapter 2

Principles and Values of Breakthrough Agile

> Correct principles are like compasses: They are always pointing the way. And if we know how to read them, we won't get lost, confused, or fooled by conflicting voices and values.
>
> **Stephen R. Covey, Principle-Centered Leadership**

A look inside:

- Why principle-based organizations experience challenges with transformations
- Understanding that resistance to change and transformation is a natural output
- All transformation platforms are principle based – the common thread
- Introduction of the five principle-based cultural processes of Breakthrough Agile

Let's take a deeper look at how principles influence the actions of an organization and how the culture is shaped by the five cultural business processes (CBPs). As mentioned early, with any transformation platform, the way of working is defined by its principles. On a broad level, the more robust platforms, Lean and Agile, use customer centricity as its starting point. In particular, Agile transforms the organization with a mindset shift from internal efficiencies to an external focus on the customer's need, wants and motivations. Breakthrough Agile takes this a step further and asks that organizations to put customer centricity not only in key discussions across the business but also

 DOI: 10.4324/9781003335702-2

embed this enabling principles of customer centricity into the critical business processes that shape its culture. It is imperative that the organization takes the time to understand the principles of the Breakthrough Agility and connect the dots as to how they influence the output of the 5 CBPs.

As the organization starts to gain a better understanding of the Breakthrough Agile's principles, a natural growth is tension across the organization. Tension will manifest itself through employee resistance, competition of focus areas, defining the transformation language, and understanding what capabilities are needed to deploy the systems. The focus of this tension is on the transformation systems (Scrum, Kanban, 90-day planning cycle, etc.). Why the tension surfaces is the elephant in the room and one that gets lost in the efforts to do what is right for the organization. The elephant that gets ignored is the knowledge gap between understanding the transformation systems and their deployment, and the capability level of the organization's personnel to how to deploy and utilize them to deliver value for the organization. For an organization to be successful on this journey, a sense of vulnerability and self awareness needs to exists that reflects this knowledge gap. By approaching the transformation with a sense of vulnerability, people in the organization move forward on the learning journey with the transformation. A common mistake in transformational journeys is to glaze over this elephant, believing that people will get it, the capability and knowledge, after a while. Even those who are accountable for leading the transformation tend to put this tension into the shadows of the journey. Unfortunately, not recognizing and acknowledging the gap, this tension turns into conflict between the old school and the new school of working. Those who sense they are in the knowledge gap of learning a new business system now become critics of the transformation and its foreign (outsider) way of working. The strategy for a successful transformation is to deal upfront with the knowledge gap. With Breakthrough Agile, we start by building up people's confidence with the transformation's principles and how they play a part in the daily business processes. By starting with everyone understanding the transformation principles at the start, and showing how they impact the 5 CBP, then as the systems of the transformation are deployed, people feel tension, but it is the healthy tension of learning a new and more efficient way of working, versus one where people feel belittled or minimalized because they don't understand the what, why, or how. The 5 CBPs will resonate with the general population of the organization and by focusing on the relationship of Breakthrough Agile's principles to the execution of the 5 CBPs, then adopting the transformation systems, reduces the tension and eases the barriers to change.

As the journey starts, emphasize to everyone that the principles for Breakthrough Agile are agnostic to the personalities, history of the organization, products, and local cultures of a company. The core principles are distinct and tied to the framework itself. We live in a world that works like this. Take any holiday from any culture. Each one has specific symbols and ceremonies that define it based upon the principles of the holiday. Examine Chinese New Year, where the main principle of the holiday is to "reconnect with family." This principle leads thousands of people to travel and visit their parents, siblings, and other family members during 2 weeks of each year. Yet, you don't have to be Chinese to celebrate this holiday or live in China. People across the world, of different nationalities and races, celebrate this event and follow its principles. Another example is Christmas. One of the principles for this holiday is the act of gift giving. Regardless of where you are and what nationality, race, or even religion, a person who is celebrating Christmas will follow this principle of giving a gift to someone in the spirit of the holiday. As you can see from these two examples, the principles of the holidays are agnostic to the region, personalities of leaders, and other societal influences that we assume drive the actions of the holiday. Another example, closer to the business world, is when a company creates a vision that has the tone similar to "Be the Toyota of Consumer Goods" or even more current "Work with Amazon like speed." When a company commits to this vision, they are preparing themselves to embrace the principle of the transformation platforms that has made those companies the benchmarks for their industry. For some of these companies, they feel the passion and excitement of creating this change, but what they don't anticipate is the tension between the legacy work principles and the new transformational principles. If a company decides to transform itself to work at the speed of Amazon, there is a sense that they are changing their culture based on what made Amazon successful. The principles of Amazon's operating model are embedded in its cultural business processes (CBPs) and this creates the company's culture. A company might not duplicate the same systems that Amazon works with, but, through their CBPs the company will think how automation and speed can improve their competitiveness. Additionally, there is a strong understanding that internally, the company doesn't have the capabilities or resources needed to embed the new principles into the organization. Amazon has grown their capabilities over time and with successful role modeling from the highest level leaders. To work like Amazon, a company needs to have this type of sponsorship at the start. To change a culture is a challenging task. Even more challenging if the organization has a strong presence in the market. This undertaking is embedded with traps. Without a doubt, tension and conflict will occur at the beginning and in the sustaining steps of the transformation. A transformation following the approach of Breakthrough Agile will generate this tension and managing the tension is a key learning discussed in this book.

Too often, organizations fail to learn and repeat their experiences with attempting transformations. As a by-product, disillusionment and reticence precede the implementation of the next transformation effort. This is seen and heard when employees stand their ground and boast phrases like "we have done that before," "isn't this just like the last time," or "we are already doing this." As the change journey continues, it is important to address these sensations from the organization because it is the manifestation of the resistance within and ultimately the friction that slows down the pace of change and adoption of the new way of working. What I have seen in organizations is their inability to deal with the resistors to the transformation efforts. One reaction by a transformation team to resistors is to request the organization's senior most leaders to make bold statements to gain everyone's buy-in through a top–down directive. Other times, the organization adopts the "fit-for-purpose" model. The important point to note here is that when this type of resistance appears, the organization displays its inability to resolve conflict. As one of the Breakthrough Agile's CBPs, conflict resolution can help the organization manage this event within the transformation. However, if the organization's skills at conflict resolution are basic, then it will find it hard to move resistors to supporters. Examples of basic conflict resolution are escalating issues for resolution to a higher authority, or top–down directives. Other tactics include avoiding conflict or the resistors and just working with people that are open to the transformation. Regardless, these manifestations of tension and resistance need resolved during the early stages of the journey.

Taking steps to meet this resistance and addressing it as it occurs is needed by the transformation team. There are times when resistors to the new way of working do not buy-in. At this point, steps need to be taken to manage these people. It should be noted that even if these are high performers, or star employees, they need to adopt the new way of working principles for the transformation to be successful. The different scenarios of resistance by individuals within an organization are endless. As a summary, by focusing on teaching the organization's employees the principles of the transformation platform first and how they would impact the execution of the 5 CBPs, then the fuel that drives resistors is reduced. You are no longer asking people to adopt a new work system that they have little to no experience with. With Breakthrough Agile, you are asking people to become better at something they have experience with and can relate easily to. The transformation is focusing on changes to decision making, conflict resolution, strategic planning, project management, and performance management.

Resistors understand the company's old principles are being threatened by the transformation framework's principles. Change and transformation are two discomforting experiences for individuals and, especially when time and resources have been rushed to get the transformation up and running. The first stage of the journey is designed to train and educate people on the principles of the transformation's framework and more importantly how they influence the 5 CBPs. At the broadest levels in the organization, it is critical that clear and recurring communications about the transformation happen. The frequency should follow a pattern that everyone understands – monthly, quarterly, etc. Additionally, role modeling across the organization needs to come from the most senior level leaders to the recently joined or most junior level employees. Individuals and teams need recognition when they step up and embrace the change creating the environment that will move the organization toward its new culture. At times, it means allowing space for those who do not fit in the new culture an opportunity to leave. If you hit a point during the transformation where a few people decide to leave the organization due to the transformation efforts although an unwanted experience, it might also be an indication that the organization is changing to the new way of working. These individuals see that the old principles of work are being replaced with a new set of principles that require a relearning. This generates anxiety and fear within individuals, especially those who were able to manipulate the old ways of working for their own personal advantage in terms of self-promotion.

Let's look at a transformation framework's principles and determine why these simple statements can result in outstanding business benefits and impact people's ways of working to the point that some might leave the organization (Figure 2.1). To set the context for Breakthrough Agile's principles, let's first examine the more well studied and known transformation frameworks within the business world today. Figure 2.1 contains the core principles of each transformation framework.

- Lean transformation framework has been one of the most holistic and robust frameworks with thousands of companies embracing its principles as a way of working. Its potential to change a culture within an organization is great. From some perspectives, Lean has many additional principles and values. However, the intent of the table is to show the differences between Lean and Six Sigma.

■ **Six Sigma has embedded itself within many industries today, and at times, it has been seen as a robust transformation framework. After working years within organizations that use the methodology, I tend to view it as a fixed and very rigid approach to transformational change. Culture changes little by applying a Six Sigma transformation. In an organization that follows Six Sigma principles, the organizations can remain traditional and hierarchical. In practice, Six Sigma finds its way into the project management office of many organizations whose projects have an underlying reliance on basic statistics. This can be helpful to some and with broad and sweeping promises on paper appears to be credible at delivering results. Many organizations continue to support the Six Sigma approach. In my experience, it was supported mainly due to the low impact to the culture of the organization and the promise of high impact in theoretical savings.

Transformation Framework	Principle and Values
Lean*	Reduction/Elimination of Waste Built-in Quality Just-In-Time Inventory Error Proofing Equipment High Value Add Ratio Build to Customer Demand Standardized Processes Problem Solving Creating Value Stream Organizations Lean Leadership Respect for the Employee
Six Sigma**	Reduction in Variation Methodological SME Hierarchical Subject Matter Expertise Following a process to get a result Statistical Aptitude Project Management Aptitude
Lean – Six Sigma	A combination of the two above. Depending on the industry and leaders of the transformation effort, the transformation focus will be focused on one of the other.

Figure 2.1   High-level overview of transformation methodologies principles.

In the typical transformation journey, only the transformation team/ leaders understand and can apply these principles to the content of the work for creating value. Black belts are individuals that can apply a statistic model to provide theoretical savings from quality or process improvements. OE Leaders, or Lean Practitioners lead kaizen events and apply tools like SMED or Standard Work, to shorten change over time, or cycle times. Again, strong individuals that are leading others to change a process. Even within one of the best business models for operational excellence, the Shingo Model, there is a segmentation of knowledge for deployment. In the Shingo criteria, you will see three broad areas of knowledge. There is the tool level, system level, and principle level. Applying these broad areas to the people in the organization, those at the principle level are fewer, than those at the tool level. For me, the Shingo model is very good, and I applied its approach many times in my Lean work experience, but I also see how it can lead an organization to transform through top–down directives. As mentioned, with Lean and Six Sigma, only a handful of people can apply the principles to the work of the organizations. With both of these platforms, the common starting point is to use the tools and get fast results (low hanging fruit). In these transformations, the organization misses the point of building up its capability on the principles and how they impact the 5 CBPs.

At first, the passion and enthusiasm to apply the transformation platforms systems and tools blur the effort to make a sustainable change over the long term. In other words, the organization applies only a cosmetic level change to the way of working. Leaders talk the talk but have a knowledge gap on what it takes to walk the walk. In order to make the organizational change to be sustainable and for an organization to realize the benefits of the transformation platform, everyone, not just the transformation team and a few leaders, need a clear understanding of the new principles and how they will impact the 5 CBPs.

Having personally repeated this cycle more than once and seeing other organizations follow the same path, I tend to believe it is how businesses have been conditioned to act when launching a new transformation. In most cases, even the brightest and finely tuned deployment plan gets the nod to start with the tools first. Accordingly, we need to accept the experiences and learn from them. With Breakthrough Agile, the approach is different. Education and training on the principles of the transformation are the starting points. The transformation team then connects the dots between how these principles will then impact the execution of the 5 CBPs.

Time and resources are taken to ensure that people understand how the 5 CBPs currently operate and what will change as a result of the transformation. As this effort is underway, then the systems and tools of Agile began to be introduced into the day-to-day work of the organization. As momentum builds from this approach, then agile champions step-up and articulate the future vision of the company as an Agile organization. In the early stages of the journey, it is critical to start building awareness and understanding of the principles of Breakthrough Agile and linking these to the 5 key CBPs. The next step is then to link the outputs of the 5 CBPs to the execution of Agile systems or tools. Once the employees of the organization can visualize these relationships and articulate them in discussions with their teams, then the impact of the transformation on business outcomes grows and benefits the organization. This will lead the organization to being more competitive within its industry. To help illustrate this relationship between principles, CBPs, and systems of the transformation are illustrated in Figure 2.2.

Transformation Framework	Principle and Values	Cultural Business Process
Lean*	Reduction/Elimination of Waste	Decision Making
	Built-in Quality	Project Management
	Just-In-Time Inventory	Strategic Planning/Decision Making
	Error Proofing Equipment	Project Management
	High Value Add Ratio	Strategic Planning
	Build-to-Customer Demand	Strategic Planning
	Standardized Processes	Project Management
	Problem Solving	Project Management
	Value Stream Management	Strategic Planning/Decision Making
	Lean Leadership	Strategic Planning/Decision Making
	Respect for the Employee	Decision Making/Conflict Resolution
		Performance Management
Six Sigma**	Reduction in Variation	Project Management
	Methodological SME	Performance Management
	Following a process to get a result	Performance Management
	Statistical Aptitude	Project Management
	Project Management Aptitude	Project Management
Lean – Six Sigma	A combination of the two above. Depending on the industry and leaders of the transformation effort, the transformation focus will be focused on one of the other.	

Figure 2.2 Overview of principle-based business processes with transformation methodologies.

Diving deeper into Lean as a transformation framework, it continues to deliver superior benefits to organizations across the globe. When Lean's core principles are linked to the company's 5 key CBPs, the value generation for the customer, employee, and company is substantial. The list of companies that use Lean to achieve this is long – within every automotive industry in any country, the idea of single piece flow, takt time production, and error proofing equipment exists. BMW, Volkswagen, Toyota, and the American Big Three have all benefited from the practices of Lean over the years. As these companies role model the principles of Lean, their business model impacts their supply chain. Tier 1 and beyond suppliers adopt the principles of Lean to be better equipped to meet the demands of the automakers. Lean has impacted aviation, food service, consumer goods, and many others organizations in both manufacturing and service industries. The companies that are using Lean as a way of working have changed their principles and how they work day-to-day using the 5 CBPs.

For instance, while working for a US Tier 1 automotive supplier, I witnessed the effects of Lean thinking on both a broad level and then at a specific one. To the case in point, the entire design of the plant had a U-shaped product flow. Product entered the plant as raw material and was staged within feet of the manufacturing center. Storage or warehousing didn't occupy any space at the site. Just-in-time (JIT) included not only the raw materials that we received but also the finished goods shipped to the customer. From the staging area, the raw material entered its first processing step and then traveled by a Kanban cart to the following processes. As the WIP traveled throughout the plant to various process steps, the Kanban carts served as scheduling and inventory control systems. Color coding of carts designated the product type, and at what stage the product was in during the MFG process. Here again, the principle of JIT being used within the plant between operations as well as visual controls to monitor WIP levels to schedule and control production. Across the plant, each piece of MFG equipment had electronic sensors in them that would shut down the machine when an abnormality in the product was detected (error proofing/ poka-yoke). Each piece of equipment had an Andon light with stop/go light indicators. The plant was designed with excellent visibility from one end to the other. Visually, anyone in the plant could see how the product was running based on whether they saw more green lights than red. Quality control was built into the equipment and when critical process parameters didn't meet specifications, alarms were activated and the equipment stopped.

Here are examples of error proofing and quality at the source. The final assembly lines were within feet of the racks that were by the shipping docks. As the finished product was packaged into a reusable tray, it was staged for next day shipment. Externally, a shipping company had "milk runs" between the plant and customer. The trucks that came to pick up the finished goods also returned the packaging trays from the customer so that we could reuse them for the next day's delivery. Based on the number of empty trays returned, we had an idea of how many cars were being produced. These trays served as a visual indicator of inventory between us and the customer. Here, we can see how Lean's principles influenced the design of the plant, internal processes, and the shipping of finished goods to the customer.

Reflecting back on Breakthrough Agile's approach, let's see how the principles of Lean impacted the 5 CBPs with the output being the way the plant operated (Figure 2.3).

CBPs	Principle	Evidence
Decision Making	Just-in-time	Raw Material Inventory
		Kanban Carts
Conflict Resolution	Build in Quality	Error Proofing Equipment
	Error Proofing	Andon Lights
Rewards & Recognition	Respect for the Employee	Error proofing equipment – for both safety and quality
		Minimized transportation of raw materials/equipment
		Level flow of production using Kanban
		Scheduling by Kanban

Strategic Planning	Waste Elimination Value Stream Organization	U-shaped product flow Kanban Milk Runs
Project Management	Standardized Processes	Equipment designed for its purpose – inclusive of error proofing and safety features

Figure 2.3   Example of how principle-based business processes are applied.

The Tier 1 company illustrated above had strong roots with Lean. The plant itself was a green field operation and its parent company was a Japanese industrial company that worked with Toyota in Japan for years. From my experience working at this company, I carried the principles of Lean to the other organizations in my career. There are always great wins not only with creating value for the company in terms of top- and bottom-line growth but also with employee morale and respect for the employee.

In one experience, I was a Value Stream Leader at an industrial manufacturer. The company manufactured large industrial values that were used in refinery, chemical, and other types of processing plants. One main work task was to move large raw castings that needed machining from a pallet to a CNC work center. Each work center was equipped with a small crane that employees used to pick up the casting and load them into the CNC machine. The end-to-end process for this step was as follows: A certified forklift driver had to navigate a narrow corridor, component racks, as well as the operators after picking up the pallet with the casting on it. Once the pallet was placed in the machining cell, the operator used the crane's hook and attached it to the casting through a bolt hole. Afterward, the operator had to pull the crane's ratchet chain to raise the part high enough to position it in the machine. As the operator was continuously bending over to reach the casting on the pallet and then standing up to operate the crane to lift the casting into the CNC, there was continuous strain on their back, shoulders, and legs. One result was that the company had paid hundreds of thousands in worker's compensation and insurance from this process as over time operators became injured. Using the principles of Lean, respect for the employee, I made a decision to implement a new material management process for this step. With a team from the shop floor, we introduced Kanban carts into the process, not just with the machining cells but between every step from warehouse to shipping. This eliminated the need for the forklift operator to move parts. Now the machinist or supervisor could stage carts for the day's production. The carts had a storage tray that was at waist height (32″) and had robust casters to move the heavy castings. The cart's height eliminated the need for the operator to bend down and attached the crane hook to the casting. The empty carts served as a visual indicator for production and inventory control. This simple Kanban system and applying the principle of respect for the employee ended up creating enormous value for the company. In the end, the entire Kanban system increased to the top line of the company by 10% since inventory was kept at a minimum for machined castings. We were able to reduce our order lead time to 24 hours for most orders and ship products sooner which increases the number of invoices being fulfilled sooner. However, and more importantly to me, it stopped the injuries to the operators. Imagine an employee who worked years at this plant, having recurring back pain nightly and then with a simple Kanban technique having the pain go away. I had employees tell me this after the implementation of the Kanban System. This is the type of reward I appreciated the most from practicing Lean for many years.

The intent of using the Lean example is to help the reader understand how the principles of Breakthrough Agile need to be practiced. Within the software industry, principles and values of Agile are well documented. A quick search on "Agile" will lead a reader to discover the "Agile Manifesto." This document contains 12 principles and 4 values and serves as a quasi-contract for a software company's way of working when designing products and delivering on projects. Here is the Agile Manifesto (Figure 2.4) as known today and the principles behind it.

Like the Agile Manifesto, Breakthrough Agile requires that an organization follow its principles and apply them to the 5 CBPs to enable the transformation of the organization.

One of the main features of Breakthrough Agile is it's holistic approach to using Agile than practiced by software developers. Agile, as used by software developers focuses on the Scrum Process. For these organizations, Scrum activities are Agile. Even as it scales up to an enterprise level, delivery products through value streams or trains via sprint activities is the backbone of Agile. Scrum is an effective system to use and we will discuss it in 1 of the 5 CBPs in Breakthrough Agile – project management. However, with Breakthrough Agile, an organization needs to apply Agile principles to the 5 key CBPs that intrinsically shape the culture of the company. With this approach, the outputs of the 5 CBPs leverage Agile systems such as Scrum, Kanban, OKRs, design thinking, self-management, etc. These 5 CBPs impact the organization at every level within every function. All employees need to understand and adopt the principles of Breakthrough Agile as they practice the 5 CBPs. The Agile Manifesto is the original set of principles and values for Agile and has its own power in terms of influencing the process for results. We need to respect this document for what it is and realize that it wasn't intended as a set of principles for an enterprise wide transformation but for organizations that want to get better at delivering on projects. For an organization that wants to go beyond Scrum, they need a deeper

Individuals and interactions over processes and tools
Working software over comprehensive documentation
Customer collaboration over contract negotiation
Responding to change over following a plan

Agile Manifesto

1. Our highest priority is to satisfy the customer through early and continuous delivery of valuable software.

2. Welcome changing requirements, even late in development. Agile processes harness change for the customer's competitive advantage.

3. Deliver working software frequently, from a couple of weeks to a couple of months, with a preference to the shorter timescale.

4. Business people and developers must work together daily throughout the project.

5. Build projects around motivated individuals. Give them the environment and support they need, and trust them to get the job done.

6. The most efficient and effective method of conveying information to and within a development team is face-to-face conversation.

7. Working software is the primary measure of progress.

8. Agile processes promote sustainable development. The sponsors, developers, and users should be able to maintain a constant pace indefinitely.

9. Continuous attention to technical excellence and good design enhances agility.

10. Simplicity–the art of maximizing the amount of work not done–is essential.

11. The best architectures, requirements, and designs emerge from self-organizing teams.

12. At regular intervals, the team reflects on how to become more effective, then tunes and adjusts its behavior accordingly.

Figure 2.4 Agile Manifesto and principles.

understanding of what truly influences the way people work. How are decisions made in our organization? Who should make them? How do we deal with conflict? What projects/initiatives do we need to resource first? What do we need to stop doing? What is a way to recognize people who reflects their commitment and role modeling of the new ways of working? This is what Breakthrough Agile will provide the reader.

The 5 CBPs of Breakthrough Agile are derived from the work experiences of thousands of leaders and employees whom I have worked with throughout the years. These processes occur on every level of the organization, and whether big or small, publicly traded or a Mom & Pop organization, they exist and shape the culture of the organization. Here are definitions of each cultural business process:

- **Decision making:** Decision making in an organization is a singular person or a team of people, choosing an option that impacts the work that has to be done within an organization.
- **Conflict management:** Conflict management is the process of individuals, teams, or organization units resolving differences or conflicting priorities.

- **Strategic planning:** Strategic planning is the process of looking forward, and with the support of data, deciding on the future of the business. What will the organization do and how it influences the operation(s) in the future embody this process.
- **Project management:** Project management is the process of prioritizing, selecting, executing, and monitoring initiatives, both large scale and small scale, that are designed to impact the business to the most favorable outcome in the future.
- **Performance Management:** Performance Management is the process of managing the talent of the organization. Performance management identifies and provides opportunities for growth and development of people for the sustainability of the organization. A second part of Performance Management is the recognition and rewarding of people, teams, or organizations that exceeded in delivering results to customers, employees, or the company. It is a process where individuals are provided an additional monetary enumeration based on their skills, abilities, experience, and contribution to the organization.

On the surface, many may assume that the principles for each of these CBPs are the same. It is true that every organization, whether small or large, has these 5 CBPs. Down to one of the smallest organizational units, a family, each of these CBPs exist. When a family decides to go on a vacation, a child decides to join the military or choose a college, or play sports, the decision-making process is activated. How families resolve conflict among themselves, save and plan for the future, and how parents develop themselves and children all are practices of the 5 CBPs. It is helpful that everyone has had experience with these five processes when starting a Breakthrough Agile transformation. How easy is it to engage people, when you can apply the approach to how a family might buy a house, send a child to college, or groom their children in a talent. It is the intent of this book to help people recognize the impact of these processes in the work environment. We take this a step further by diving deep into how they are practiced and executed day-to-day and ask people to reflect on how principles shape the culture of the organization.

This practice of the 5 CBPs is what is referred to as the ways of working in Breakthrough Agile. The main theme of this book is to help people identify that the 5 CBPs shape the way of working or culture at any organization. And that the principles that an organization uses shape the way the 5 CBPs are practiced. Figure 2.5 illustrates this point.

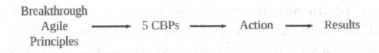

Figure 2.5   Breakthrough Agile's transformation model.

When an organization starts a transformation journey using Breakthrough Agile, tension is created between the old principles and Breakthrough Agile's principles. Organizations may not even realize that their decision-making process is driven by a principle of cost reduction, because it is ingrained so deeply within the culture that people are subconsciously practicing it. This is a tremendous challenge for organizations that want to transform to an Agile organization. It is also one of the factors that impede change and, in some cases, squash the transformation journey's purpose. It is highly recommended that once an organization starts on the Breakthrough Agile journey that the vision and purpose of the organization change to reflect the new principles of the organization. It is also critical that strong senior leaders in the organization champion the vision and purpose of the organization.

Summary and Key Takeaways

Principles are the underlying forces that shape how an organization works. In order for any transformation to be successful, the transformation's principle needs to be understood and then applied to 5 CBPs that every organization practices. The 5 CBPs are as follows:

1. Decision making
2. Conflict resolution
3. Strategic planning
4. Project management
5. Performance Management

At the start of the transformation, all employees need to understand how these processes are currently practiced. This gives the organization a baseline for them to measure their transformation progress against.

As the transformation moves into its first few phases, tension or conflict is a natural output. Inherently, as with any change, the employees who have excelled using the old principles will feel threatened by the new principles and the changes in behavior and mindset that they bring. This tension needs to be addressed and conflicts made transparent to create an environment for the transformation to succeed. Addressing this tension can take the form of the following actions:

1. Awareness campaign on the new principles and 5 CBPs
2. Clarity on current state of the 5 CBPs
3. Constant and recurring communication on the transformation and why the organization is transforming
4. Changes in organization structure to support the transformation
5. Development of a transformation team to "hold the helm" in the early stages of the transformation
6. Coaching by champions, early adopters and senior leaders on how to deal with the transition after the change has been deployed
7. Addressing resistors through appropriate channels of conflict resolution

Chapter 3

What Is Breakthrough Agile?

Nearly all men can stand adversity, but if you want to test a man's character, give him power.

Abraham Lincoln

A look inside:

- Introduction of cultural business processes
- Identification of the cultural business processes that influence an organization's culture
- Traps to transformation – what can derail a transformation
- Principles of Breakthrough Agile

In this chapter, we introduce the principles of Breakthrough Agile and demonstrate how they impact the five cultural business processes (5 CBPs). It is key that people who are leading the Agile transformation efforts have a clear understanding of this relationship between the principle-based cultural business processes and the organization's culture. Breakthrough Agile is a transformation platform any industry can use to deploy Agile ways of working to achieve higher performance and competitiveness. From this point forward, start to think that "Agile isn't just for software or IT companies anymore" but a way of working to achieve superior business results.

As mentioned in the preceding chapter, Agile started off within the software industry as a better way to manage projects and deliver new products. Exploring the genesis of Agile starts with the frustration software project managers experienced in the late 1980s in delivering projects

DOI: 10.4324/9781003335702-3

through the traditional approach to project management – the waterfall approach. This frustration fed a desire to work differently and produced a new way of working around project management. The outcome was to create a project management approach that delivered superior quality products to the market faster. The Agile manifesto and Scrum were outputs of this new way of working and still today remain a key feature in an Agile organization. What the original Agile practitioners understood was that the principles of traditional project management weren't effective when being fast, flexible and adoptable was needed to develop and design projects. As companies continued to utilize the waterfall project management approach, poor results and execution were constantly experienced. These early Agile pioneers realized that a new approach was needed to stay competitive. They also recognized this problem as being systematic of a traditional organization's principles and could not be solved through "brute force" or additional human capacity. The pioneers saw that a new project management approach was needed. As a result a new approach was born: Scrum methodology. Today, Scrum is one of the most widely known systems of Agile and most people view Agile as Scrum. Breakthrough Agile incorporates what the software industry discovered and expands the thinking to all areas of the organization through the 5 CBPs. This is where Breakthrough Agile starts and expands on current Agile thinking as designed by the manifesto pioneers.

Breakthrough Agile promotes that all parts of the organization benefit from Agile ways of working. On a closer examination of any organization, 5 CBPs defined by Breakthrough Agile define the ways of working for an organization. The ceremonies, rituals, roles, and structure of these five business processes define the culture of the organization. This is what a new employee would experience, see, and hear as they began to learn how to adapt to the culture of the company. Regardless of the organization's products or services, an organization's culture is shaped by the execution of these 5 CBPs.

Every day, employees make decisions, resolve conflicts, strategize, execute projects, and performance evaluated in the spirit to advance their organization's competitiveness within their industry. By understanding what factors influence the execution of these 5 CBPs, Breakthrough Agile offers a powerful transformation model for an organization to develop high performing teams and individuals to meet the demands of the customer, stakeholders, and employees. At the tip of the spear of Breakthrough Agile is the concept that an organization needs to clearly identify what the customer is truly desiring – what are the needs, wants, and motivation of the customer. Once this is clear, then setting into motion actions that will transform the organization through better execution of the 5 CBPs will lead to better outcomes that separate the organization from its competition. Once the organization builds up its capabilities on using Breakthrough Agile principles, the Agile ways of working best systems to identify and create value for the organization. Agile practices are the sustaining element that sustain the organization's competitiveness and uncovers value both internally and externally. The challenge however is getting started. The organization needs a departure gate, and resources to sustain the growth and development of the transformation through the journey. Whether an organization is a market leader or looking to create a new business segment, the transformation's principles and agile systems will deliver the outcomes it seeks to realize. Transforming a company is a hard undertaking and one that takes some time. Those organizations that do take the challenge begin to see the results of the cultural change. When starting a transformation using the Breakthrough Agile approach, the cultural business processes need to be understood by all and the link to how Agile principles will change the methodology and output of them. By adopting Breakthrough Agile, an organization will create an culture where employees continually learn on a daily basis on how to transform themselves, their work processes, and deliver higher value adding outcomes.

When the transformation journey starts people in the organization need to adopt a different way of thinking and mindset. The agile systems will teach teams and individuals a new approach to identifying and realizing higher value adding outcomes in a shorter period. The illustration below offers a view on Breakthrough Agile's model. When applying the platform's principles directly to the execution of a cultural business process like Decision Making, then the actions and results that are created are more closely aligned with the customer and their needs. By fulfilling the customer's needs, the outcome is a product or service that delivers value over time. From the Model T to mobile phones, this model reinforces the impact of principle based business processes. As results drive a higher value, employees begin to experience how their actions contribute to the success of the business. Over time, the approach becomes self-perpetuating as better results lead to people more firmly experiencing how principles influence the output of the cultural business processes. At this point, the organization becomes a learning organization as more people in the organization close the knowledge gap on how principles influence results. The Agile

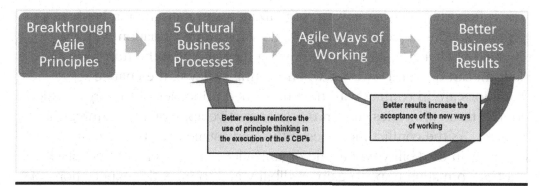

Figure 3.1 Breakthrough Agile's model including self-sustainment and relearning.

ways of working become the mechanism for the delivery of the value and breakthrough results for the customer and patient. After continuous application of this model (Figure 3.1), the culture changes to an Agile organization that embraces the principles described by Breakthrough Agile.

From the diagram, it is clear that starting with the principles and the 5 CBPs is key to a successful Agile transformation. As people adopt Breakthrough Agile's principles, the organization will experience levels of tension and conflict that need to be addressed. At times, leaders in the organization need to view the start of a transformation much like the way a child learns to ride a bike. At first, there is a need, want or motivation on the part of the child to ride the bike. At this point, resources, a bike, is provided for the purpose. Usually, the bike has stabilizer wheels on it. After the child becomes proficient at riding with stabilizer wheels under the observation of their coach (parent), then, the next stage of the transformation journey starts. The bike is redesigned without stabilizer wheels. With a guiding hand from the coach on the bike, the child begins to pedal and find their balance on their own. As this journey is underway, the child then becomes proficient at the other needed activities to ride a bike. The child learns to get on and off the bike without help. As the journey to ride a bike enters the final stage, the child is learning to use the wheel brakes, ride long distances, make sharp turns, and going over different terrain. The guiding hand in this analogy is the transformation team, and early-stage champions of the transformation. As the child then begins to ride on their own, they become teachers and coaches themselves. Gaining the experience and skill at understanding the system (bike riding) and explaining it to those who need assistance. This evolution of skills and abilities is self-perpetuating in a robust system that fully practices and adapts the principles of the transformation model.

It is important to note how an organization can miss the mark when getting started. Frequently, organizations start a transformation with the intention of changing its culture knowing the value that the transformation platform can deliver. However, when starting at day 0, the change champions are in conflict with the entrenched principles of the organization. Usually, these principles sustain the conservative approach to running the business. As the conflict increases at this early stage and the champions seek to gain credibility within the organization, the movement finds itself in a transformation trap. To gain credibility and to meet the expectations of the "old school" culture, the transformation is forced to deliver the "quick wins." What this means is that the current organization's leaders require the transformation to lead with action and results first. This trap occurs most frequently in organizations that embrace a principle of cost cutting in their cultural business processes. In this scenario, the effort to transform isn't the focus but winning short-term gains is the output of the transformation. The transformation's principles are not introduced and limited resources are assigned to help the employees understand them and how they impact the way of working in the organization. Simply stated, the why of the transformation is overshadowed by the zeal to show short-term results.

In the low hanging fruit approach, employees are required to learn and implement the systems and tools of the transformation to achieve the short-term win. The long-term outcome and future culture is sacrificed to maintain the current traditional principles that define the current culture. As employees are spending thousands of hours in training and attempting to learn the new transformation systems, the organization is still practicing the 5 CBPs as before. Ironically, the organization although in a transformation state, is still working as it did in the past. Small scale changes, improvement to processes that are removed from the core business processes, and limited transformation resources are evidence that this approach is being used by the organization. In this situation, there are two journeys that are underway. The first journey is the Transformation Journey that has been broadly marketed by the organization, the second journey is the resistant journey comprised of those in positions of power and control who are maintaining the current organization structure to retain their status

As this dual system of work continues within the organization, "camps" develop and silo's thinking becomes stronger. One camp is made up of the champions of the transformation. These individuals have a clear vision as to how the organization can change its culture and that this would benefit the future of the organization and its sustainability. The other camp is in favor of the old way of working. This camp means well and reflects the risk adverse and conservative side of the organization. Within this camp are people who continue to believe in the principles of the traditional leadership, hierarchical control, and command principles. This group continues to practice the 5 CBPs as they did before and fear changing. This is reflective of a culture that seeks to maintain the status quo and avoid taking risks. Creation of value escapes this camp, but protection of the current state of the business is guaranteed. Here is where fear mongering around the transformation can take place. Statements like, "do we risk our business" or "we don't have time for this" begin to echo from the conservative camp on transformation activities. These conservative voices are a powerful force within the organization. They generally are the ones in positions of power and influence. Ironically, they usually are the people that are responsible for introducing and launching the transformation at the start. The duality in thought, and conflicting polarities that exist are driving factors in how far an organization will go, and the pace of change. At times, if feels as if the success of the transformation is a contest over which of these two camps gets their way.

Most transformations are derailed as the old way of working camp overtakes the new way of working principles. One purpose of this book is to show you why this happens. The derailment starts at the early stages of the transformation. A reactive strategy from the old ways of working is to lull the transformation champions into the quick win scenario or focus their time and energy on applying the transformation systems before spending time educating the organization on the new principles that drive the transformation. This strategy emerges because people continue to practice the 5 CBPs using the traditional principles of the organization. For example, performance management doesn't change at the start of the transformation journey. A key cultural change as a result of the transformation is for people to be empowered, take risks, and fail fast. How do you think the project lead shows up when they are aware their bonus and merit increase is tied to the output of their project? How big of a risk will the person take? How empowered will they be to make their own decisions without getting endorsement from their seniors two or three levels up within the organization? In my experience, very few people jump onto the new platform when they know their personal pocket book might get smaller as a result or their career may be shortened.

As a result, project leaders behave and think like they did before. Project teams create a perfect waterfall chart for the project's deployment. The plan goes down to the number of hours individual will spend over the next 2- to

3-year period. The strategic output for the plan is prioritized on how much budget is available and what are the key performance indicators (KPIs) that need to be maintained or improved. Compounding these realities is the mindset of the project leader. The project leader may have less interest in the value generated for the customer, and be more focused on how the project makes them look and increases or decreases their advancement opportunities. The project leader's focus is to keep the team and the project in the comfort zone of the higher level review committee, and avoid being a target for criticism. The project leader then spends hundreds of hours preparing slide decks that will be presented to a committee or review team made up of senior leaders for their endorsement (approval). This review body is a decision making governance team that serves to minimize risk. Generally, a consensus of this group is needed for a project to move forward. In the end, group consensus is usually achieved after the project's innovative actions are minimized to a level that doesn't cause disruption or the threat of instability. This slow moving process was a catalyst for the original Agile pioneers to create Scrum and recreate how projects move within the organization. This process is then repeated for each high profile project, and round and round the organization goes with its old way of project management under the banner of transformation.

This model gets minimized within Breakthrough Agile. The approach recognizes that to make a change from within, the organization needs to educate and practice the principles of the transformation methodology. Without first adopting new principles and educating people within the organization on how they influence the 5 CBPs, the organization is at risk of being derailed by the old school of working. As the review committee approach repeats itself with every cycle, the change champions become fatigued. They sense that the organization is challenged between how work should bne practiced and how it hasn't changed from the past. To minimize the impact, a compromise is communicated within the organization on how to work. As stated previously, this is where the "fit for purpose" or "nice to have" approach is adopted for the cultural change. As the momentum shifts to more people working as they did before the transformation, organizational demands are made of the transformation champions. Their roles change, and their job scope moves further away from the original intent of the transformation. At this point, the transformation team that started the journey begins to feel the pressure to conform and try to generate a safe landing space for themselves. They start to bend and give in by modifying their actions to meet the expectations of the resistors.

As this continues, they stop advocating the new ways of working in the organization, and go back to an older model of continuous improvement or operational excellence.

As a result, the transformation journey becomes a nice to have but a lower priority on every employee's agenda. It is a scenario that I have experienced, seen, and heard about many times. That is why it is critical that organizations start with changing the principles of the company when starting the transformation. This is to ensure that the organization doesn't create the dual working system which leaves the proponents of the transformation without the support they need when the transformation begins to take root within the culture of the organization.

When following the roadmap of Breakthrough Agile, people will sense a change in how the cultural business processes are executed. The output from these processes will be different from what it was in the past. Mindsets and behaviors of individuals across the organization reflect the changes. Leaders state to talk more about empowerment, and letting go. Questions about accountability at the lower level, and coaching for performance start to happen. Leaders make it a priority to attend calls, or meetings that specifically focus on the new systems, or Agile ways of working with the transformation. This change in mindset and behaviors indicates the potential cultural shift to an Agile organization.

In a Breakthrough Agile organization, people will experience decisions that are more customer centric and employees will feel empowered to take decisions that impacts their work. These actions encompass solving problems, creating solutions, prioritization, and interactions with customers. Even the interactions between teams will change and reflect the principles of the new culture. Employees begin to innovate on solutions that enhance their engagement with its customers. Leaders let go of control and find a different purpose to their role as a leader. In the transformation, leaders realize their impact and contribution to growing and developing teams and individuals through effective coaching. Their role may be characterized as a role model that practices the Socratic method of teaching. Through a curious and questioning behavior, the leader will help teams understand what is the most impactful action to an opportunity or problem. By teaching and sharing stories of their experiences, by asking what, and how questions, and by showing up as a humble listener, the leader will influence the content of how teams complete their work. It is a core understanding of Breakthrough Agile that once the organization starts the journey, leadership changes 180 degrees from the command and control model. Success will be experience through the delivery of higher valued-added actions and the creation of an ecosystem that fosters everyone learning how to transform the organization on a day-to-day basis.

For example, in Breakthrough Agile, partnering relationships over transactional relationships is a principle found in decision making. By consciously focusing on being a better partner, both internally and externally, employees will decide on actions to create solutions, make proposals, and create strategic visions that are different from a company that focuses on cost control or efficiency. This principle will positively influence the quality and value of the actions taken by the team or individual. To experience this principle to the fullest, we need to understand how we have been groomed to think and act in a transactional way across the world. All of us have been groomed by institutions such as our education system, government services, or being consumers to associate value as a transaction. We study and pass examinations to move from one level of education to the next. In the end, we receive a diploma that designates us as a subject matter expert in a certain field. Or with a government service, after reaching a certain age, being able to receive a license to operate a motor vehicle after paying a fee. For people who fly frequently, there is a value seen in the purchase of a certain class of travel. A business class passenger expects meals served on porcelain plates and a selection of wine for the price of ticket. The economy class passenger expects crowded and cramped seating for the duration of the flight. In Breakthrough Agile, the transactional behavior that we've learned a lived with for years is minimized, and the new culture moves towards employees that use a growth mindset, and teams that practice psychological safety. This change in how we relate to each other also gets transferred to how we engage with the customer.

Employees need to develop empathy skills when communicating with their colleagues and customers. Learning from failure, being aware of one's own limitations, and realizing that individuals are imperfect is the basis for building high performance relationships and teams with Breakthrough Agile. Growing one's sense of self-awareness brings people closer to being more empathetic to others in the organization and customers. In traditional organizations, the principle of knowledge is power is at the forefront in how people interact with each other. In a partnering organization, information is not withheld, or altered to control the reaction of those in the discussion. In a transactional organization, people would limit information flow between teams, departments, and business units to control reactions and direct others. At times, even creating falsehoods that are used to invoke fear or motivate others to act in a certain way. Many times, I have been in a meeting and heard someone say that they were speaking on behalf of the senior most person in the organization in an attempt to persuade others to take a certain action. Afterward, it is then discovered that the statement was false and only used to control others.

In a transactional organization, information is disseminated through the hierarchical organizational structure by leaders with the intent to release only what they feel is needed. Those at the top are seen to have the critical information and knowledge of the future. The *few controlling the many* through information bites invokes images of tyrants and dictators, but this is happening in today's business organizations. Whether done with good intentions, or as a result of a leader's ego, this is a power play that repeats itself daily in the business world today. Managing information flow is seen as a skill and has a perceived value to it by a traditional organization. Those that practice it understand this fact, and know how to hold on, or control information to maintain the current power structure. Have you ever been in a conversation where someone said what they are talking about was confidential? Didn't that make you feel like you had additional power in the organization? Or that you were working within the inner circle of those with power and control.

In my travels, I have worked in countries that limit internet access. It confirms my observation that those who have this transactional mindset, view information as power. One reason why Agile appeals to businesses today, is due to the principles of openness and transparency of what is important for the business. Most industrialized countries today have unlimited access to all information. With this dynamic change in how easily accessible information is to anyone, organization's find it difficult to control information that was previously used by individuals in power plays over their team. Think of government regulations and laws that cover the marketing and distribution of product within the country's geography. In the past, this was seen as specialist knowledge, but in today's business world, it is widely available on websites sponsored by the government. And if information is power, then why wouldn't we want it to be shared with everyone. Shouldn't everyone be as informed as possible on how to work with a customer, build partnerships with colleagues, and create value for the organization. Breakthrough Agile will empower customer facing personnel with the skills necessary to uncover the needs, wants, and motivations of the customer. This information will be used to help the organization build a partnering relationship with the customer. In the end, the company looks to increase their presence and gain more interface with the customer through communications, but it also implies that if the company isn't in opposition to help the customer as a broker or middle man in meeting their needs. This is how we want to build partnering relationships within Breakthrough Agile. The principles will help an organization build long-term relationships and better business outcomes. This partnering relationship promotes a culture that listens and cares for the needs of the customer. Employees, whether dealing internally with peers or externally with a customer, see success as helping others be successful through the sharing of knowledge, skills, and insights that are needed at the present moment. By practicing this behavior, being open with information, and developing empathetic relationships with our colleagues and peers, productivity and value will increase in the future. A customer will more likely be open to meet and hear about new products or services when the relationship has been built on this partnering framework. Breakthrough Agile's principle of partnering would enable the organization to achieve more with its customer both in the short term and long term. This leads to the question, where does an organization start when deciding to utilize Breakthrough Agile.

Where and how an organization starts their journey can influence the success of the entire effort. In my career, I have experienced many approaches to change an organization's way of working and the culture. Prevalent in most of these experiences is the approach to start with the mindset first. In these organizations time is spent on raising awareness of what it is meant to be a team leader, team member, and work in a team environment in the new organization. We ask people to self-reflect on how they lead or work currently and what impact the transformation will have on the current state of operations. Leaders are usually the primary target for this approach. The belief is that they currently uphold the current way of working, so changing their belief system first will lead to a successful transformation. The hypothesis is stated, "If we are successful at changing the mindset and behavior of the people's leaders, then they will role model the mindset and behaviors for others to follow."

Results are mixed with this approach and for some organizations, this is a good starting point. Also, it is a low-risk approach as it doesn't impact directly how the organization builds its product or receives revenues for the product or services. The drawback with this approach is that there is no consequence for a leader being non-compliant with the new leadership framework or principles of the transformation. Most transformations introduce a set of behaviors that are loosely defined enough that a leader can easily fit their current way of working into the new way without really changing anything at all about their leadership style. For instance, being a servant leader is a popular model for a leader today. A servant leadership has clear descriptions as to what it means to be a servant leader. However, leaders will follow a more intuitive approach to the leadership model, and begin to think that actions like opening the door for employees to enter first or serving them breakfast in the cafeteria defines them as servant leaders. These are fond and gratuitous gestures and I think very polite but they are far from the mark as to what a servant leader should be doing. I have even seen leaders who feel they are servant leaders because they leave the parking spots closest to the entrance door free for lower level employees to use. Again, if the true principles of a servant leader were applied to organizations that say they practice servant leadership, many would fall far short of the standard. This type of false practice is the type of role modeling that can occur with the leader's first approach.

In my experience, the leader's first approach and efforts to change generally stalls as the pull to see leaders change more dramatically into areas that are outside their comfort and knowledge zone is challenged by the ever present need for short-term results. This later pressure is too great for leader's to manage and instead of working through the struggle, leaders fall back into the command and control leadership model – hierarchy and positional power deciding what to do and when. At this point, the transformation team realizes that their deployment strategy is at risk and they start to rebrand or self-correct the strategy, most likely to a more conservative and less disruptive approach. The dynamics at this point are complex. Leaders are acting more and more like they did before the transformation. The same meetings and business processes are executed the same as before. The transformation team is still active in its efforts to change the organization for the better. And the majority of the organization's population is looking to the leader's and the message they are sending. In my experience, this leads to an organization that becomes good at talking the talk but isn't walking the walk of being Agile.

Another drawback of the leader lead approach is that the organization never moves past the training on mindset. In the leader led approach, the leaders are told that they are giving up part of their power and authority. Through empowerment, delegation of decisions, deploying self-management techniques, and moving away from leader led initiatives, it is understandable that this group of people will resist and slow down any changes. What typically happens is that decisions on the pace of change, or scope of work for the transformation is consensually decided upon by a group of leaders. I have seen leaders delay meetings for months because they couldn't align everyone's calendars to meet to discuss a transformation topic. What is telling in this example, is that the leaders didn't prioritize the transformation meeting over routine daily work in order to get everyone together and discuss a path forward.

Many other stalling and undermining tactics can happen. With the leader led approach, after a year or two of sounding boards, huddles, town halls, and other deep discussion types of actions, people begin to question what value is the transformation delivering. Where are the results that were promised with adopting Agile ways of working that were communicated to everyone at the initial roll out of the program? In other cases, as the "mindset first" approach continues, the organization becomes fatigued with the underperformance of the transformation. The enthusiasm for the new ways of working evaporates. Within this scenario, a few events can catalyze this drop in momentum. The original experts and champions of the effort find new roles as they start to see the resistance of leaders to the transformation and how the organization continues to bargain on change. More people continue to work as they did prior to the transformation roll out. Or the organization reduces the current resources or fails to add the needed additional resources to continue with the transformation. The decision makers will rationalize the additional resource request in this way, "Why invest more in a transformation that isn't showing a major contribution or impact to the organization?" Another sterilizing scenario for the transformation is that the senior leaders who originally championed the approach leave the organization. To their credit, they know how to market themselves for a higher, better paying position. When they are interviewing for the next big role, they can fall back onto their experience when the question comes up, "what changes did they bring to the previous organization?" with the initial roll out of the transformation at the current or prior company. What better self-promotion tactic for a higher level role than to claim that they lead an organization transformation for the last few years. For these leaders, after just a year or two, is usually enough evidence in the "result column" of the leader's scorecard for the leader to support their promotion into the next higher pay grade. As one can see, many things can happen to derail a transformation effort.

Seemingly, random organization changes displace those who were key change agents in the transformation efforts. Discontinuation of transformation roles or combining them with traditional roles is another way to slow the pace of change. In one case study, a senior leader who was an excellent transformation champion and senior leader within the organization took a global role on the transformation team. The intent and the promise in the new role was to take the transformation to the next level of performance across the organization. Once the person was in the new role, the global team reorganized with a change in reporting lines for this senior leader. In the end, instead of sitting in the same meetings with the senior leaders where their influence would have been much greater, the transformation leader was reporting one level down to a senior leaders. In a traditional organization, imagine the limiting impact that this reorganization had on influencing others at a high level to adopt transformation mindsets and behaviors. As you could imagine, with this change, the senior leader was piqued and after a few months, left the organization to pursue their career with a competitor. The way this particular story ends is that the global transformation team practically dissolved after this person left the organization, as did the enthusiasm across the division for the transformation. Imagine the scars the organization has from this action on the current and future efforts to transform the organization. A lack of trust develops within the organization for any future transformation efforts.

The design of Breakthrough Agile is different from the previous ways of deploying a transformation effort. It has a different starting point to build this trust in the platform and show the organization results that impact the competitiveness of the organization. In essence, when starting with the mindset first, the culture of the old organization continues and it dominates over the fledgling new way of working. Another way to state it, is that the 5 CBPs of the old way of working derailed the transformation efforts.

If the mindset first approach isn't used, then an alternative is the system first approach. What we are saying here is to start with the systems of the transformation platform. For a company with the intent on being an Agile organization, that would mean adopting the Agile ways of working first. In other words, have the organization start to use Scrum to solve problems and meet the needs of the customer. Using this approach, I have seen quicker growth on the transformation journey as it generally produces physical changes in the organization. By starting with the systems first approach, people within the organization learn by doing. This is an excellent way to gain traction in a transformation. Let's follow the journey of a systems first Agile Transformation. Most would start with Scrum as the Agile system. Scrum, in a concise way of speaking, is based on using a small cross-functional team, with user requirements or stories, that follows a sprint approach to developing a minimal viable product (MVP). The MVP is an outcome that contributes to the development of a scalable solution or service that the organization can generate value off of. By starting here with the transformation, senior leaders and employees alike see how the new way of working delivers value-adding outcomes for the organization. This then generates an enthusiasm and commitment from people in the organization to work using the new ways of working. If done well, then the process repeats itself, and scales up and across each business unit or team. Along the way, the transformation team then starts a parallel campaign on building the Agile mindset for leaders and employees. Scrum is one system to start with, additional systems to consider when starting with the system's first approach are visual Kanban board, Objective and Key Results (OKRs), and Self-Managed teams. Generally, a system's first approach produces good results. In this systems first approach, the expectation from the old school organization is met, by showing quantifiable results, and a broad cross section of the organization experiences the new way of working. Also, people began to sense that the organization is changing since there are physical changes to the work environment.

One story I enjoy telling people about happened while I was leading a transformation at a medical device manufacturer where I used the system first approach. The business was a pioneer in the development of the particular medical product and over the course of years grew in size and revenues. The founders were loyal to the geographic area they lived in and kept their growing company within this location when I started with the company. As the company grew to an organization with hundreds of millions in revenue, the company retain its local color. Even at the time I joined, there were still people who remembered working with the founders and told stories of going on sales calls with them to doctor's offices to sell their devices. Within the MFG areas, certain pieces of equipment were named after the engineers who designed them. The inline washers for product carriers were designed by an engineer who worked for their entire career with the company and it bore his name. My role when I joined the company was to lead this brownfield organization through a Lean transformation. The GM at the time wanted to turn the company around to try and avoid a plant closure. His thoughts were that if the company can show higher productivity through lower costs, then the decision to close would be delayed or reversed. My approach was to start the transformation by using kaizens for process improvements that were identified through the analysis of value stream mapping. The organization's first major kaizen, a 5-day event, was on a production line that had much of its equipment designed by in-house engineers, in a clean room that looked more like a storage room, and ran at an efficiency rate of less than 60%.

As the planning for this kaizen was underway, the leader of the kaizen team met resistance from the production manager. As it turned out, even though we were starting with a system's first approach, key decisions by the production manager and other senior leaders were made based on the principles of a command and control and hierarchical organization. I remember heated discussions with the production manager about the start date for the kaizen event. The goal of the kaizen was to improve the production line's yield and quality through a pull system and standardized work. The production manager agreed on the goal; however, he wanted to work overtime to build up inventory before shutting down the line for the kaizen. Time and again, he delayed the start of the kaizen because he didn't have the inventory at the right level. The traditional principle of risk aversion through higher inventory. My position was that we were trying to improve the process to gain a better yield, and when we were successful, he would produce more good products on regular time than on overtime. A cost saving in my mind. I was following the Lean principle of quality first.

After taking a hard stand with this manager, the kaizen team was given a firm date to start the kaizen. The team executed the kaizen and the results showed an increase in yield by 15%, reduction in inventory by over 40% and a more organized and cleaner working environment. The kaizen team introduced a pull system within the line, created an in-line inspection cell and linked primary packing to the manufacturing of the product. After the kaizen, the line was running at over 80% efficiency, the cost to produce a product had been reduced, and employees in the plant were overwhelmed with enthusiasm to be part of the kaizen event. The senior leaders including the production manager all became champions of the Lean transformation. So much so, that the next few kaizen events were completed in the quality labs to increase their efficiency and throughput.

This is one example of starting with a system first approach to build by-in and move the organization down the transformation journey path quickly. The resistance doesn't end even when the systems produce outstanding results. In this same plant, the company was faced with a health authority warning letter over a high volume of customer complaints. In order to remediate this product risk, the equipment to the assembly line needed modified. There were a few senior leaders that didn't agree with my assessment, and wanted to build an entire new assembly line. In order to resolve this risk and remediate the quality issue raised in the warning letter for at the company, I had to move forward with my problem-solving analysis with little senior level support. The problem analysis and following solution for the problem was to modify the washer equipment to perform at a higher standard. To meet this goal, a small team of myself and two engineers conducted experiments on the washer equipment to optimize it capability. In the end, the modification showed a substantial improvement in cleaning, and after the proper documentation was completed, the change went live, and the plant saw a reduction in this customer complaint. As a change champion, being persistent is a needed behavior. With this Lean Journey, the system approach was successful. After a few years, the organization had a working Lean Culture. The site received recognition from the Association of American Manufacturing Excellence, and the next milestone was to apply for a low level Shingo Award.

After a few years of value stream mapping, kaizens, and gemba walks, the culture of the organization changed. To me, when I think of evidence of a cultural change, I like to hear it from those who experienced it. To that point, one day at this company, a senior maintenance supervisor pulled me to the side for a quick chat. I will always remember what he said to me. He stated that he was extremely grateful for the work that I was doing with the organization. In his opinion, by introducing the Lean systems into the organization, he started to see changes in how people worked. He and his team realized that there was a different way to approach work using the Lean systems. In his comments, he stated that prior to the transformation, he hated coming to work because no one would listen to his ideas or try to fix inefficient processes. With the Lean transformation, we introduced the Lean system of kaizen and started to address issues using a team-based approach. Through the kaizen events, Lean visual management system, and the efforts to eliminate waste, this supervisor recognized that we had changed the culture of the organization. By starting with a system first approach, this organization changed its way of working, and through the journey, the mindset of employees at the company. The organization's culture changed as a direct result of the Lean transformation. But with this approach, the journey doesn't reach the full potential of the change.

As the culture started to shift, the anti-patterns that derail a transformation grew stronger. Unfortunately, the roots of Lean didn't get firmly entrenched. As mentioned earlier, when deploying a transformation, two camps develop. In this case, the old school camp took advantage of the new school's lack of internal networking. As the success of the Lean efforts grew, a few senior leaders complained to their global counterparts about the perceived additional work and reorganization. Reaction with a conservative mindset, the global community became skeptical of the site's Lean efforts and the risk that it introduced to a regulated product. As you can imagine this additional pressure, and scrutiny, derailed the future plans for the transformation. In the end, the VP of operations followed through on the plant closure decision as a priority. The Lean efforts were sidelined and the plant's biggest priority was to manage the transfer of the technology to a low-cost region.

In the end, the plant was decommissioned as part of a global footprint reorganization. All employees, some with other 30 years of service were given retirement/exit packages and others offered roles elsewhere if they wanted to relocate. The product moved to a low-cost country (LCC). After the technology transfer and validation, the device is still available to customers across the world. In light of the transformation successes, the organization still made decisions, developed their strategy, managed conflicts, practiced performance management, and managed projects based on the traditional way of working.

Another short-sightedness of companies is to start with grassroots activities. This is a slightly different approach than the systems first approach. *Just do it,* has been a motivational phrase when applying the grassroots approach. Although an effective way to generate some early successes and momentum, the drawback to the *just do it* approach is that it allows leaders to hand off the responsibilities of the transformation to less empowered employees across the organization. Leaders direct employees to, just do it: Mindset or behaviors, systems, discussions, whatever the employees feel is needed. Sort of a bottom–up approach that generates early interest in the transformation. This approach leads to sparks of innovation within the organization. What is generally seen when applying the Just Do It approach to an Agile transformation are pockets of people getting certified as scrum masters, product owners, and design thinkers. In lean or six sigma transformations, people become Lean experts, green belts, black belts, or other types of roles or subject matter experts. Since budget dollars are usually spent on the certification, managers then want to see a return on this investment. This leads to a scattering of sprints, kaizens, continuous improvement activities, bottom–up suggestion systems, and off-site workshops that people misconstrue as being transformative. The belief of the *just do it* approach is that more of anything and everything is better.

In the "just do it" efforts, there is a sponsor at the senior level who permits or delegates the space to transform. With this stamp of approval, leaders within the organization construct a strategy that is the least disruptive to the current daily operations. At times, I have seen where the transformation becomes the responsibility of an entry level engineer or junior level finance business partner whose passion is in the right place but lacks the skills and abilities to manage the politics in the organization. As you can imagine without the key resources, structure, and commitment of senior leaders, the transformation efforts will fall short of delivering any significant value that reinforces the transformation's systems. A learning to share is that when the organization does not educate and train its employees on the principles of the transformation platform, the changes and results of the activities are usually at the superficial level. In these superficial transformations, how the organization is structured, how product is manufactured, and delivered to the customer remains the same. Similar to those companies that bolt on the transformation's framework to the traditional organization, in the "just do it" approach, there is a gap between how things worked before, to the way things could work under the new transformation platform.

When there is a clear understanding and adoption of the transformation platform's principles, an organization will see changes in the output of their 5 CBPs. In Breakthrough Agile, start with the transformation platform's principles and embed these in how the 5 CBPs are executed. To realize the value of the transformation's potential the cultural business processes need to compliment the Agile Systems. Additionally, the organization will scale up quicker after the initial kick off and on-board future employees into the new culture of the organization by starting with the 5 CBPs. Following Breakthrough Agile's approach, a broader and deeper level commitment to change is generated. Everyone starts by understanding the principles and how that will affect the work they do daily. At the same time, the organization is practicing and experimenting with the principles through the 5 CBPs. People begin to experience, see, and hear themselves behaving differently and seeing better outcomes for the customer. In Breakthrough Agile, what an organization experiences is that once the principles are embedded within the organization, they will influence the outputs of the 5 CBPs, then adopting Agile ways of working is easier. This dynamic combination drives the organization into moving quicker on actions that deliver higher value adding results. Figure 3.2 helps us understand the relationship between these different parts of the organization's ecosystem.

Here is how starting a Lean transformation looks when starting with principles and value.

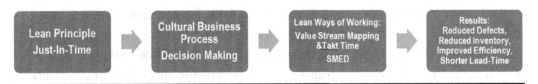

Figure 3.2   Breakthrough Agile's model.

In this case, the starting point is to ensure that everyone understands at a basic level the principle of Just-in-Time. As this principle is better understood, then in daily meetings with topics like product availability, inventory, and operational planning, Just-in-Time is embedded in the decision-making process. To increase the satisfaction of the customer, teams would utilize lean ways of working such as value stream mapping, takt time calculation, Kanban, and 1 pcs flow. As the organization experiments with a Just In Time mindset, its culture begins to change. As the culture changes and the Lean systems are better understood, then better actions are developed. This leads to better results for the organization. In this case, improvement in quality, inventory costs, and lead time are realized.

This point is articulated and emphasized as being critical to the success of Breakthrough Agile. When the organization fails to learn the principles of the transformation platform, then they underutilized the effect of the platform's systems. Too often, companies will start a transformation by deploying the systems (ways of working) of the transformation platform either through actions or mindset, without fully establishing the foundation of getting people to understand the frameworks principles and how they influence the organization's 5 CBPs. When starting at the transformation's systems, the company continues to practice the 5 CBPs as they did before. This creates the dual culture within the organization. This duality within the organization leads to confusion, lack of focus, and competing priorities. In the end, a poor foundation is built for the deployment of the transformation ways of working. Figure 3.3 illustrates were most transformation start.

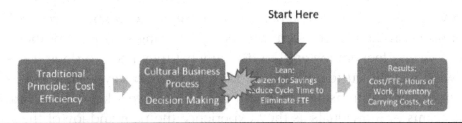

Figure 3.3   High risk of failure transformation deployment.

As you read more about the Breakthrough Agile and how it relies upon this foundation of using principles to change the 5 CBPs, it is apparent that the impact to the business is tremendous. The model above (Figure 3.2) may be interpreted by some that top- or bottom-line improvement isn't an outcome of the model. That is a misconception that needs to be addressed at this point and it reflects how the traditional principles influence our thinking unconsciously.

When changes happen with an organization's 5 CBPs, the results of the actions come from Agile systems or ways of working. By adopting Breakthrough Agile, the organization will identify, define, and deliver the highest value adding solutions or products to the customer through an Agile system. By adopting the platform's principles, the organization changes the fundamental processes that shape its culture. For example, senior leaders in the organization will have to learn to let go of their control in the decision-making process for actions that directly impact the customer. When all leaders take this step, a major shift in the culture of the organization occurs. Teams feel the shift in responsibility and start to take ownership over their work and its results. Leaders play a different role with their teams. They no longer direct and control their activities. They now become coaches and seek to understand how their teams are performing and operating. Senior leaders provide their guidance through open-ended questioning and thought-provoking discussions. The initial feeling for everyone in this new culture is one of uncertainty and this is natural since this is a new way of working that didn't exist before. Both leaders and teams alike need to relearn how to work in this new environment and the organization needs to allow this experimenting and growth to occur during these first few phases of the transformation journey. As the entire organization starts this journey, then people will start to experience success that they couldn't achieve under the traditional organization. New ideas, different solutions, and teams working more collaboratively will all produce better results for the organization and higher quality service and product for the customer. The outcome is that the organization has discovered the key to unlock the full potential of their employees' experience, skill, and innovation. Employees start to experience being in control of their own work and feel empowered to decide what they need to do and how they will meet the customer's needs. Leaders need to stay visible and present during the transformation journey. They serve a key role as coach to the teams or individuals as they experience the pain and joy of the transformation.

Let's look at an example of how Breakthrough Agile's framework operates with 1 of the 5 CBPs. In Breakthrough Agile, conflict resolution is a cultural business process that has the potential of developing talent and creating stronger relationships within the organization. In most organizations, when a conflict occurs between two people, it gets resolved at the next higher level in the organization if the two people are unable or unwilling to work it out. By escalating conflict to a higher positional authority for resolution, these two individuals avoid the pain of growing and developing a way to cope with personal conflict. They delay their ability and minimize their communication and empathy skills. Having effective conflict resolution skills is a key behavior for Breakthrough Agile. When an organization adopts Agile as its transformation platform, one of the key Agile ways of working is Scrum. Scrum, with its different ceremonies and sprints, focuses a team on producing a product in a short amount of time. In a Scrum event, it is critical for people to speak up, challenge each other, say no to activities, and have meaningful conversations that impact the quality of the MVP that comes out of the Scrum. Healthy tension should occur in a Scrum to help the team design the best MVP. When the organization educates its employees on the principles of conflict resolution and how to manage conflict at the lowest level, then this knowledge transfers into the Scrum activities and teams are able to hear diverse opinions and respond to the idea versus reacting to the person who stated the opinion. This moves the team forward faster, and opens up many more possibilities for solutions for the customer. As a result, the team's MVP is of higher quality to the customer. The solutions that come out of the Scrum will be more focused on the customer needs, wants, and motivations. As more diversity of opinions, challenging ideas, and synergizing on decisions occur, then the team produces an MVP that will meet the success criteria and definition of one of the Scrum.

The flip side, not educating people on principles of conflict resolution will result in a lack of diversity and challenging ideas in the MVP. Most likely, the Scrum event will have one or two outspoken people who may end up monopolizing the brainstorming activities or be threatening to others on the team that have diverse opinions. In the end, limited ideas are heard and discussed for the MVP. The final ideas that go into the MVP reflect those on the team that felt safe to speak up or those who were the dominating players on the team. Others avoided conflict by withholding their ideas. Since the organization did not start with building the foundation of conflict resolution with its team members, the Agile system (Scrum) produced a semi-optimal result. As a one-off event, this might not derail an Agile transformation. However, if left uncorrected, then the organization starts to see enthusiasm and support for Scrum events wane. People stop volunteering or even participating in sprints. Common or routine activities are prioritized over the Scrum, which is a derailing experience for the transformation. Scrum is a defining characteristic of an Agile organization and if this becomes an unused system in the organization, then the organization has fallen back on its old ways of working for generating new solutions for its customers.

This chapter is setting up the reader to understand that the transformation's principles are key to unlocking the potential of the organization. Let's look into the principles of Breakthrough Agile. These principles are based upon the current thinking on how an organization will succeed in the future. The principles are compiled from research into areas of management including self-management, various leadership models, the Agile manifesto, and observations on what organizations are in need of improving to achieve breakthrough results. The principles (Figure 3.4) reflect holistically how organizations set its standard for execution of the 5 CBPs. Figure 3.4 depicts the principles of Breakthrough Agile.

Figure 3.5 depicts the starting point for successful transformation.

As you review these principles, it is important to realize that they are the basis for change within the organization. Adapting them will

Breakthrough Agile Principles	5 Cultural Business Processes
Equal Power among all employees. Avoid Hierarchy Single decision making at all levels Decision-Making speed correlates to delivering results Experiment to learn, grow, and experiment Start with the customer need, known or unknown	Decision Making
Develop capacity to empathize Listen to understand. Discuss the idea, do not respond to the person Diversity supports growth and development Deal with conflict. Avoid escalation	Conflict Resolution
Empathize from customer's needs, wants, and motivations Transparency of work produces high performance Plan for the long-term value, execute for short term delivery MVP thinking for every solution	Strategy Planning
Less is more, Prioritize Speed of design, development, production, and delivery is key Change is welcomed and wanted People contribute through scope of work, not positional hierarchy	Project Management
Team first-individual second Peer feedback drives high performance Level playing field each cycle. Avoid Confirmation and Halo Bias Team objectives are clear, focused and challenging	Performance Management

Figure 3.4 Breakthrough Agile's principles as related to cultural business processes.

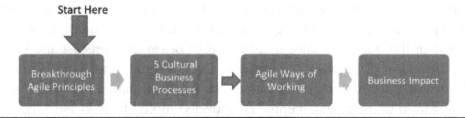

Figure 3.5   Starting point for successful transformation – Breakthrough Agile's deployment point.

change how leaders lead, the conversations and discussions between individuals, team work routines, and the way people grow and develop. The language, actions, and behaviors of the organization will change to reflect the value that is inherent in the principles. This change symbolizes the transformation and its desired outcome of being customer centric and a partner in society. As the transformation takes roots, then the organizational structure and focus on the customer changes. Over time, the organization sees products and services change as a result of adopting the principles and changing its practice of the 5 CBPs. Here the impact of Breakthrough Agile (Figure 3.5) grows exponentially to a point that customers see the change and are drawn to work with the organization. How many companies do you know where customers state it is a pleasure or joy to work with? Breakthrough Agile delivers this value to both the organization and its customers.

When you understand how principles and the 5 CBPs impact the ways of working, the reader will appreciate that this type of transformation takes time. Along the way, expect to experience the highs and lows that come with any change. Organizations, teams, and individuals will struggle with the transition towards the better culture. At times, people may voluntarily leave and in their exit interview take aim at the transformation efforts. This instability is part of the growth process and the organization needs to prepare themselves for these types of experiences. For any transformation to succeed in its early phases, it takes a disciplined and committed set of leaders who passionately believed that their organization has the capacity and capability to change their ways of working to those of the transformation platform.

Take for example, a commercial operation that has adopted Breakthrough Agile and is working its way through the struggles of making decisions differently and embracing a new organization structure that reflects a network versus a line and staff hierarchy. After a little more than a year of working through the tactics that are changing the structure, the leadership team experiences a sour monthly financial meeting. In the meeting, it is relayed that the quarterly sales numbers were below the forecast and short of the aspiration of growing the business. As the senior leadership team analyzes this information and discusses the financial gap, a few of the senior leaders started to make statements that sounded more like leaders of the past. Under this financial pressure, the majority of the senior leaders fell back on their micromanaging tendencies.

As their coach, I experienced this when I started to hear leaders state they needed to be consulted on all the activities that the sales team was doing. The senior leaders wanted to take back the empowerment given during the transformation and require all decisions to be routed through them for approval or fine tuning. The financial pressure triggered the fear of failure and as a result, the leadership team resorted to placing blame or fault on someone or in this case, the transformation organizational structure. The senior leaders mistakenly sensed that the new way of working was the cause of the drop in sales. Since people weren't being watched and micro-managed, then they must not be doing their jobs right. That was the collective rationale of the senior leaders of the organization. It reached a point where some leaders stated that they needed to stop the transformation efforts and go back to the old way of working. All of this fear in the senior leader team was directed at the principles of decision making and the new way of working (empowerment) for the sales teams. The senior leaders wanted to go back to having sales representatives go over their script for sales calls with the manager so it can be endorsed. This also included the senior leaders asking sales representatives to provide them with a detailed plan of who they plan to meet with, the ways they communicated with the contact and how, i.e., email, phone call, etc. The spreadsheet that captured this information would take sales representative hours to complete for all their contacts for a week. Imagine the wasted time on the part of the sales representative to fill out this spreadsheet, when they could have been building better relationships with their customers. This was all triggered by a monthly financial sales report that had disappointing information.

A principle of decision making in Breakthrough Agile is to enable decisions to be made by an individual at the lowest level possible or closet to the customer. In this event, the leadership team wanted to reverse this direction and require all customer related decisions to be made by them. In a traditional organization, all decisions roll up to the manager or senior leaders to make. For whatever rationale, this gives the senior leaders a feeling of security and stability. In this case, the tension generated by the financial report highlighted the senior leader's lack of faith in leading the transformation using the new organization structure. As many have experienced before, the conflict between the new and old ways of working is tenable during a transformation and without strong leadership from the senior leaders who champion the vision of the transformation, an organization will slip back into the old ways of working.

As the team's coach, I used this opportunity to think more deeply about the financial gap. I ask them to investigate what else might have caused the poor performance for the month. What analysis did they have that showed the transformation efforts were causing the sales representatives to miss their targets? In this case, the team started to reflect more strategically on the gap and soon they realized that outside factors due to the recent changes in COVID 19 social distancing had more impact on the sales numbers than the reporting line and job role changes occurring as a result of the transformation. The leaders were then able to focus their attention on an action that would address this problem, continue with their transformation activities, and find a better way that they can show up as a leader for the frontline sales staff.

Let's put a finer point on Breakthrough Agile. Breakthrough Agile is a holistic approach to an Agile transformation that provides an organization with the growth and development to compete on any level. It is designed to help teams' focus on external and internal system issues that accelerate innovation and creativity. Whether it is the design of new products or solutions, the improvement of technical and business operations, or the commercial end of the value chain, Breakthrough Agile provides the organization a framework that delivers results.

Summary and Key Takeaways

- Breakthrough Agile starts with understanding the principles of the transformation and then applying them to the 5 CBPs.
- The organization will develop novel and robust actions to address customer needs, wants, and motivations.
- When the organization reaches critical points in its transformation journey, the efforts to sustain the growth of the transformation will be challenged by the old principles of the organization.

- By reinforcing the principle first approach and using Agile ways of working, greater benefit and competitiveness for the organization is experienced.
- Organizations need to be aware that false starts to the transformation are a reality.
- Most conflicts will occur as the knowledge gap between what it takes to change the culture and the purpose of the transformation platform becomes clearer, especially to people leaders.
- Being clear at the start and focusing on the approach defined by Breakthrough Agile will create the right ecosystem for all employees to grow and develop through the transformation journey.

Chapter 4

Decision Making

Most discussions of decision making assume that only senior executives make decisions or that only senior executives' decisions matter. This is a dangerous mistake.

Peter Drucker

A look inside:

- 360 model on Breakthrough Agile
- Current state of decision making in organizations
- Breakthrough Agile's decision-making process
- Stages of the decision-making process
- Different methodologies of decision making
- Breakthrough Agile's principles on decision making

Breakthrough Agile is the implementation of a transformation methodology that focuses on first educating employees on the new principles of work, then coaching them through the change on how the principles affect the key cultural business processes (CBPs) of the organization. These processes are called *principle-based cultural business processes (CBPs)* in Breakthrough Agile. In the second phase, Breakthrough Agile focuses the organization on understanding and becoming proficient in how the new principle-based CBPs work when applied to the systems of the transformation platform such as Agile, Lean, or Six Sigma. During this phase, new behaviors and mindsets are developed to enable the organization to achieve the higher quality outcomes it seeks. In the third phase of Breakthrough Agile, the organization identifies novel and unique

DOI: 10.4324/9781003335702-4

opportunities and value from the transformation platform's systems. Phase three includes the execution of actions to realize the value that was identified and deliver it to the customer. This creates a cultural that allows continuous learning and transformation on a daily basis through the execution of the CBPs. As an outcome of this approach, the customer benefits from a delivery of more customer-centric products and services that gives the organization a competitive advantage in its industry. As customer satisfaction and engagement increases, then the future of the organization is more stable and rewarding.

This model (Figure 4.1) reinforces itself as the results of the actions validate the use of principle-based CBPs. As an organization becomes more capable at deploying this method of working, the Agile ways of working mature and show the organization the enormous potential and value they can create for the customer. One key point that needs emphasized is the importance of the execution side of the model. The difference between a successful transformation and a so–so transformation is found in the third phase of this model. Allocating resources, time, and attention to the Agile ways of working and actions is paramount in tapping into this wealth of value. As we go through the five cultural business processes (5 CBPs), we will see how decision making, strategic planning, project management, conflict resolution, and performance management all deliver actions that focus the organization on achieving breakthrough results. However, acting on and realizing the benefits of those actions by everyone is what that separates the good from the great transformations.

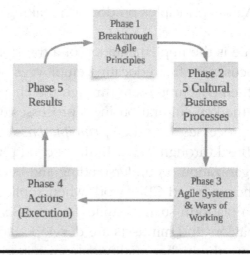

Figure 4.1   Breakthrough Agile's operating model.

In prioritizing the 5 CBPs, decision-making surfaces as the one business process that has the greatest impact on culture. In my experience, decision making is one of the most talked about CBP across organizations and at the same time, it is one of the most misunderstood CBPs. Large organizations will spend tens of thousands of hours in meetings, discussing issues such as budgeting, resource planning, M&A, strategy, product life cycle, and then fumble through a decision on what to do. The inability and inadequacy of an organization's decision-making capability inevitably leads to issues such as lack of trust, bias and stereotyping, reinforcing positional and hierarchical authority, and exclusion of customer-centric solutions. The best of companies spend time on understanding decision making but still end up with a decision-making process that lacks empowerment and speed. In a majority of companies, decision making takes on a paternal/maternal ethos where the senior leader/highest paid person (HPP) graciously guides the team or organization with their final vote of confidence or veto on decisions. As people within the organization struggle to deal with this personality-based type of decision making and seek stability for decision making, the customer is impacted as poor decision making becomes a barrier for growth and innovation. The poor decision making impedes the organization from moving fast and delivering better outcomes, being high performance, capturing value for the customer and itself. The consensus style of decision making, where the senior leaders has veto/single decision-making authority inhibits the empowerment of people to reach for bolder and greater levels of performance. All new or potential innovative actions need to have a 1 up or higher stamp of approval before acting on it. How the organization executes decision making internally strongly influences the way employees think and act,...or another way to state it, defines their culture. People across every level of the organization, throughout every function, will emulate the paternal/maternal aspects of decision making in their day-to-day in a traditional hierarchical culture.

When I coach teams on decision making, I have a question that I ask at the beginning of the working session. I ask the participants, "how many decisions do they make in a day?" When I did this the first time, I was expecting people to give a very low number. However, to my surprise, I had people stating that they made hundreds of decisions a day. When I ask them to explain the type of decisions they made, they were quick to respond. What to eat in the morning; What food to buy; What activities to do on the weekend; Who takes the kids to school; Where to go on holiday with the family; What house to buy; How much money to save; etc. From this simple ice breaker type of question, my hopes were high that people understood decision making and its impact on their daily work. However, what became interesting is when I asked the follow-up question of, "how many decisions do you make it work?" Here the reverse occurred. The numbers were much lower and a high number of participants did not even acknowledging making a decision about their work. I found this observation disconcerting, and I wasn't sure if it was a reflection of the culture of the organization or a capability of the individual. In the exercise, I would then continue to ask questions to the participants on why they see themselves having little if no control over their work. As it turned out, most of the time, people intuitively responded by saying all the decisions are made by the manager or next level leader. In some cases, people responded by saying that decisions at work needed a committee or team to make the decision. Keeping up with this line of thought, I asked what is the context of work decisions. To my surprise, most people responded that most decision at work were characterized as being large, heavily invested projects that required millions of dollars and thousands of hours of work. This set the context for me to unravel the disconnection people displayed – why are they able to identify decisions on a personal level yet struggle to identify or make decisions that affect their day-to-day work. It led me to ask, "do people understand the process of how a decision is made?" Why are decisions that impact their personal life so easy to identify, yet at work, there seems to be a fog that obscures the process? How transparent is the decision-making process to people on their day-to-day issues?

After having done this exercise with a few hundred people and different teams from different cultures, it leads me to believe that decision making is strongly tied to positional authority and hierarchy. A person with a high social status on the organization chart or an authoritarian job title are seen as the decision makers for teams and they define way of working for the organization. I call this the paternalistic/maternalistic method of decision making. Additionally, people easily recognized a decision-making event when it contains a high dollar amount either for investment or operating costs. In summary, decision making is experienced as an event where there is an element of a high dollar amount investment or resource planning (FTE redistribution/hiring) or when there is a need to prioritize ad hoc work assignments (one off assignments that span across a large segment of the company, e.g., modifying existing company-wide benefits, policies, or programs). This leads to those in control being seen as the decisions makers.

In reality, decisions are made on activities at all levels and have numerous scopes that impact both internal and external stakeholders. The examples briefly discussed above fall within the scope of decision making, however, what I found interesting time and time again is that people seemed to think the large scope and high investment decisions defined the boundaries of decision making. When I asked them about who decides how long a meeting is, what day to have it on, or what will be the agenda for the meeting, the gray shadows of organizational hierarchy creep into the discussion. Even moving to the point about assigning work to team members or developing a proposal or solution for a customer, the belief was that the people who did the work or those who would be impacted the most from the decision are not the decision makers. In these cases, the decision reverted to a traditional way of working or the paternalistic/maternalistic model of decision making. In these cases, teams deferred the decision-making authority to the senior most person in the meeting or on the team, to make the decision. A non-surprising correlation is that usually the senior most person is also the HPP for the team. Even as a team's coach, I was occasionally asked to make the decision for the team on when to meet and what the topics for the discussion should be. Even though I wasn't the senior most person in the room, the team didn't understand how to take ownership and make a decision. There is inherently a fight, flight, or freeze attitude when someone is asked to take ownership over a decision. Test this theory in your next meeting. When the time for a decision maker is to be assigned, nominate the person who would be the most appropriate person for the assignment. Try to have the senior leader let go and not endorse or veto the choice. Observe their reaction to letting go of power and control. How might their reaction reflect the culture of the organization? To me, this reinforced the belief that people see decision making as someone else's responsibility, whether the manager, the manager's manager, or the Agile coach.

Surprisingly, people are happy to go along with what someone else decides for them. This element of personal disengagement and hierarchical compliance in terms of decision making continue to challenge organizations that seek to change its culture. As I researched this more, it became clear that people only have a basic understanding of decision-making methodologies and need to improve their capabilities on what is decision making. In Breakthrough Agile, this is the starting point of understanding principle-based CBPs.

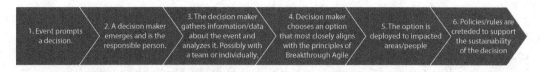

| 1. Event prompts a decision. | 2. A decision maker emerges and is the responsible person. | 3. The decision maker gathers information/data about the event and analyzes it. Possibly with a team or individually. | 4. Decision maker chooses an option that most closely aligns with the principles of Breakthrough Agile | 5. The option is deployed to impacted areas/people | 6. Policies/rules are creteded to support the sustainability of the decision |

Figure 4.2   Decision-making life cycle.

To help understand this point, let's examine the life cycle (Figure 4.2) of a decision. A decision is made up of a series of stages that involve a decision maker and stakeholders. The table in Figure 4.2 is a basic example of the life cycle of a decision. The first step involves an event that triggers the organization or individual to make a decision. This could be an investment of the company's money, a new project, absenteeism within a department or function, or an emergency (act of God). As a side note, the speed at which the organizations move through these stages is in direct correlation to the benefit the decision will have on its impacted stakeholders. For example, in an emergency situation, a quick decision could be life-saving. A doctor's 2- to 3-minute assessment in deciding what treatment to give a trauma patient, might be the difference between life and death. Whereas, in the pharmaceutical industry, decisions by health regulators on product approval take much longer due to the unknown risks or side effects the product may pose to thousands of people who will consume the product. Health authorities rely upon a legion of information and data from the manufacturer to prove the efficacy of the drug product, its repeatability in manufacturing, and it will be commercialized. Unfortunately, this conservative and risk averse process, delays potential life changing products to presently ill patients. The trade-off that health regulators across the world take to deliver safe and efficacious treatments.

Within the broad ranges of decisions, universally either an individual or a team makes the a decision on what action needs to happen. It is a key learning in Breakthrough Agile that decisions are either made by an individual or a team in the new organization. Organizations need to clearly understand that both of these types of decision-making approaches will impact the output of the decision. When evaluating the velocity of delivering value to the customer, a single decision making approach or team decision making approach each affect the speed. In the cases above, the single decision maker, the doctor, quickly makes a decision that delivers immediate impact. Whereas the team decision of the health regulator on approving a new drug requires mountains of data, consensus from internal government functions, and continuous clarification questions that need answered by the one seeking marketing approval for the drug. This process delays the product's impact on sick patients for years and at times, due to the risks of guarding public safety, results in those that need the product to suffer as it awaits approval by committee.

Breakthrough Agile's framework implies that the process of decision-making impacts the fabric of the organization's culture. When thinking of the thousands of decisions made daily by teams or individuals, how decisions are made shape the behavior of people. The way people work and act reflect the pace of decision making. In theory, when an organization is slow to make decisions, the culture suffers from a stifling its innovative spirit and employee engagement. Many times I have had discussion with employees about bringing new ideas up in their teams and the common response is that employees realize that any new idea will need numerous endorsements and approvals from higher level managers before it even gets started. Even when a committee endorses an action, then most likely the next hurdle to execution arises – budget dollars to support the innovative idea. In these types of organizations that are slow to change strategies, that view novel with a conservative mindset, reward consensus thinking, and seeks a perfect outcome to any decision, the pace of work lacks behind the innovation curve. Performance isn't measured by delivery of value to the customer, but measured by how well one adapts to the conservative decision making culture. Without questions, these cultural of the decision-making will influence how employees think, act, and behave toward each other in all aspects of their daily work.

If you think of a government agency or a religious institution, the connection between how they make decisions and their culture is closely related. Take the timeline to bring a new drug to market. Going from laboratory to commercialization under the FDA's guidance (Figure 4.3) takes from 10 to 14 years.

In working with the FDA over the years, the principles of public safety and risk avoidance results in a governmental body that has a very precise applications processes, timelines, and decision milestones for new drug applications. Although there are innovations such as fast tracking, breakthrough and priority reviews, these amendments to the original process generally impact the overall timeline by no more than 20% for new drugs. Generic drug approval is much quicker since the branded drug already underwent the lengthy review by the government agency, so the rationale by the health regulatory agency is that it can use the branded drugs clinical data for the generic drug, as long as the generic product is

Example of Timeline of Drug Development

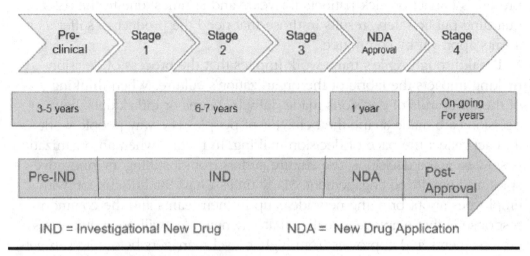

IND = Investigational New Drug   NDA = New Drug Application

Figure 4.3   Drug development timeline. (Information from: FDA, Office of Professional Affairs and Stakeholder Engagement)

identical to the branded product. This process can still take 18–24 months for approval.

Likewise, in an organization that takes risks, experiments, and empowers individuals to innovative, the speed of making decisions is much quicker. By making decisions quicker with the right level of information and expertise, the organization is able to deliver value to the customer faster, and in turn, increase their competitive position in the market. Possibly, the most widely known principle for decision making that fits this description is Amazon's two pizza team rule. By applying this rule, Amazon keeps team sizes to a maximum of ten people. This small team retains its autonomy and is empowered to make a decision on the topic. The two pizza rule helps Amazon to keep its customer-centric focus, and constant drumbeat of bringing innovation to its business and value to its customers. The two pizza rule eliminates the bureaucratic structure other organizations have with a decision-making process that includes committees, countless endorsements, and consensus from all stakeholders. The two pizza rule allows teams to quickly make a decision that can deliver higher value to the customer.

In a traditional organization, stages 2–4 (Figure 4.4) of the decision-making process have the greatest impact on shaping the culture of the organization.

Stage 1	Stage 2	Stage 3	Stage 4	Stage 5	Stage 6

1. Event prompts a decision.	2. A decision maker emerges and is the responsible person.	3. The decision maker gathers information/data about the event and analyzes it. Possibly with a team or individually.	4. Decision maker chooses an option that most closely aligns with the principles of Breakthrough Agile	5. The option is deployed to impacted areas/people	6. Policies/rules are creteded to support the sustainability of the decision

Figure 4.4   Decision-making life cycle by stages.

Stages 2–4 require that the single decision maker or team is identified to take accountability of the decision from that point forward. During these stages, collaboration with experts, research on best practices, and/or the development of options occur to understand what to do. These are the stages where the traditional way of thinking can creep into the decision-making process and influence the mindset of the decision maker or team. In these stages, those with the responsibility and accountability for the decision feel the pressure from the internal stakeholders on how the decision should be made. Normally, these internal stakeholders are the next higher level leaders or people within the organization. Additional pressure within the traditional organization is that the single decision maker or team feels the stress that the result of the decision may affect their career or at least their pay and bonus at the end of year. This promotes a sense of self-preservation on the part of the team to be less bold and innovation. From my experience with decisions that are high profile or priority, the organization's senior leaders will micro manage the decision maker or team as they go through the life cycle of the decision. This may take the form of a committee or sounding board body. In the end, it is a way for senior leaders to keep the decision-making power in their control for the activity.

As the decision maker (Single or team) moves through the decision-making process, they will always keep an eye on pleasing the higher ups with the decision that is made. I've lost count of the number of times I have been in a sprint and heard the product owner quote a senior leader's expectation as a reason to move in a certain direction or prototype a certain idea,.... "This is what the VP or director wants decides for the sprint team what path to take, or MVP to work on. Even if it is a power play by someone trying to get their way, by making it, you can assume that the focus is to keep the boss happy. To me, this is a signal that the sprint team is not fully empowered and the team is creating something for their line managers versus what is best for the customer. Other times where I see decisions made by sprint teams that are influenced by senior leaders' stakeholders is when the sprint team consists of all the organization's high potentials. In these cases, the individuals are assigned to the team merely for show and to allow them to get some spot light time with across the organization. Usually, these teams end up with too many chiefs and no one to complete the work. The high potentials are on the team to "tick the box" as being part of a sprint. Since these are individuals within the organization that have high aspirations on career progress, they generally seek out their boss' opinion on what to do for the sprint team. In both cases, the activities self-perpetuates the hierarchical command and control organization. Decision making remains conservative with a high level of risk avoidance that ends up stifling innovation.

Early in my career, I was told an axiom that still holds true today, "Likes like Likes." Meaning, a senior leader will like someone just like them working for them or on their team. How might this reality affect the decision-making process? When a single decision maker or a team leader needs assigned, then the senior leader will select a person who they feel will do what they would do. Those individuals who might have a different mindset or approach, are not given the same opportunities as the "Likes." Unquestionably, people see this cultural rule being applied and adjust their behavior to try and fit in with the "like-minded people." Once employees realize that this is how their senior leaders work, they understand that to advance in their career, they need to adopt a mindset like their bosses. This gives them an advantage when development opportunities arise. The feature of decision making has a significant impact on the culture of the organization. It can change how people work, behave, and think critically. Breakthrough Agile starts with developing people capabilities on decision making so that anyone can be a single decision maker within the organization. With so much at stake, decision making needs to be understood by everyone before launching Breakthrough Agile.

Within the traditional organization, as the decision maker gets closer to making the final decision, the output or options to the decision are reduced to being less disruptive and more conservative to gain support. Being bold and aspiring is left for the committee to decide and introduce to the final output of the decision. In large projects, the team accountable for the decision is doing nothing more than implementing a fixed solution. The project has a solution, and the team is there to complete the pre-planned tasks that have been orchestrated by the project management office, or an outside consultant. This occurs when there is a high investment level, or sunk costs of the project. In these cases, the decision becomes more and more influenced by internal requirements versus the customer's needs and wants. Inevitably, the organization loses sight of the value the decision will bring to the customer due to the cloud of bureaucracy in the internal decision making process. In terms of performance, the decision maker isn't evaluated on the decision impact to the customer, but more on how well the decision maker presented their project plan during a committee meeting. In other words, how big the promise of value delivered to the customer overshadows the actual results or execution of the value delivered.

Once the option or output is made final, and the decision made by the individual or team (or is it the committee?) happens, then the final stages of the decision-making process come into play. Depending on the scope of the decision, the need for a formal roll out of the decisions action might be a step. Communicating to the impacted stakeholders or customers is another possible action at this point. Skill building and training of customers, employees, or other impacted individuals could occur. To sustain the output of the decision, an organization may need to modify its current procedures or policies. Internally, alignment with other teams or departments occur and people need to adopt the new way of working as part of their daily work. In some cases, this is when the discussion turns to the post-decision behaviors of the organization. How well will the decision be supported by others? Even though HR changed its policy of diversity, how well is the organization following the new policy? Does the new policy have an impact on the demographics of recruited candidates, and do the newly hired candidates improve the business impact of the organization on the customer? Decisions have multiple spin-offs across the organization. In hallways and lunch gatherings, people discuss and debate the solution from the decision. Some may be supporting, other not. In an effort to keep the organization stable in these times, generally a mandate is delivered to help ingrain the decision's solution. This mandate generally comes from the top of the organization with the tone that everyone needs to support the decision maker and the solution. This is a common practice when a decision changes how people work.

The speed to move through the stages (Figure 4.5) of the decision-making process makes a difference in competitiveness. Slower, more conservative organizations lag behind customer needs and preferences when it comes to decisions on types of products to produce or services to provide. Companies that are quick to adapt to the changing environment and make changes to products and services will grow and gain customer's approval and dollars sooner. Apple products showcase this speed of

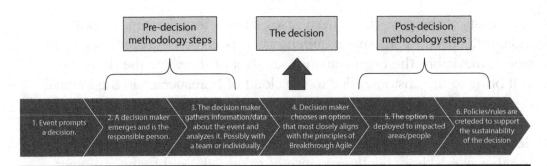

Figure 4.5   Anatomy of a decision.

decision making with its evolution of the iPhone. Throughout each feature, the iPhone has adopted or discontinued features that focused on meeting customer's need. Changes in size, speed, memory, operating system, camera and video quality, and other features reflect a company culture that makes decisions quickly on its products and services to meet its customer's needs and as a result, experiences extraordinary growth rates. Newer features that are meeting the customer needs such as biometric security features are enhanced with each innovative cycle, whereas other features become discontinued such as a separate port for a headset. These changes to the phones features impact iPhone sales and Apples overall revenues. The chart (Figure 4.6) shows the growth of the iPhone even in a product market that is considered highly saturated and competitive.

In my experience, organizations stumble when trying to improve their decision-making process. At the start, usually a group of leaders create a new list or "rules of the game" for decision making. Typical rules that pop up at this stage are decisions will be made with fewer people, not everyone needs to be involved with the decision. Or everyone needs to support the decision when it is changes a process or way of working. To bring everyone to the same level of understanding a change management plan supports the output of the decision that impact internal operations/employees, and emphasizes that people shouldn't criticize the decision maker(s). On the surface, these are good rules to have but the organization still avoids leaning into understanding the decision making methodology. Its decision-making process still reflects the traditional organizational culture of top–down, highly bureaucratic decision-making bodies. There is a lack of focus on restructuring and relearning for the organization toward understanding the types of decision making methodologies. It is unfortunate that most organizations spend more time focusing on controlling the organization's reaction to decisions, then spending time understanding the methodologies of decision making.

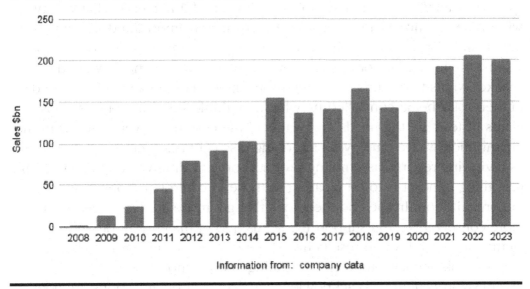

iPhone Sales from 2008 to 2023

Information from: company data

Figure 4.6   iPhone sales. (Data from https://www.businessofapps.com/data/apple-statistics/.)

In my research, I have discovered that internally there is a clear gap in employees' willingness to take on decision-making authority without having the positional authority to enforce the decision. This behavior reflects the level of control that an organization gives its employees on details of their work. The more employees resist taking on this empowerment with decision making, the more the organization has a micro-managing, controlling leadership that results in stifled productivity of its employees. This characteristic of a traditional organization's culture will derail an Agile transformation. Breakthrough Agile is designed to dismantle the traditional mindset about decision making and cultivate the power of the organization's employees to build a more competitive organization through more effective decision making.

In an Agile organization, decision-making authority sits with those who are closest to the impacted stakeholder whether it is an internal or external stakeholder. By anchoring decisions on Breakthrough Agile's principles, then decision making enhances the value and benefit of the decision's output for the organization. I find it interesting that the impact that the decision-making process has on the culture characterizes how people work within the organization at all levels and in most situations. It is so common to hear in a problem-solving workshop, the leader of the team making a statement such as "this is what the boss/manager wants" or "this is what the project's sponsor wants." Here, the psychological impact of a higher level authority within the organization influences the person or team in the decision(s) that they make. For anyone on the team, the fear of falling into disfavor or going against the higher authority brings everyone into alignment on what the speaker wants to do. It is a chilling proposition that people work day to day in their roles being controlled by what they think their boss or boss' boss wants instead are the needs and wants of the customer. Even at levels in the organization where employees are doing discreet task-oriented work, such as reviewing reports, assembling products or providing walk-up services, the prevailing mindset is to be pleasing to those in control and power within the organization. In the end, decisions that get made are less aspirational, more conservative, and support the status quo of the current organization. Getting to breakthrough results from here is a very challenging task.

Let's look deeper into decision making and its impact on an organization's culture. To acknowledge a fact, most organizations are good at two types of decision making. The first type is what we will call a single decision-making authority. This is when decisions are made by one person. For most organizations, this is the manager, leader, or the most senior person (HPP) at the table. As practiced in a traditional organization, we will call this single decision-making methodology the directive method of decision making. Anyone with any professional or work experience will easily identify that they have seen this type of decision making methodology at one time or another. The directive style of decision making has a few identifiable characteristics. Micro-management, finding fault, and always reworking proposals are the common characteristics of the directive style of decision making. In some instances, the directive style of decision maker will always spur fear into the discussion. They approach the decisions as if the impact of making a mistake or failing to meet the senior management's expectation is a career destroyer. Or, the ego of the decision making takes on an air of superiority on the team where people are stating that the higher level leaders trust this decision maker more than others because they have delegated the role of decision maker to them. Imagine an organization where trust is defined by whether or not people are given decision making accountability. These examples showcase the worst side of directive style of decision making.

More skilled leaders who use directive style of decision making obscure their authority over the decision by bringing a team together under the pretense to help make the decision. What normally follows is the decision maker then introduces the final output of the decision at a team meeting. Although the team is presented the final output of the decision, the team is asked to endorse the decision-maker's choice. Maybe a discussion starts on the topic and different points of views are discussed but the directive decision maker skillfully defends their choice. Usually in these situations, the decision maker is the supervisor of the team members. With this dynamic, endorsement is usually given by the team. Many justify this compliance as a means of survival in the corporate world, why risk your next pay raise over giving critical feedback or a diverse opinion on your boss' work. In the end, the directive decision maker feels they used a collaborative, team based methodology in making the decision.

In reality, most employees don't challenge their boss' thinking or decisions. Agreeing is a much safer tactic than refuting or questioning the boss' solution. This consensus/compliant approach to decision making proportionally gets more firmly rooted as one progresses up the organization ladder. When the perception of going against the boss' opinion or the collective team's thinking, results in loss of status or positional influence, rarely will someone take a diverse opinion or provide constructive feedback. In these situations, the discussion quickly shifts focus from the decision making process, how the decision was reached, to the post decision stages. At this point, the team's conversation shifts gear into the implementation and change management approach. When a leader orchestrates this process with their team, unknowingly, or with intent, they have created a top down directive decision making methodology. As this unfolds they team understands this as the decision making process for the company's culture. When in reality, the team is there to carry the leader's decision forward to the employees of the organization. In this situation, people feel they are part of the decision-making process through suggestions on how to implement and the ways of communicating the decision to the organization. For some company's this is their decision making culture.

Directive styles of decision making can negatively impact the culture of the organization through a false sense of engagement. At worse, people do what the boss wants out of fear of losing their livelihood or future career progression. Directive decision making creates a culture of compliance to hierarchy and social status position, versus doing what is best for the customer or organization. Generally, a person who uses the directive decision making fears losing their sense of control over the team. There are many variations and situations for decision making. This is why it is such an important lever to understand and then appropriately develop capabilities around it as the transformation starts within the organization. As you reflect back on decision making ask yourself, how does a decision get made in your organization? How do the outputs of decisions get translated into everyone's day-to-day way of working?

Single decision making is one of the methods for making decision within the organization. The other method of decision making is the team-based decision-making methodology. This second type of decision-making methodology in traditional organizations is practiced through a consensus team-based approach. With consensus decision making, no one person is accountable for the output or results of the decision. The accountability and responsibility of the decision's impact is spread over the members of the team or multiple functions. Consensus decision making will end up creating a culture that fails to hold people accountable. Without clear ownership of the decision to single person, team's are buffered from learning from failure. When the outcome of the decision has a positive impact on the organization, then the team celebrates and acknowledges the work that they completed. When the outcome is so-so or maybe not implemented, then the activity or decision gets pushed into the shadows and comes to a end without any review of its impact. Consensus decision making spreads the responsibility and accountability of the decision across many people. When things go well, then many can celebrate in its success. However, in the cases when the decision fails to deliver its intended outcome, consensus decision making deflects direct feedback or criticism on an individual.

Ironically, consensus decision making is especially prevalent in organizations that take a punitive view to decisions that are viewed as being failures. In organizations where individuals and teams are shamed or embarrassed for an "off the mark" decision, then people rely upon the consensus approach to soften any criticism from senior leaders or others. In a toxic culture of placing blame and tearing people down, any decision that needs made will either follow a consensus approach or get escalated to the highest level possible for their decision. When a tough decision needs made or there isn't a clear idea of how the decision's output will affect the organization, why take a chance of being target and risk your personal safety. Why put additional pressure on an individual or team to appease everyone, knowing anything short of "greatness" is seen as a failure.

In an organization that views anything short of a "grand slam" impact on the business' short-term objectives as a failure, then people begin to take conservative steps to decisions. Risks are avoided and every stakeholder's opinion gets incorporated into the decision's output. Teams and individuals are coached on what not to do to avoid being showcased as a failure in the eyes of leaders and others. Normally, employees manage this polarity of being risk adverse versus being innovative by taking and learning from mistakes. If this polarity is a feature of the company's decision making approach, then its impact on initiatives or projects will limit the innovation and competitiveness of the company now and in the future. Consensus decision making is detrimental to the company and its culture. Why would a team tackle a problem where they didn't already know the answer or risk public embarrassment for trying to do something novel or experimental in the organization? Generally, as the consensus mentality for decision making shapes the culture. Strategic objectives and initiatives start to lack boldness, authenticity, and the impact to drive a change with the customer's behaviors. Consensus decision making will lead most teams to see self-preservation and viewing their self-worth as more important than learning or developing the organization's future. Consensus decision making will lead the organization to the opposite end of the innovation spectrum. Utilizing Breakthrough Agile' approach to decision making will support the organization as it captures the value its employees can bring to the organization through a thorough knowledge of how decision making works.

Directive and consensus-based decision making will deceptively appear collaborative and inclusive when practiced by an experienced person. Both seek to gather input from individuals and stakeholders and hear their feedback. However, as practiced, both approaches have pitfalls. The directive approach limits collaboration and input from impacted stakeholders. And the consensus approach is slow due to a belief that all suggestions or feedback need incorporated into the final output of the decision. Even for the directive decision maker, if they are seeking input from a team, they might not move forward on a proposal until everyone on the team has their issues incorporated in the final solution. In Breakthrough Agile, the approaches to single and team decision making find that right balance of getting a diverse set of opinions during the processes, yet not slowing the cadence of the decision down due to bureaucracy. The goal is to make the best decision possible and getting key people's input into the process quickly to make a good decision. Other methods of decision making will give an organization this opportunity to make decisions but with the loss of speed and agility. In Breakthrough Agile, the output of a decision is to have a good quality decision quickly. Breakthrough Agile contradicts the traditional mindset about decision making. In companies that support the hierarchical approach to decision making, the belief is that a good quality decision cannot be made quickly. This need for perfection in decisions causes the organization to delay the introduction of new ideas or novel solutions to help the organization grow. It is a barrier for innovation. Both the directive and consensus methods of decision making will either limit diverse solutions or insist on perfection before implementation. As a result, companies that practice both methodologies of decision making have cultures that are slow to change, insensitive to customer needs, and are protecting their traditional ways of working. Breakthrough Agile provides a way for an organization to become unshackled with the traditional decision-making methodologies and tap into the greatness of its employees.

In organizations that have an Agile culture, people have adapted principles that give it speed and flexibility in the decision-making process. Breakthrough Agile embraces the principles of minimal viable product (MVP) thinking, empowerment, and lowest level decision making to enable the organization to deliver value to the customer at a faster rate than previously experienced. Organizations will need to relearn their decision-making process and connect the principles of Breakthrough Agile's to the process to realize how the change delivers value. By applying Breakthrough Agile's principles to decision making, the organization will experience a swell of new ideas and solutions that would have been untapped using the traditional decision making methods. Before deep diving into Breakthrough Agile's principles on decision making, lets summarize the types of decision-making methodology (Figure 4.7) that we discussed so far.

Type of Methodology	Single Decision Making	Team Decision Making
Name	Directive Style	Consensus Style
Decision Maker	Leader/HPP	Team/Group of Peers
Cultural Impact	Low Empowerment Low Trust & Psychological Safety Favoritism Micro-management	Same as Directive plus: Slow to Act Perfectionism

Figure 4.7 Decision-making approaches in traditional organizations.

As we move forward with Breakthrough Agile, let's look at the principles of the framework with regard to decision making:

1. Equal power among all employees. Avoid hierarchy
2. Single decision makers at all levels
3. Decision making speed correlates to delivering results
4. Experiment to learn, grow, and experiment
5. Start with the customer's need: Known and unknown

The infographic below demonstrates how learning the principles at first and then applying them to the cultural behavior process (CBP) impacts the use of the systems within the Agile transformation framework. In this example, we take the principle of "equal power among all employees." Avoid hierarchy and apply it the decision-making process (Figure 4.8). Now an engineer or technician is empowered to make a decision on a production or maintenance schedule that was routinely done by the manager. This decision happens in the daily stand-up for each department with the team's leader present. The leader acts as the coach for the team

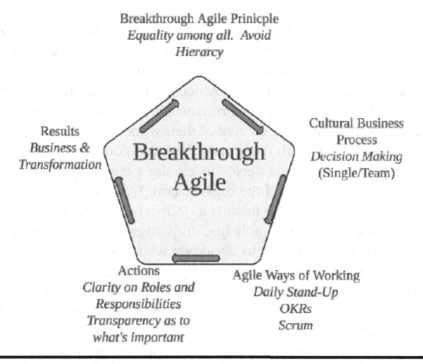

Figure 4.8   Breakthrough Agile's approach to decision making.

as they make decisions on what work needs to happen, who will do it and when it will happen.

As the team continues to practice the Breakthrough Agile principle, people on the team feel more of a sense of belonging and less of a sense that it is a team designed to make a manager look good.

Equality in Power among All. Avoid Hierarchy

In one regard, a decision maker exercises a certain amount of power in their position. When we think of iconic roles like the president of the United States, CEOs of companies, board members, and other high-level people, there is a sense that these are powerful people because the hierarchical system is set up to support them in their decisions. Their authority and positional power is palpable for everyone, and the social structure around them is design to reinforce their presence at this level. They exercise their power by the decisions that they make. As a society or organization, we recognize that the impact of their decisions can change the course of history or the future of a company. In an Agile organization, the decision making power is distributed equally among everyone. The power that comes with decision making is shared among all employees. That is to say, all employees are decision makers when it comes to the "what" and "how" of their scope of work. There is no longer a top-down directive decision-making method within the organization. All employees, whether those with the broadest of roles like CEOs, managing directors, owners, or those with the most specific job scopes such as engineers or technicians are empowered (weld power) to make decisions that affect the content of their work. The characteristic for this empowerment rests with the scope of the decision. For instance, a CEO in an Agile organization might decide to acquire a company for the future growth and competitiveness of the organization. While at another level, a production employee might be making a decision on what product and how much to produce on their assembly line. In both cases, the employees own the decision and has the power to decide on what and how of the decision's output. We would slide back to the old way of thinking if we allowed for the manager to make the decision on what product to run in the assembly assembly operation without including the operator of that equipment as part of the decision-making process.

In the Agile decision-making processes, employees are required to collaborate and seek advice from others when making a decision.

In Breakthrough Agile, final decision-making authority is assigned to one person. Employees are coached and mentored to build their capabilities on the decision-making process and the intent of being a single decision maker. This coaching comes from Agile coaches, peers, and the employee's leaders. Employees are coached that the single decision-making methodology is called the advice or consultative method of decision making. In essence, decision makers are required to seek advice from others when starting the decision-making process. One segment of people who need included for advice are the impacted employees of the decision. Seeking advice from this group gives the decision maker and the advice process its customer-centric element that needs embedded in an Agile organization. For example, a company that might be changing its health benefits might designate the director of HR as the single decision maker. Then this person would seek out the advice of exerts, colleagues, and the affected employees of the change on how to proceed. Engaging with the impacted stakeholders early in the process is key to making the advice process work. Imagine the feedback a group of affected employees would give to the director of HR if their benefits were changed with them being consulted on the new product? What if they were included on the team from the start to give their advice? Wouldn't the feedback be different? Doesn't the later approach resonate with a more quality, and customer centric output to the decision. The Information that the impacted employees would give, would certainly help the decision maker to form a solution that is more customer centric. In this example, the decision maker is being transparent, diligent, and authentic in how they make the decision on the change in benefits. In our other example, the machine operator would seek the advice from their supply chain partners on future customer demand and product mix, as well as other machine operators on what is needed to make the production operation run more effectively to meet customer demand. Engaging others early in the process and seeking advice from those who are impacted the most from the decision is how organizations realize the value of being Agile.

As mentioned earlier in this chapter, all organizations understand the decision-making process when it involves a large investment or purchase. There is standard operating procedures (SOPs) and Designation of Authority (DOAs) to guide the organization on these decisions. For decisions that are day-to-day in scope, the organization tends to have a blind eye to these decisions. However, these day-to-day decision occur in the thousands and here is an opportunity for organizations to build their decision-making capabilities. Leaders need to help employees identify that daily activities include decisions that follow a decision making methodology. In transforming the culture, decision making has to be addressed at all levels of the organization and for all scopes of decisions. A misstep would be to only apply Agile decision making to the large investment type of decision, which happen less often and maintain the command and control directive style of decision making in the day-to-day operations. This duality will slow down and derail the cultural transformation journey of Breakthrough Agile.

As a leader, it is necessary for you to let go of the decision making authority that was previously a part of the role. The leader needs to encourage their team and others to take accountability of decisions, and apply the single decision-making methodology. The leader may not be excluded in the decision. In fact, at the start of the transformation, leaders should coach employees in the decision-making processes as it unfolds.

Leaders should ask such coaching questions as:

■ What is their research or investigative plan to gather data to make this decision?
■ Who will they consult with on the decision?
■ What barriers are they having to completing their work?

By taking this coaching step early in the decision-making processes, the associate's leader prompts the decision maker to gather data and seek advice on the action that is being considered. This also provide a leader a way to engage the employee. Being a coach to an employee will enhance the leader's coaching capabilities as well as build up the capabilities of the decision maker on decision making. The key to realizing the value of this principle within Breakthrough Agile is that an associate understands that they are empowered to make the decision for the action assigned to them. They should not be escalating decisions or seeking their leader's endorsement of their decision.

Letting go of the decision making authority is a challenge for leaders within an Agile organization. As the journey begins, the previous principles of the traditional organization will filter through the decision-making process. Employees will seek to gain approval or endorsement from their leader/manager prior to finalizing the decision. This is a self-preservation behavior of the employee and one that is driven by fear or confidence. Leaders in the organization need to be clear on the new decision-making principles and create the environment for any decision maker to feel safe to make the decision without fear of retribution, adverse action, or any other organizational method to stifle the decision-making process.

In the beginning of the journey, leaders need to be careful not to endorse or confirm decisions when the employee has been assigned as the decision maker. They might even need to state to the employee that this is their decision and they are responsible for it. This is especially difficult when the associate engages the leader in the late stage of the decision-making process. At stage 4 of the decision-making life cycle, a leader can be approached by the employee to seek that final confirmation that they made the right decision. At this time, the associate has already developed their solution and made a decision. To a leader, this is a tricky spot to engage and coach the decision maker on the process. The associate may genuinely be asking for feedback from the leader or, and this has been the case many times, the associate is transferring the responsibility of the decision to the leader or manager. They did all the heavy lifting for the decision, now as the employee's leader, you are asked "what would you do or did I choose the right option?" As their coach, the leader needs to reinforce the new way of working on decision making and provide the reassurance to the employee that they are the decision maker. Creating the environment for success in the early phases of the transformation is a key objective for the organizations leaders. Each decision making event, when handled through the approach described in Breakthrough Agile, will propel the transformation forward. Employees of the organization will start to say that leaders are talking the talk and walking the walk. If the expectation of leaders within the organization is to endorse all of their subordinates/team's decisions, then the organization hasn't truly bought into the Agile principle that power is shared equally and avoiding hierarchy in the decision-making process.

When power is shared equally in the decision-making processes, the Agile method they are practicing is called the consultative or advice decision-making approach. With this approach, the decision maker has the authority and power to make the decision that they determine is best for the customer or group that is impacted by the decision. Decision makers are empowered to decide how the decision will impact the customer and organization. When we say that people are all equal, what we are stating is that people own their own work and are responsible for the results. There isn't a decision maker, a person with veto power above them, or a person who needs to endorse a decision. If we want to have accountable employees, then naturally they should be making the decisions that impact their work.

When we think of an Agile organization and compare Breakthrough Agile's principles to those of a traditional organization, how do they stack up? How does empowerment, and pushing decisions down to the lowest level, fit with an organization that in the past required "pitches" and "committees" to decide on actions before moving forward. Taking this a step further, in an Agile organization trusting an engineer or marketing team to make decisions about their work on a day-to-day basis becomes hindered by an organization that makes decision by committee. The principles of Breakthrough Agile are opposing to those decision-making principles of an organization that makes decision through bureaucratic systems.

Living the principle of "all have equal power" in the decision-making processes is hard to practice and live. However, the results of the principle and way of working will deliver outstanding value to the company when practiced. As the principle grows during the transformation, people in the organization will start to experiment and become more innovative. Leaders will seek ways to become less bureaucratic and allow more employees to take on ownership of the details of their work. Leaders will start to fill the role of coaches and invite team members who have decision-making authority into more informal settings to discuss how the decision is going. This first step into building better relationships between people at work through less organizational hierarchy and status will start the momentum toward a more empowered culture at work.

Understanding the methodologies of decision making will bring the organization further along this empowerment principle than it has ever been before. There are also additional actions that will accelerate achieving this output of equality across the organization. One of the more transformative steps would be changing the organizational hierarchy. A command and control hierarchy will be an anchor holding the organization back from change, as it tries to increase its level of empowerment and shared power. Adopting a network structure will require everyone to shift their mindset, especially leaders. Leaders will move from being controlling to that of a coach creating an environment where the concept of equality is a reality. By adopting the network structure, new roles for past leaders are created. There will still exist positions with leadership responsibilities to develop teams of employees and coach them on their performance. However, other leadership roles might be more consultative with a broader reach than a team or function. These additional roles might be converging specific topics or business processes and cover a geographic area with multiple teams. In the network organization, self-managing teams would be responsible for meeting daily needs and objectives. The 5 CBPs show up as governance processes within the network organization and illustrate the new rules of working within the organization.

Single Decision Makers at All Levels

Single decision making at all levels is a principle of Breakthrough Agile that requires the organization to allow individuals to take on decisions that affect their tactical as well as strategic work. It complements the principle that power is shared equally and defines to a greater detail how a network structured organization will increase empowerment and promote better decision making. The best single decision-making methodology for Breakthrough Agile is the consultative or advice process. With this approach, the decision maker is required to seek advice, feedback, input, and opinions from peers, colleagues, and people from across the organization on the details of the decision. Following the model introduced early (Figure 4.2), before reaching a decision the single decision maker would have researched, collected data, and interviewed impacted stakeholders both internally and externally before reaching a decision. The role of the leader in this process is to support the decision maker when faced with with barriers. This new coaching role would displace their previous role as endorser or "veto" person.

Readers may find it discomforting to hear that single decision making is a core principle of Breakthrough Agile. When practice as designed, this principle will lead to faster delivery of value to the customer. In most cases, readers may think that decisions are usually too high a level for a frontline person to make. Or, the risk is too great for the organization for a person not positioned high within the organization. However, when practiced as designed, the intent behind a single decision maker for all decisions is to train the organization to breakdown vague or large tasks into smaller more discreet activities. When this occurs, the decision and resulting actions are much clearer and a single decision maker can take ownership for the impact of the decision. For instance, if an increase in demand for a product triggered a manufacturer to buy a new piece of equipment with a capital investment in the hundreds of thousands of dollars, in traditional organizations, this would take months and numerous approvals. At the least, the fiscal policies of the company would require that before buying, the decision has to be approved by every key leader linked to operations, finance, safety, and quality. In this practice, each leader could make suggestions, or recommendations as to the equipment design and use. In the end, there would have to be consensus between this ad hoc team on the purchase of the equipment before moving forward. By applying the single decision maker principle, the trigger would still exist; however, at the beginning, the responsible leader would identify a single decision maker, who is closest to the equipment, to make the decision. The decision maker could be an experienced production employee or a supervisor to make the decision within a given timeline. At this point, the decision maker is responsible for engaging people who have a stake in the purchase and collecting data on their thoughts and concerns. For instance, by interviewing the safety manager, the decision maker may discover the need for interlocking safety features on the equipment or other types of guard. Through an interview with the maintenance manager, the decision maker would discover what brand of equipment the department is better able to service. The decision maker would discuss with the technicians who would run the equipment and what was their needs and wants. This might include features such as larger switches or buttons, brighter control panels or better lighting with the equipment. The decision maker may interview equipment manufacturers to hear about differences in equipment that is available. All of this information then would go into the research that the decision maker conducts on selecting the right pieces of equipment. The decision maker would then seek to find the right equipment. After the research and interviews are done, the decision maker would select the option for the equipment. This way of working would be quicker than having multiple meeting with committees of managers and sign-off documents circulating through the organization waiting for signatures from busy people. One person, with the right guidance, reaching out and collecting the data and then making the decision would end up with a solution that would create more value for the manufacturer by meeting the customer demand quicker than through a consensus team-based approach.

Another benefit of using a single decision-making methodology is to ensure that an appropriate decision maker is assigned to the decision based upon the scope of the decision. For example, if an airline decided that they were planning to use only one type of aircraft, the decision making should be the CEO or COO of the company. As this would affect the image and reputation of the company as well as the capacity of the organization to carry travelers. After deciding who is the decision maker, then that person would seek the advice of passengers, pilots, on-board flight staff, gate staff, ground crew, maintenance personnel, and airline industry to gather as much data about the right type of plane to use with the company. If a decision for the airline was to choose a coffee to serve, then this decision might be with someone who serves on the flight staff and has firsthand knowledge of what customers want and need for a good coffee. The same process would then be followed, where the decision maker for choosing coffee would seek the advice of colleagues, passengers, coffee experts, and others before making their decision. The scope of the decision helps in deciding the right person to be the single decision.

As the organization transforms itself into an Agile organization, the network structure will support the principle of a single decision maker for all decisions. As triggers for decisions occur, it is key that an individual is assigned to the decision and that the individual fits the scope to make the decision. What this implies is that large broad sweeping decisions for the organization need to be simplified into smaller scopes. Similar to the concept of 1 pcs flow in Lean, decisions need to be broken apart into manageable pieces and single decision makers assigned to each piece to speed up the delivery of value to the customer. When the scope of the decision is simplified, then individuals with closer contact to the customer are responsible for the decision. For instance, an airline wants to enhance its reputation as a premier carrier. At first, this might be seen as a CEO or COO decision on what and how to enhance the reputation. However, by breaking down the decision to smaller scopes, then a wider group of decision makers can be engaged to make this goal become a reality. Diving deeper into this example, let's assume on-board meals are seen as a way to create this reputation. Then the decision maker for what type of food to serve, in each class of airline service, would be a chef in the airline's kitchen. If on-board amenities, blankets, pillows, etc. are seen as a way to improve the reputation, then an on-board airline staff should be the single decision maker for these features. The process would repeat on and on with each simplification of the broader scoped outcome. With these smaller decisions, each one is independent of the other and can be implemented when completed to start the value creation cycle quicker for the airline. Meals become better on its own timeline. Amenities has its own timeline. Entertainment enhancements its own. When summed up, all the simplified scoped decisions increase the value generation that the airline creates through these efforts.

Decision-Making Speed Correlates to Delivering Results

This principle is an outcome of a company practicing the first two principles. Since industrialization became a foundation of the business world, time has been the constant key performance metric (KPI) to become the market leader or most competitive. Both speed and time are two constants that all companies are attempting to control to become the best they can be in their industry. From R&D, to MFG, to commercialization, to competitive intelligence, being fast is a key to success. In an Agile organization, there are no perfect solutions. Instead, organizations empower people to take risks and make decisions based on their current knowledge and data on the topic. By allowing shared power and a single decision maker methodology, the organization will become quicker at taking action delivering superior value to the customer and generating greater value for the organization. In recent times, the impact of fast decision making has been observed by how vaccines were being approved by the United States Federal Food and Drug Agency. The COVID pandemic saw two pharmaceutical companies surge ahead of others and the FDA making the decision to approve their products for use quickly and to the benefit of society. Although the standard for efficacy remained the same, the FDA saw the urgency to accept smaller sample sizes of clinical study data to give emergency approval to these companies' vaccines. For both Moderna and Pfizer, being Agile meant being able to deliver quickly on their drug products' clinical data to the health authority to gain their approval. Researching the space of COVID vaccines, other pharmaceutical companies failed to meet the same speed to gain FDA approval as these two companies. Maybe a more effective decision-making process within these organizations would have given them a quicker timeline for approval with the FDA and other world health agencies. It is imperative for an organization to reap the benefits of Breakthrough Agile, that decision making is quick and robust. By adopting this principle, an organization starts to become innovative. They shed the idea of being perfect or pleasing everyone. Meeting the needs and demands of the customer with the best product they have at the time, minimal viable product, is how value is generated and earned in Breakthrough Agile.

Experiment to Learn, Grow, and Experiment

Decisions spurs action. That is the intent behind this principle. In an organization that has adapted the principles of Breakthrough Agile, decisions are made with the right amount of information and in the spirit of experimentation. Teams need the freedom and ability to try different ways of working in order to get a better understanding of how their product works, what the customer thinks, and how the market will behave. This repetitive cycle of allowing single decision makers to own their work and holding them accountable for the results embeds in the organization a drive for doing more. This habit of looking for better ways to meet the customer's needs leads employees to try new and more innovative solutions. This in turn allows for more opportunities for employees to learn and grow. As they see the good and bad of their decisions, this will inspire them in their next assignment to challenge what works best. The Experiment, Learn, Grow, Experiment (ELGE) cycle is similar to that of the Plan, Do, Check and Act (PDCA) cycle. An organization decides on a course of action and executes on it. From deployment of the first MVP, the organization experiments with customer behaviors and reactions. Through this experiment, the organization learns more about the customer, process, product, and buying forces in the market. These reflections result in knowledge growth of the decision maker and those on the team that are linked to the experiment's deployment. This new knowledge then leads the decision maker and the design team onto their next experiment. The decision-making process gets the cycle of experimentation started. The old adage is learn from failure but that falls short as it doesn't imply that you continuously restart a new experiment and try again.

Start with the Customer Needs, Known and Unknown

Breakthrough Agile has an *outside-in* mental model when implemented. When and how decisions are made will vary widely across an organization. The range of decisions could be from a production team lead deciding what product to manufacture on a given day to an executive board member deciding to divest or merge with another company. In both cases, the needs of the customer have to be the focus of the decision. By looking to the outside and understanding the customers' motivations for the service or product, the organization will identify value opportunities that trigger decisions for value creation. At times, the customer needs may come from market research, customer feedback, forecasting, benchmarking, or other investigative work that yields relative business insights. When the organization uses this data and acts on it, then more than one decision-making event is started. In each of these cases, meeting the customer needs has to be the driver for decisions. As one organization I worked with started their transformational journey, they decided to put a nameplate with "customer" in each of the conference rooms where employees discussed and made decisions. The intent behind the nameplate was that during daily meetings or discussions, the presence of the customer was in the room and needed considered for the decision that was being considered. Organizations that lose focus on the customer's needs and motivations tend to fall back into the traditional mindset of looking inside out.

Summary and Key Takeaways

- Decision making is a strong cultural influencer in Breakthrough Agile. Most organizations have a lack of understanding decision-making methods and need additional education and coaching on developing this skill.
- How leaders show up and empower others will greatly impact the transformation change in decision making and results that affect the customer. Leaders who don't let go of this power and control will continue to inhibit innovation and the unleashing of the organization's creativity.
- Decision making in an Agile organization is free of fear of failure. There is a constant learning cycle at work in an Agile organization and this learning comes from trying something new and seeing how it delivers value to the customer.

Decision-Making Sensing Guide				
Principles of Breakthrough Agile	Experiencing	Seeing	Hearing	Anti-Pattern
Equality of power among all employees. Avoid Hierarchy	Leaders speak less, and ask more questions. All team members are treated equally in terms of assignments and opportunities. Ideas are farmed from all team members without regard to seniority or social status	Leaders observing and listening to team members discuss their work in group settings. Team members taking ownership of a project or initiative and sharing responsibility within the team. The team's success is greater than individual success	More open ended questions like, "what is the outcome? What have you tried? What are your next steps? How did the customer respond? What did you learn? How can we improve upon this idea?	Favoritism and work politics influencing work assignments, or permissions within a team. Controlling behavior and micro management of a team's work by a leader. Individuals making decisions on behalf of a team. Team members not sharing information among themselves.
Single Decision Making at all levels	People feeling the weight of ownership on projects and initiatives. Clear focus on what success looks like for a decision. Absence of fear in the decision making process. No more right or wrong decisions. Individuals making decisions on behalf of a team.	Performance boards and projects where responsibility for decision making is clear for everyone to see. Leaders allowing team members' freedom to make their own decisions. Team members taking accountability for decisions and the results.	People saying phrases like, "this is my responsibility, I am accountable for this action, let me prepare to make the decision by gather input from experts, let me discuss with the decision with those that are impacted the most."	People looking for endorsement from managers and leaders on their decisions. Leader's surreptitiously making decisions for the team through manipulation of meeting agendas. Everything turns into a team decision with the leader present and giving their opinion. People judging others decision choices.
Decision Making Speed correlates to delivering results	Achieving results at a faster pace than before. Fewer team meetings for simple decisions. Quicker data collection on decisions.	Moving forward on decisions without having all the facts. Higher expectation on making decisions quicker by leaders. Leaders supporting individuals throughout the process with professional coaching.	Phrases such as let's build on this momentum. Let's self-correct and try again. Celebrating small wins and incremental progress.	Constant delays caused by leaders that expect more data collection or review by committee of decisions. Decision outputs being dismantled by a senior leader because they feel it is too risky.
Experiment to learn, grow, and experiment	Iteration of solutions after first testing. MVP approaches to new opportunities. Piloting of new solutions to understand customer better. Trying something new, and unknown by the organization. Building of new skills as a result of trying to do something new.	Teams refocusing, self-correcting, and becoming more creative in their solutions. Resilience of teams to bounce back when things get off track. Rewarding failure and learning from failure.	Stories of teams failing and restarting. Team members telling stories about overcoming barriers and achieving stellar results. Talk about re-starting and self-correction on strategic and tactical OKRs	Teams working as implementation squad for a solution. Teams and team members being shamed or reprimanded for taking risks. Ideas only coming from senior leaders within the organization. People taking direction from leaders as a way of working.
Start with the customer's need: Known and unknown	Outcome and OKRs to define strategic projects. Value adding projects being worked on instead of routine activities.	Customer motivations are part of goals for organization. Language in presentations and decks have a customer centric focus.	Less about internal processes and structure. More discussion on delivering value to the customer. More external goals that focus on better outcomes for customer.	Internal focus activities to decrease costs. Doing activities that only benefit the P&L. Delaying innovation for the sake of cost savings.

Chapter 5

Conflict Resolution

> In case of dissension, never dare to judge till you've heard the other side.
>
> **Euripides (484–406 BCE)**

A look inside:

- Origins of conflict resolution approaches
- Current state of conflict resolution at work
- Tomorrow's work ecosystem and conflict resolution
- Escalation doesn't work for conflict resolution
- Conflict versus tension

Conflict and conflict resolution is a topic that every reader relates to. Whether on a personal or professional level, each of us has had the experience of being in conflict with another person or organization. As you reflect back on your own conflicts, think of what the end goal was for you or the other person. Most likely, it was to gain an advantage or win a point of view. As we entered and worked through conflict, our egos dominated our emotions which determined how we thought and behaved. The resolution is usually a zero-sum game. Either, we get our way or don't. This engrained approach to conflict resolution permeates our professional lives and ways of working today. Even when blanketed by pleasantries and masked generosity, conflicts are usually about one person getting things done their way versus a competing way. Have you ever worked for someone who has a narcissistic and micro manager tendencies? Did you ever say "no" to them? What was the aftermath? Did tension enter into

DOI: 10.4324/9781003335702-5

the relationship? Unfortunately, people will avoid conflict because it is unpleasant and demoralizing. People avoid conflicts at work because they also fear the risk of jeopardizing their next career step or year-end merit and bonus payout. In today's organization, people will intentionally avoid conflict. The method to deal with conflict or disagreeable events, is to put them in the shadows of one's own working space. Does anyone ever bring up the lack of senior leader involvement in leading a transformation during a senior leadership team meeting? We know their involvement is key to a successful transformation, but we avoid bringing it up at these times because it will trigger a conflict within that team. We rationalize it, justify the lack of involvement as being not in the interest of the organization, and then park it in the shadows to keep it out of sight until either the transformation fades away or the next new "flavor of the month" develops.

Over the last 20 years, seeing how individuals manage conflict and try to achieve a mutually respectable resolution reinforced the idea that organizations need to develop their employee's capabilities with conflict resolution. Whether people acknowledge it or not, people spend valuable time in conflict with each other over topics related to their work. Whether on an individual, team, and organizational level, conflict permeates the ways of working in each of our daily lives. At one extreme, we can conclude that conflict is the driver for what people say and how they act on a daily basis. Everything, from who does what, to prioritizing projects, selecting products, managing budgets, and creating a vision, conflict at some level is present. It might be a simple disagreement on priorities, or it may be opposing points of view or opinions that define one's personality, but the simple fact is that conflict is present and shapes decisions, actions, and our relationships at work. How people deal with conflicts and manage it influences the culture of the organization.

Being in a conflict at work dramatically changes how a person performs their job. When in conflict, people stop being themselves and imitate behaviors that they have seen others use in similar situations. This might include staying silent, becoming passive aggressive, retaliating, or some other form of behavior that inhibits a team from performing at a higher level. From a cultural perspective, conflict at work defines the boundaries for what is acceptable behavior when in a disagreement or challenging situation. How conflict is managed by individuals and leaders becomes the standard for what is acceptable in situations of disagreement. The behavior(s) takes on both verbal and non-verbal communication toward others and within the team. In multiple cases, having been on teams where conflict affects the behavior of the team, the verbal and non-verbal clues are omnipresent.

People getting cut off during mid-sentence, people being overlooked when ideas are suggested, even excluding certain people from meetings to avoid having their ideas or opinions discussed are tactics that might arise. This conflict-induced behavior and communication then becomes features or elements of the organization's culture. As mentioned, conflict can be highly confrontational, or acted on through passive aggressiveness actions such as non-committal to a team's decisions. After spending years in meetings and observing the behavior of colleagues, I am convinced that passive aggressiveness is becoming more and more a norm for business today.

How passive aggressiveness shows up can come in many forms. For me, I have personally experienced passive aggressiveness as a coach and facilitator. An experience I will share here occurred to me early in my career. At this company, I performed the duties of a facilitator for large team off-site type of workshops to build capabilities for individuals. Usually, these were part of the organization's efforts to transform the organization. The topics of each workshop would focus on ways of working such as the strategic planning, problem-solving, and other features associated with the transformation. At my first workshop, I noticed that the workshop participants routinely returned late from their breaks and lunches. I didn't think much about it at first, and eventually I brought it up to a co-facilitator who had worked at the company for more years than I. He confirmed what I was experiencing from the behavior of the participants. I assumed that the participants were networking during the breaks, and getting to know each other better. Made sense to me at that time. On the surface, I could accept this rationale, especially if it happened once on the first day or two. However, over time I noticed that this habit seemed less about networking and more deliberate about irritating the workshop facilitators. Even, when extending the breaks and lunch times to allow for the networking element, people still returned late and disrupted the workshop's flow. As a result, the facilitators were tirelessly re-inviting people from the break area back to the training room. Over time, my observation about this habit led the facilitators seemed to agree that there was a resistance or passive aggressiveness on the part of the workshop participants. I even saw this in workshops where I was a participant and a peer of mine was facilitating. People intentionally wanted to upset the facilitator and disrupt the workshop design by being late. I found this behavior to be very odd considering the time and resources that went into the workshop. What was more puzzling is that I noticed people would joke and deliberately ignore the invitations to rejoin the workshop at the cost of irritating the facilitators.

After witnessing this for a year or more, another reason was given about the "late" tactic for these workshops. I was informed by my leader that my reputation as a good facilitator was judged on how effective I was at bringing people back to the workshop on time after breaks. The participants knew this, and as stated, would passively wait until they were ushered back to their chairs. As it turned out, this minor confrontation or performance conflict was part of the culture of the company. Everyone from the divisional leader to individual contributors played the game, and would be a participant in the action at times. Since it was viewed as part of the culture of the organization, it seemed to make it the right thing to do. It made me annoyed, and I began to ask how the tactic adds to the value of the workshop. It also made me think that people didn't respect the time spent by the facilitators to prepare their material. This activity could easily be written off as a type of corporate hazing or jesting; however, even these small conflicts create an image of the company and its culture.

Conflict resolution at work has deep roots in all industrialized countries. If one looks at the United States and the National Labor Relations Act (NLRA) of 1935, the idea that a day at work was harmonious with people being vulnerable and accommodating toward each other is far from the truth. Because conflict at work ended up with violence and bodily harm in most industrialized countries, governmental regulation was introduced to manage the conflict. It is the NLRA in the United States. Within this law, the primary feature was to make it lawful for employees to join a union and participate in collective bargaining. In addition, to these two features, the law also introduced a process to resolve conflicts at work. It is called a grievance/arbitration process. This process describes how a person working in a hierarchal organization resolves serious conflicts between employees and management. In the European Union, countries like Germany and Switzerland have worker boards that serve as a committee to oversee changes to workers' conditions of work as a pre-emptive system to minimize conflict between the two working groups. Although both of these examples illustrate a macrocosm of how unilateral and broad sweeping conflicts are resolved at work, it also provides insights into the foundations of conflict resolution for individuals on a daily basis.

Generally, if more than two people are on a team, then conflict will occur. It happens within teams over assignment of work, setting of priorities, development activities, or perceived favoritism of one employee over another by the manager. From the personal conflicts to conflicts between business units or divisions, within any organization conflicts occurs. We take for granted that conflicts at work are a normal occurrence. And we are also at the point, where we accept poorly managed conflict resolution procedures as the norm. How many times have you heard someone was upset or didn't like a decision, and then stated that they weren't going to do anything about it, because nothing would get changed anyway. This shows a lack of faith in an organization's skill at conflict resolution, both procedurally and individually. If serious enough, meaning a law is being broken or a code of ethics violation, then most organizations have a formal appeal or conflict resolution procedure. Typically, this policy has escalation steps as its procedural feature. An employee follows the policy when they perceive a company decision or individual within the company has treated them unfairly or capriciously. Although most company policies are not as codified as the NRLA, nonetheless they are policies that provide an outlet for an employee who feels aggrieved by the actions of a co-worker or manager. In a simplified definition, the aggrieved employee will seek to gain remediation through a series of steps starting with the supervisor and up to the highest, senior most official in the company. In the end, the aggrieved employee is given a "verdict" on the issue with the hopes of settling the dispute. More serious accusations may take a legal route.

Conflict resolution will continue to be a part of an organization's culture regardless if it's a traditional organization or an Agile one. Being Agile will not prevent conflicts from occurring at work. As we discuss conflict resolution in more detail, I want to steer away from the conflicts that contain legal ramifications or those who require professional interventions. These are far too few to shape culture. I want to focus on the conflicts that people live with day to day. Through the lens of transformation, this book will focus on conflicts that occur when an organization undergoes a transformation. Conflicts that we want to focus on in Breakthrough Agile are the ones that will occur when the old principles of work converge with the new principles and two people or groups both feel they are right about the future ways of working. Whether the conflict is between two people, departments, functions, or divisions, the skills that employees need to manage and resolve this conflict at work are vital to a successful transformation.

In Breakthrough Agile, it is key to build an employee's skills at conflict resolution to achieve breakthrough results in the workplace. Instead of training employees on how to follow a procedure or policy, train employees to recognize when they are in conflict and how to manage the conflict to resolve it on their own. By taking this step, an organization creates a culture of collaboration, trust, and transparency that leads to higher levels of performance and innovation. When conflicts are present and at the point where they do influence the way people work, Breakthrough Agile provides an alternative to the traditional conflict resolution approach.

In my experience, conflict resolution has normally been a line manager's responsibility. In other words, if you have an issue with someone or something, then you seek guidance from your boss. This may or may not resolve the conflict but it complies with the company's conflict resolution policy. Although this seems straightforward, what I have experienced is that people will avoid talking to their manager about a conflict. This could be for a few reasons, but in my opinion, it is due to the lack of skills on both the employee to articulate the conflict without fear of retribution and the lack of skill of the manager to listen and create a sense of security for the aggrieved employee. To state it simply, employees don't speak up because they see the organization (manager) as being a part of the problem. As a result, individuals push their conflicts into the shadows of their work. Then, when stressed or pressured, the employee will talk with friends or close colleagues about the issues to reduce their stress, still avoiding taking any steps to remediate the conflict. I've heard people make statements like they took a new role, changed jobs, or waited for someone to leave the company, as a resolution to their conflict. Doesn't this sound damaging to how the employee does their job on a daily basis. Other times, people wait out conflicts to see if some organizational change eliminates it. For instance, maybe structural change, or realignment of teams eliminates the conflict. If a person is in conflict, then there are endless ways that a conflict might be managed by some organization random action. The one way that seems missing is that the two in conflict discuss and seek to understand each other's way of thinking. By appreciating the diversity of opinion instead of feeling threatened by it, two people can resolve most conflicts that hinder the performance of a team.

Managing conflict and conflict resolution is one of those realities that hide in the shadows of the organization. Everyone experiences conflicts and see them occurring within their teams. However, since employee's capabilities to deal with conflict are rudimentary, conflict becomes a cultural norm. To some, working with perpetual conflict is the way the company works day to day. Since everyone has ongoing conflicts, so why begin to single out conflict and conflict resolution as a cultural business process. There are unspoken rules or rationalizations about conflicts. For some, facing conflict might generate a fear of being seen as weak or incompetent. If an employee raises the conflict out of the shadow and seek to resolve it through discussion or conversation, then the outcome might affect them professional, or on a social level that deals with their credibility.

Another point of view on conflict is that the outcome of a conflict is characterized by the saying, "only the strongest survive." If one doesn't think they'll win the conflict or have the upper hand in the conflict, then why try to resolve it. As a leader, how many of your direct reports come to you with a conflict that includes you? This is what I call the Industrial Darwinism belief. Rather than exposing the conflict to light, and trying to resolve it amicably, it is better to leave it in the shadows and keep your ego and personal social status intact. This is how one survives in today's organization. On the other hand, some may find that by keeping it in the shadows, the unresolved conflict gives them a boost of energy to be more directive towards their antagonist. As the unresolved conflict stays alive in the shadows, it shapes the way decision are made, and work is prioritized for the team. Maybe development opportunities get steered away from the instigator of the conflict. Or in a toxic culture, the conflict gives individuals the courage to shame or humiliate the conflicted individual in a public setting. The "throwing under the bus" mentality happens between the individuals in the conflict. This "tit for tat" type of activity goes round and round in an organization that works and lives with unresolved conflicts. I have seen at times, that people consider this to be the competitive spirit of the organization. To me, this seems pretty far away from how I see a high performing team operating.

In my career, I have met a few leaders who like to create conflict between two people on their teams, as they think it as a way to get things done. One case, the vice president told two team members that they each were up for the same promotion, and that over the next few months, he would be evaluating them to determine who would get the job (the VP was the decision maker for the promotion). Having sat in the meetings that followed this set up, I can assure you that the damage this created within the team and possibly long-term impact of the individuals was measurable. In this case, the two team members spent time attacking the others' credibility and undermining each other's work. It reached such a stress level that in the end one of the two left the company. Afterward, this behavior was so well established as the norm at the site, and people knowing it was approved by the VP, it became the normal way people treated each other. The VP artificially created the conflict thinking it would create a competitive environment to get more innovative work done by the two individuals as they vied for the higher level role. It was a monumental disaster, and one that affected the mindsets and defined a value that was damaging to the team, and organization. In the end, neither were promoted to the higher role, with, as stated earlier, one of the affected people resigning from the company. To me, this is another twisted example of someone who has power over others, and looks at the organization as if it is a survival of the fittest contest – Industrial Darwinism.

At times, I think most people downplay the importance of conflict resolution, or how conflict shapes the company's culture. If you believe that employees are the greatest asset for an organization, then why do we permit, encourage, and/or create an environment that pits them against each other. This is where Agile is more characteristic of a 21st century mentality than a postindustrial mentality of the 1950s. The whole management/labor classification, leaders believing that their purpose is to stress the organization and create tension through fear of job stability. Employees idolizing hierarchy and status, all creates the environment for conflict to be a dominate feature of a company's culture. Agile gives an organization a chance to break-free from this past, and work with greater collaboration, trust, and collective efforts. Breakthrough Agile will create an environment where employees feel safe to speak up and raise ideas or opinions that are new and different. Agility is about getting people to collaborate and work on a team that handles its own conflicts. Being capable at conflict resolution will separate the good from the great companies. People skilled at conflict resolution generally do not show up as the strong-willed leader or someone with thick skin. Usually, people who excel at conflict resolution are excellent communicators and able to let go of opinions or positions at the right time. People with good conflict resolutions skills have resilience and bounce back with renewed energy after setbacks. Skilled professionals at conflict resolution demonstrate how being empathetic and vulnerable is a strength rather than a weakness. Since most organizations work around the issue of conflict resolution, it becomes a barrier for a transformation. A business culture that has poor conflict resolution skills will easily derail a transformation effort to change the way people work.

Everyone can reflect back on how they learned conflict resolution. Whether it was a child learning to play with others or as adolescents maturing into young adulthood. A teenager navigating the complexities of their school or college learns the basics to solve a conflict. Science has added its theories as well stating most people follow three approaches to a threat or conflict – flight, fight, or freeze. This might seem justifiable for an animal, but as human beings, we have a higher cognitive element that helps us to deal with conflict on a reflective level. This is what separates us from other primates who have limited cognitive abilities. It is our ability to self-reflect and communicate using a non-threatening language or behavior that gives humans that competitive advantage in the animal kingdom. As you look back and think about how conflict is handled in your organization, how is it dealt with – flight, fight, or freeze? Or is the fourth approach used – do people communicate respectively with each other and try to reach an understanding of what is the source of the conflict and how the two people might resolve it in an amicable and sustainable way.

My first experience with a formal conflict resolution process occurred when I was a college student. During my undergraduate years, I studied English and History. This meant loads of reading of everything from European and American writers to histories of Asia and Africa. One class I took was in Victorian Literature. The Victorian era generated a list of classic authors who are still studied today due to their contribution to English literature. Their poetry is used today as a standard for modern day writers. I took this course as it looked challenging and would improve my writing and critical thinking skills. However, I soon realized that the professor and I didn't mix well. I couldn't seem to complete an assignment that met his standard. Even after applying due diligence in research and rewrites, I never had a paper that was passing. To my surprise, I soon found out that almost half of the class had the same experience as I did with this professor. This seemed to ease the sting, but I was still concerned as I knew that I had good skills at writing and interpreting literary works of art. I became concerned about what seemed like an evitable failing grade in the course and midway through the course, I approached the professor and sought his support and guidance. Trying not to be confrontational, I explained how I researched my opinions on my papers. To the point of showing him the references in a published textbook. I also made it transparent to him, that other students had told me that they were in the same situation as me. However, the professor didn't want to hear my story and he felt that he didn't have to hear my appeals over my grade as it was his interpretation of my work as a writer, and he commanded the large office with the distinguished literary title.

The professor continued to flunk me and half of the class. At one point, I would go to the professor after receiving a failing mark and try to persuade him that he didn't grade me fairly. In these situations, there would be silly arguments or discussions on the use of a word in a particular sentence that was interpreted by him one way and myself the other. For instance, in one case, I used the word "rod" to imply punishment to an individual, i.e., spare the rod and spoil the child. However, in the discussion, the professor seemed to think, the context of the Victorian writer was to indicate that the passage wasn't about punishment but about authority and the rod as used in the story was more of a holy septure or religious symbol. In his opinion, I had used it wrongly in my sentence and the interpretation of the literature. Therefore, the score I received was justified. Even though both were correct, his definition ruled and I received the failing mark. I was in extreme conflict as I realized my grade point average would suffer and the credits for the course would not go toward my degree.

As the semester continued, I became stressed. Other classes didn't get the attention needed as this class because of the conflict. Could this happen to a work colleague who is experiencing a work conflict? The conflict led me to spending hours researching ways to appeal the treatment I was receiving from this professor. In my investigation, I discovered a formal student rebuttal process to address a case like this. It was a formal process when a student had a conflict with a professor and the student perceived that the actions of the professor were arbitrary and/or capricious. As someone who didn't have another option, I started the process of rebuttal. As part of the rebuttal process, a third party reviewed my assignments and discussions were held with the professor and myself independently. Surprisingly, in the end, I came out with a satisfactory result to my issues. However, there was no resolution to the conflict between the professor and me. When I would cross paths with him on the campus, you could sense the feelings of negativity and distrust coming from him. In the end, this experience shaded my view of the university's academic culture and how professors use the system to create good or bad grades that weren't always objective. I also want to make it clear that I had outstanding professors at this university, many of whom helped shape my thinking and critical thinking skills that I use to this day. I am deeply grateful and indebted to them for their service as outstanding teachers and mentors during this stage of my life.

Today, this example illustrates how most organizations manage conflicts. They use an appeal or rebuttal process where the two parties seek to find satisfaction in an arbitration or judgment from a higher authority. In the end, many times the conflict never gets resolved and what happens is that one person gets their needs meet and the other loses out. The approach doesn't ask the conflicted individuals or groups to gain a better understanding of the true issues underlying the conflict. In today's organizations, those issues remain and continue to creep into the daily life and work of employees as the conflicts remain unresolved. Another model for conflict resolution that has been perfected by one of the oldest organizations in the world is found in most military branches. It is known as the escalation model. In a traditional organization, the escalation model is seen as the effective way to resolve conflicts. In the military, the pathway of conflict resolution is clear – follow the chain of command.

What this means is that a soldier brings the issue to their direct supervisor, and if the issues isn't resolved satisfactorily, then it moves up to the next level of authority. In a culture based on hierarchy, command and control, and following orders, this method of conflict resolution is called escalation. Escalate the issue to the higher authority and have them decide or judge the conflict. To me, this is a disempowering approach to take as the means to resolve the conflict are taken out of the hands of those who are in the conflict. Very similar to a judge handing down a verdict, the escalation process requires the conflicted parties to ask someone else to resolve their conflict based on stories from each side. The accountability and skills needed for conflict resolution are not developed and in essence are a feature of the position one holds in the organization. Based on one's social status in the hierarchy, the escalation process assume that the higher the position, the better equipment that person is to judge or resolve a conflict. From my experience, this seems to falter when held up to a mirror.

In traditional organizations, managers or leaders inherently believe that their social position on the organization chart gives them more essential skills and knowledge in conflict resolution. Leaders and managers may assert that solving conflicts is a major part of their role. This belief gets reinforced because a superior in an organization can tell two direct reports what to do. In my early years as a manager, my advice to two direct reports in conflict would be something like, "I want you two to work together better" or "I want you two to work together or else!" The element of fear always had a way of cooling off a conflict on the team. However, is the conflict closer to resolution? Or, are the two now still at odds and worse, affecting other team members and their performance because they continue to intimidate each other at work. The fear of losing one's favor with the manager or damaging ones career prospects shapes how conflicts are managed. These fears are reflective of how employees in a traditional organization handles conflicts internally. To become Agile and generate value from being a customer-centric focused organization, it is essential that employees resolve their conflicts without escalation. Developing this capability will increase the team's effectiveness at meeting customer's needs.

Breakthrough Agile provides principles to help individuals become better at conflict resolution reducing the impact that conflict resolution has on the speed of the transformation and generating value.

In Breakthrough Agile's framework, we build up people's capability in resolving conflicts. Instead of choosing between the normal three reactions of flight, fight, or freeze in a conflict, an Agile culture requires everyone to resolve conflicts in a timely pace through listening and empathy. This ability to breakthrough conflicts at work and have teams work more collaborative requires a high degree of self-awareness with individuals. No longer are conflicts settled to one's advantage over another. Conflicts are resolved with people gaining new insights and understandings of their co-workers and the processes that they are working on. One should feel a learning cycle when participating in a quality conflict resolution session. Resolving conflicts quickly, re-focuses individuals on the value creating work and refuels the team into developing solutions for the customer. In Breakthrough Agile conflicts will occur as a part of the transformation, and it is important to utilize the platforms principles to influence how the conflict is mitigated and resolved. The resolution of conflicts and their management is part of the cultural fabric of the organization.

As mentioned, a quality conflict resolution turns into a learning cycle for the participates. As a result, better outcomes and value can be generated by the individuals. Prior to the global "work from home" experiment driven by the COVID pandemic, businesses were and still are prioritizing the idea of psychological safety and the act of "speaking up." Even with the best of ideas, savvy IT applications and artificial intelligence, it is the person not the technology that has inspiration and creativity to drive the innovation process. Technology and its features may serve as the means to ease data collection, analysis, and presentation, but getting new ideas to work on innovative and novel prototypes are coming from humans. People test the boundaries of technology, instead of technology testing the boundaries of people. To increase this innovation spirit, people need to show up as themselves, as their whole selves, and not work in fear of employee conflicts.

This new way of working challenges the traditional mindsets. One structural feature to change this mindset is to transform the role of the manager or next level authority from a conflict resolution mediator. In the future work environment, individuals need to be able to identify when they are in conflict and work through a conflict without the need of a managerial arbitrator to reach a resolution. This will also drive individuals and teams to achieve a higher level of performance since it implies that conflict is absent in daily work allowing teams to focus on their prioritized goals. Applying Breakthrough Agile's principles, an organization will prepare itself to enter into a model where people handle conflicts at their own level through deep discussion and focusing on issues and processes. Leaders will prepare themselves to take on the role of coach and teacher to educate their employees on how to handle conflicts between each other without escalation, fear of losing/shaming, or being admonished. This becomes increasing important as the work of the transformation journey is hard and challenging. People need to have this psychological safety in order to work in this new pattern of work created by the Agile ways of working.

Breakthrough Agile principles will sustain the Agile organization as it transitions and re-shapes how conflicts are resolved. As you can imagine, during the transformation, conflicts will surface between the old and new mindsets. Conflicts will develop at all levels throughout the multiple learning cycles of the transformation. It is on the individual, team, department, function, all the way up to division, and business unit levels that individuals need to utilize a better way to resolve conflicts to help the transformation succeed. To shed light on what might happen, we can look at conflicts that occur on the individual or team level. Within a work group, conflict is more focused on discreet activities with shorter time horizons. For instance, who does what and how it is done and by when are all sources of conflict at the individual and team level. A team leader's ego and people's pride are sometimes the root of the conflict in these discussions. When someone doesn't want to be told what to do or take on a hard assignment, this easily triggers a conflict on the team. In other cases, at the team level, conflicts occur when there is a fear that one person's assignment will generate higher recognition or personal promotion over other team members because of the scope and nature of the work assignment.

As the size of the team or organizational unit becomes bigger, then the conflict may be broader or more strategic. What is the vision of the team or organization? What is the best city to invest in across the globe? How to allocate resources or assets, and what are the future products of the organization? How will a poor performing business unit be managed by the CEO of a company can create conflict between the CEO and the senior leaders of that business unit? All of these events happen within today's business world and it is key that people within the organization role model and demonstrate Breakthrough Agile's approach to conflict resolution. In the boarder and larger scope conflicts, the impact grows exponentially. Let's take an example of a case study that I experienced. In this example, the global organization had decided to close a manufacturing plant to reduce its operational footprint across the world.

As one leader of the business unit tells it – during the final stages of a site's history, the local leadership team and the global team entered into a conflict. As a plant closure project entered the first phase of personnel layoffs and product transfers, leaders within the closing site started to question the rational for the closure. The plant had shown excellent productivity gains over the last few years, the employees were extremely loyal and easy to work with, and the management team had been together for years. The conflict the local team had with the global operations team focused on their belief that the local team was being treated irresponsibly and weren't given investment opportunities to grow the product pipeline. This lack of new products, and the draw of a low-cost region manufacturing site resulted in the decision to shut down the operation and move the technology to a low cost region. The objective of the global team was to close the plant down to save money and move the product to a region that would lower product cost. Overshadowing the closure, was the knowledge that the technology at the plant was becoming obsolete, and a newer design for the product was already on the market.

In a final attempt to slow the plant closure project, the GM and leadership team started to implement efforts to increase productivity and reduce quality issues. Their belief was that this would show how an aging plant with a small product portfolio can be successful even when the parent company had identified financial savings by closing the site. The local team was successful at increasing productivity and reducing its costs through a Lean transformation over 2 years. However, the problem became worse when a new VP of Operations came on board, and he steadfastly pushed to keep the plant closure project moving forward. The conflict heightened and the lack of trust between the two groups grew. The global team's perspective was that its strategic alignment with the CEO and that office's strategy for a smaller manufacturing footprint was the priority for the division and this site. The local team saw the impact of this project on the lives of the people at the plant and the end of the plant's history within the community. As a reaction, the local team resisted and slowed the closure project down through various means such as claiming personnel shortage, health regulatory guidelines for transferring of product, and other credible actions.

This organization practiced the escalation method of conflict resolution. As a result, the VP of Operations was the final judge and his intention was clear. The local team didn't have an avenue or the skills necessary to manage the conflict. Since escalation was the rule for how conflicts were resolved, the balance of power was in favor of the global team, as the final arbitrator was the VP themselves. The local team was unable to move past this point in the escalation process. As can be expected, the conflict ended with the plant GM being removed and many of the senior leaders leaving for new roles during the closure. Personnel at the site saw the inequity in the conflict between the local and global team and sympathized with the local team. In the end, the organization lost key talent, developed a negative reputation with its employees and the local community, and lost customers from the fallout. The transfer took two additional years and ran over budget before the plant and technical transfer was complete. How the two teams communicated reflects how conflict resolution when done poorly impacts the business. If the two sides were able to have worked through the needs and wants of each other and not just focus on their own needs, then the impact described above would have been minimized. The local team's resistance and subterfuge may have been prevented resulting in an on-time project; as well as the collateral damage done to the people and community could have been minimized and talent that left the company could have been transferred to another location. In the new ways of working, it is especially important that the organization builds up conflict resolution capabilities as it starts on its transformation journey toward Agile.

One difference to highlight at this point, is that conflict and tension are different. Conflict generally is characterized as individuals or groups having opposing or contradictory views on a decision or action. Tension on the other hand is a feeling of nervousness or uncertainty in an event or preceding an event. Tension within a team is the result of the team being challenged to work outside their comfort zone on outcomes. Tension is beneficial as it is a signal of change that people are stretching themselves and challenging the status quo. Innovation, experimentation, and taking a risk are the triggers for tension, as opposed to an argument that attempts to minimize someone's work or contribution. Tension to perform, find a better solution, or to drive for a higher level of satisfaction with customers are beneficial. This is where we will find inspiration from employees to become better than their current situation. In one of the discussions I had with a team leader that implemented OKRs for the first time with their team, this tension became real for them. As a coach, I encouraged the team to be bold and challenging with the key results. The team, when we discussed the key results, felt uncertain about setting a too high target. However, at the end of the year, the team exceeded their key result by over 60% and the team leader told me that at the time of creating their OKR, they had no idea that they could generate as much value for the company. Tension is a natural output from an organization that is practicing Breakthrough Agile. Tension helps build stronger relationships between employees by deepening the understanding of the business processes and products. Tension is a natural feeling or sensation that occurs when a person has a challenge to perform at a higher level or achieve an outcome that will have a significant impact on the business.

People experience a learning cycle from events that have tension. Watch a child learn something new and you can see the tension in their actions, how they talk, and the way they interact with others. As a child attempts to learn a new skill such as riding a bike, the level of tension consumes the child's thoughts and actions. How they approach the task is reflected in their actions. Once seated on the bike, they slowly start pedaling until they learn that a certain speed helps them balance. They ride in a straight line until they become proficient at using the handle bars to steer the bike in turns. As they gain more and more experience riding, then their confidence grows and level of risk-taking increases. They continue taking risks in the early stages because they sense that riding a bike provides a reward or outcome that changes their current understanding of the world around them. As a parent, once the child learns riding a bike, the look of accomplish and achievement on the child's face something to behold. Although not entirely dissimilar within an Agile organization, the outcomes we strive for in our actions are similar to that of a child learning to ride a bike. With each outcome achieved, we feel this sense of pride and accomplishment that comes with failing, relearning, and then succeeding. This is the life cycle of a transforming organization on its journey to become more competitive, self-aware, and innovative.

Within an Agile organization, business tensions need to be transparent and embraced. Experiencing tension with one's work gives an employee a chance to demonstrate their ownership and empowerment of their work environment. Employees need to understand and communicate the tension to others. Leaders need to hold coaching conversations when an employee is discussing the tension of completing a project or task. This isn't a sign of weakness or skill level, but a sign that employees are self-aware of the expectations and outcomes that can be achieved. Leaders need to engage individuals and teams at these times through coaching and collaboration. By breaking through the tension to achieve a higher performance, a sense of growth and achievement is realized by the team or individual. As the transformation journey is being experienced by an organization, tension is a healthy result that everyone at all levels should feel about what is happening.

Conflict on the other hand is a symptom of an organization that is stuck between two different mindsets. It is a struggle of who has power over others or whose priority gets resourced and acted on. Conflict between two people or teams has at its core distrust, anger, jealousy, and a sense of one side losing control to the other. Traditional principles and values can foster conflict in the organization, when teams focus exclusively on department key performance indicators (KPIs) to measure their performance. A quality department that looks to achieve zero defects or zero customer complaints will hinder a production department as it attempts to produce to a rigorous production schedule. When budget performance dominates the decisions of senior leaders, then a silo mentality kicks in. Support departments cut back or take short cuts on providing support to those functions that rely upon them to sustain efficiency and productivity. Imagine reducing a budget to build people's capabilities to build the skills necessary to transform an organization, and then place expectations on the organization to work in an entirely new mindset and with a different set of behaviors. When short term, firefighting actions outweigh long-term development and growth, conflict will emerge. When a company rewards people through promotions and higher bonus' for activities that maintain the status quo and minimizes the work of people that are changing the culture, conflict becomes a daily part of everyone's life. People start to ask what is the motivation for working differently when the reward system still rewards people based on the traditional outputs that create stress and conflict. At times, a transformation is a conflict between those who want to change and those who want to keep things the same. A solution to resolve this conflict is embedded in Breakthrough Agile. The framework provides principles and systems that will enable an organization to achieve its short term goals while building the long term capabilities for the future.

A classic example when budget goals influence a decision is found in manufacturing plants maintenance and production. When equipment breaks down, there are times when maintenance may rationalize rebuilding the equipment/part, instead of ordering a new one. In a traditional organization, the principle of meeting the budget or saving money, drives the decision making on how to fix the problem. Many times, I have seen the maintenance team apply this thinking and go for rebuilding the part over ordering a new part. However, the end user of the refurbished part, the production employee, experiences the impact of a sub-performing repair part. The machine operator has more frequent machine stoppages, poorer quality of product, high usage of raw materials, as a result using a rebuilt part over a newly purchased OEM part. In the end, production ends up running overtime and increasing costs on labor, scrap, or raw materials. These two groups' maintenance and production come into conflict as a result of this traditional thinking. I have seen many arguments, almost physical fights between maintenance and production on issues just like this. How to repair broken equipment becomes the central point. Maintenance is seen as the expert in the equipment, yet production needs to run without waste. The end result, many times, is that the maintenance team meets its KPI of managing costs, but the production unit suffers on output and overtime due to the inefficiency of the rebuilt parts. At the end of the year, production fails to meet its productivity KPIs due to the poor performing equipment. Through the lens of performance, one team is recognized for meeting its budget, while that other team feels the sting of having to explain its higher labor costs and poor yield throughout the year.

Another example of how this might unfold could be seen in a daily team stand up meeting. At the standup, a team member has a Kanban card which is overdue. The meeting facilitator highlights the overdue. The team leader may recognize that this is an issue and wants to dive deeper into the details. In Breakthrough Agile, the leader would ask that the team member to stay after the daily huddle for a deeper discussion. In the pursuing conversation, the leader acts as a coach and supporter for his team member. They ask questions (Figure 5.1) around the lateness of the task. For example, "what do you think

Problem Solving	Brainstorming
What is the outcome you are trying to achieve?	Imagine if,…?
What have you tried?	What if you had an unlimited budget?
What will you try next?	How might a different company do this?
What barriers or constraints do you have?	Who else does something like this?
How have support teams been involved?	What is a similar operation?
How will you know when you achieved your outcome?	Where can we see a similar process or solution?

Figure 5.1   Typical coaching questions.

you need to do to get the task back on track?," "how have the resources been allocated to the task?," "what has been the barrier to the lateness?," "what have you tried already?," and "what did you learn from your early experiments?"

These open-ended questions surface details about the planning, time and resource commitment, and what action the team member might take to get back on track. This questioning focus the owner of the Kanban card on the work that needs to be done. Compare this to a traditional command and control scenario where immediately after the late card is highlighted in the stand up, the leader calls out the lateness in front of the whole team and criticizes the team member for not working hard enough or not doing their job well. The leader might be brazen enough to admonish the team member that the task needs to get back on track or else, in front of their peers. In Breakthrough Agile, leading by fear is an anti-pattern to an Agile Culture. Having lived through this scenario, the situation gets worse with the team member starts defending themselves, blaming others, and questioning the judgment of the leader. As you can see, leading by fear, using controlling techniques creates conflict. An simple event, such as this one described, may leave a scar or perception on the team as to what are the boundaries of their empowerment, and how conflict is used to control people within the organization. By giving employees the skill to resolve conflicts and pre-empting conflicts, the culture of the organization shifts from blaming and controlling to one of collaboration and trust.

Symptoms of unresolved conflict are seen in how people treat each other. When rumors and gas lighting techniques are present in a team, generally there is an unresolved conflict at the root. Discrediting others, tarnishing reputations, forming cliques, and picking a side are other symptoms of unresolved conflict within a team or organization. Unresolved conflict left to run its course creates a toxic work environment that stifles the innovation and creativity of the organization. Being at conflict limits the level of psychological safety that people will feel in their day-to-day work. To deal with the unresolved conflict, people will only do what they are told to do, and avoid taking on ownership or accountability for the company's strategic goals. Individuals will withdraw and contribute only when they feel physically safe and the action doesn't lead to a conflict with another team member. Within a transformation, unresolved conflict and fear to speak-up, will derail the best of transformation efforts. Conflict resolution is therefore another key business process that needs addressed in Breakthrough Agile at the principle level.

It is important to be able to recognize conflict within a team and then take steps to diffuse it. As a leader or team member, look for signs of conflicts within the team's daily interactions. This is included in the conflict resolution sensing model that is introduced in this book. As part of sensing conflict on the team, look for incidents when team members immediately judge the idea of others. Other signs of potential conflict within the team are seen in the engagement of all team members. Assess your team, ask if there is a disparity in time given to discussing team member's ideas. On the team, does each idea receive the same amount of attention or consideration? Do team members have an equal amount of time to speak and present their ideas or opinions? Or is the team only following the advice of one or two on the team? What is the ratio of ideas that go live from each person on the team? Or do only a few team members get their ideas discussed, and then acted on? Is there a streaming of ideas from select people on the team? Does every idea from the team leader get implemented? If statements like these are seen or observed, then the team is more likely working through unresolved conflict than with creative tension. These symptoms indicate the team is functioning with a sense of hierarchy between individuals or that the team is functioning with the assumption some people have more important roles than others. It could also indicate that some team members feel smarter, more in tune, or superior to others on the team.

In an Agile organization, being unable to resolve conflicts will impact the quality of work and level of innovation in teams. Unresolved conflict will derail the deployment of a key Agile system – Scrum. When design teams are created and placed into a Scrum setting the dynamic of the team and the pressure to produce an MVP will create conflicts. If the conflicts are left unresolved, then team members will stop voicing creative or unique opinions or ideas on how to create the solution. The lack of skill in dealing with conflict resolution will deaden the creativeness that comes from performing Scrums. As the conflicts reduces innovation, then the team starts to think and act like a traditional waterfall project team. RACIs start to surface, Gantt charts, project charters, and a hierarchy forms within the team. The cultural shift in mindset of producing MVPs doesn't happen and the Scrum event becomes another name for a project meeting. Even more concerning is that the Scrum team members will return to their normal roles after the Scrum with a feeling that the new Agile transformation isn't changing the organization's culture. The hierarchical culture will prevail during the Scrum. People will view the transformation as another "flavor of the month" program. In the end, the transformation team is pigeon-holed with another function, and the transformation tools are utilized in a "fit for purpose" or "appropriate" manner.

In my experience, conflict resolution is a powerful element of a company's culture and if employees do not have the skills to deal with conflict, then this capability gap will prevent the creation of an Agile organization. The time wasted by managers in dealing with people and teams in conflict takes the energy that could be focused on the transformation. Unresolved, these conflicts become a barrier to transformation activities. In Breakthrough Agile, employees are given the skills to resolve conflict at all levels. No longer do employees escalate issue for the manager to decide how to move forward. Employees now spend time in discussion/reflection with those that they have a conflict. The conflicted parties work through their assumptions of the other to reach a point where they can work together constructively without disrupting the environment of the team.

In today's business world, having employees show up as their whole selves working toward a purpose and leveraging their experience toward meeting the customer needs is a key outcome of the transformation. The untapped potential that all employees can bring to work daily is always greater than leveraging the insights of only one or two individuals. Breakthrough Agile is designed to move an organization closer toward this outcome by introducing principles on how to resolve conflicts. On the transformation journey, psychological friction will occur and create a natural barrier to cultural change. That barrier exists within the organization's ecosystems and the daily interaction between people. How people react to each other, how they talk to each other, and how open or closed the organization is to change will create conflict. To overcome this barrier, organizations need to develop their people to resolve conflicts without escalation or following an out-dated procedure. Conflict resolution as a skill, as with the other four principle-based cultural business processes will reshape the culture of the organization.

The coaching point on conflict resolution is that both sides need to listen to understand the other's needs, motivations, and wants (Figure 5.2). Each side needs to empathize first with the other individual and seek to understand the differences in perception that is creating the conflict.

Each person in the conflict needs to ask the other open-ended questions about their thought process, their wants, needs, perspective, and motivations. Once this information is transparent, then the two individuals can work on moving from conflict to tension or completely resolve the conflict altogether.

Figure 5.2 Perspective influences opinion.

In working with hundreds of teams and multiple organizations going through a transformation, unresolved conflict is the Achilles heel for future success. Inherently, a transformation effort will create friction and conflict between the transformation ways of working and people who resist and favor the old way of working. Conflict happens and is a natural output of any transformation effort. This is why educating and building capabilities on conflict resolution during the transformation efforts will speed the implementation and cultural change associated with transformation platform. Think about the amount of time and energy an organization spends on unresolved conflict or when conflicting views enter into a decision. What happens? Is there a winner in this conflict? What value ends up being delivered to the customer? When everyone begins to understand conflict resolution, and can identify when they are in conflict and have the means to solve it, then the organization speeds up its ability to learn and grow. Breakthrough Agile needs this foundation for it to deliver its benefits to the organization.

Understanding and building capabilities on conflict resolution is key to creating an environment for a successful transformation. With this in mind, conflict resolution has been identified as a key business process that needs to be addressed in Breakthrough Agile (Figure 5.3) at the principle and value level.

The principles of conflict resolution in Breakthrough Agile are as follows:

1. Develop capacity to empathize
2. Listen to understand. Discuss the idea, do not respond to the person
3. Diversity supports growth and development
4. Deal with conflict. Avoid escalation

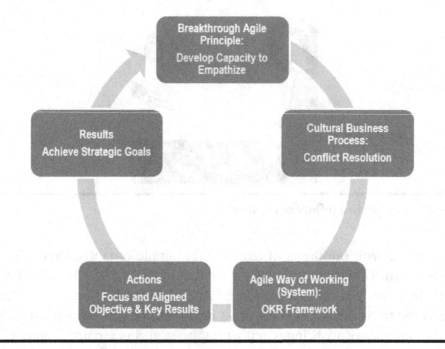

Figure 5.3   Breakthrough Agile's Operational Model for conflict resolution.

Develop Capacity to Empathize

Empathy is seen today as a key attribute for great leaders. The ability to empathize has resonates with people and they easily connect the image of an excellent leader with being empathetic. This image of a thoughtful listener and caring person who also leads the team through the challenges of a business ecosystem comes to everyone's mind when we think of an empathetic leader. Some may even think that empathy comes with the position in the 21st century; e.g., leadership roles develop a person's empathetic skills. However, once you start to peel back the layers and understand what is empathy, the true challenge of practicing empathy becomes clear. I have seen this in experiments that I use for team development. In these cases, when I start to work with a team that wants to practice Agile, I develop the team by understanding empathy through a visual exercise. In the exercise, I put two pictures side by side of the same content but different context and display them to the team (Figure 5.4). For instance, two pictures of families eating their evening meal are placed side by side but in different contextual situations, different age groups, different environment, different races, nationalities, etc. The example below shows how I set up the exercise.

Figure 5.4 Examples of pictures used to develop empathy skills.

I then ask the team to draw insights from the pictures. I ask the participants to empathize with what they see in the photos and make insights about the needs, wants, and motivations of each group. The exercise requires them to draw upon their personal experiences to create their insights. In my instructions to the team, I explain to them that insights are not the obvious conclusions that anyone would draw from looking at the photos but are conclusions or statements as to what might be motivating influences to the people in the photos. I ask the team to think about the needs of the individuals and what are their unmet needs. If they were to have a conversation with these people, what questions might you ask to get them to explain what it is that they need or what their motivations might be. Having done this exercise hundreds of times, I am always surprised at how people think they show empathy and their understanding of empathy.

For instance, usually people state what they see. Two families eating dinner or one family has lots of food, the other doesn't. Other observations come out about the age of the people or the quality of the clothes, dishes, etc. A few times, people might get into the area where they are potentially discovering what the needs of the people. This is practicing empathy. For instance, health care might be a concern for a group or education of their children. Uncovering the motivations and needs of the personas in the photo is how we empathize. The exercise would conclude with a discussion around how one would verify their assumption if they were in an interview with the people in the picture. What questions would you ask to support your assumptions, or draw out these motivations. After the exercise, people tend to gain a better understanding of what is meant by empathizing and using empathy as a way of working skill.

As mentioned, a small percentage of participants are able to step into the shoes of the people in the photos and seek to understand their motivations. Many show sympathies for the people in the photos. Statements like, I know how this family feels or this is just like my family demonstrates using sympathy to understand others. However, it isn't being empathic. Looking and expressing a shared experience with someone in a good time or bad or commiserating with them by telling them you know how they feel and things will get better is being sympathetic. Empathy is seeing someone in a hardship and drawing the insight that this person fears losing their job or not being able to feed their family. The exercise helps to awaken people's sense of being empathetic. When we begin to build conflict resolution skills within the organization, the extent to which people empathize – see the others' motivation, needs, and wants – is critical to developing the capability to resolve conflict.

Individuals using empathy will resolve conflicts easier and quicker. The ability to see the situation from the others' perspective dramatically increases a conflict being resolved to the benefit of the individuals engaged in the conflict. Throughout the transformation, especially at the individual and team level, the organization will see more conflicts as it implements the systems of Breakthrough Agility. Take for example, a Scrum event. When a sprint team is working on developing a prototype and the team has two strong supporters of a different approach, what generally happens is that a conflict emerges. In a case I coached, the two supporters had what they thought was the best idea for a prototype. Instead of working through the conflict and resolving it before beginning work on one prototype, the team decided to develop two MVPs. In the end, the sprint team was split and each MVP had half the team's resources for developing one of the MVPs. The team's focus, energy, and now sense of accomplishment was diminished since two MVPs from the same team were competing with each other. The customer centricity was lost on producing the best MVP for the customer. The conflict went unresolved and the team developed two MVPs with different features and purposes. The conclusion of the Scrum event was a little disheartening as the two teams asked the key stakeholder to decide which MVP to go with. Although there was an option of solutions, the team spirit and motivation was split in the end – one team felt right and the other wrong. If the two idea champions would have been more empathic to each other and sought to understand the motivations of the other, then the decision to work on one MVP could have been reached. Following the sprint processes, in the next iteration the ideas that were put into the backlog could have been adapted to succeeding MVP. By this approach, the team would have stayed together and been more effective in designing its MVP. When people are skilled at looking for the motivations, needs, and wants of the other, then understanding their position makes it easier to decide on what is best for the team. In Breakthrough Agile, developing the capacity to empathize leads to greater business success.

Conflict resolution can be *gamed* as well. The phrase "gamed" means when one knows what the right thing to do is, and does it to only meet their own needs. To make empathy work it requires each person to be truthful, authentic and vulnerable. When practicing empathy, especially to resolve personal conflict, then the two who are engaged in the conflict need to feel equal and have the same level of psychological safety confidence. In the end, the conflict doesn't necessarily get resolved by compromise but by an agreement where both people feel their needs are met. Once the personal conflict is resolved, then the two can focus on addressing the customer needs of the team or organization. Maybe there is still tension from points of view or opinions but it isn't a conflict associated with the personality of another person. This tension will result in a better MVP than one designed with a team in conflict between team members.

In this situation, a scrum product owner (PO) may look for signs of conflicts in how the team works together. Are some team member's ideas judged immediately? Are people's ideas not fully discussed and listed as non-viable by another team member? Is the same person getting their ideas to go forward to the next stage of the creative process? If statements like these are seen or observed, then the team is more likely working in conflict than with creative tension.

Listen to Understand. Do Not Respond to the Person

Listening to understand is a challenge that I have seen at all levels within an organization. It is a skill that needs better understood and practiced more. It requires individuals to have the discipline and self-awareness to listen. In my experience, I have a tool to test this capability with a team or individual that is quite simple. The approach is to use a video of two individuals discussing a topic that has sufficient detail and has a common business theme that the audience can relate to. For instance, I've showed a video of a job interview. In the video, the interviewer asked the candidate to explain a time when they were on a team that suffered in performance due a personality conflict. The response of the candidate, which of course is well rehearsed, describes a detailed story of an incident. The video lasts approximately 5 minutes. During the video, the training participants listen to the story, take notes, and practice their listening skills. At the end of the video, I then asked questions to the participants about the video. What was discussed during the job interview? What was the conflict? How was it resolved? In my experience, very few remember what started the conflict of the story. And very few restate the entire story in detail and can pin point turning points in the story or understand the role the interviewee played on the team. Most people remember only the last few statements in the video or the physical features of the interviewer and candidate. This exercise shows how unconscious bias influences a person when they have to listen, and what people see influence what they think they hear.

After time, I started to ask myself, "How do the workshop participants behave as they watch the video?" How do they listen?" From their body language, many of the participants looked uncomfortable. As they watched the video, I could see them struggling to follow the dialogue. Even those that took generous notes, had difficulty in following the the story and what were the significant points. The environment that they watched the video was adequate – video quality, sound, furniture to sit in. However, knowing that they were doing the exercise, and being asked to listen to understand was new to them. From the responses of the experiment, and the comments made afterward, I concluded that people, if unable to listen to understand, will apply their mental stereotypes to the video's characters – their unconscious bias. They look at the non-verbal clues instead of hearing the dialogue. They listen for changes in tone of voice to indicate a serious point in the story. There is a lack of focus on the verbal story and more a focus on physical elements of the speakers. Often the participants practice a *listen to respond* behavior. In some cases, people would hear a statement from the video, and immediately form an opinion. From that point forward, they apply the opinion to the rest of the narrative. For example, if they felt the interviewee was responsible for the conflict, the remaining dialogue had this bias to it. Or, most of their opinion was based on the reaction of the interviewer to the interviewee. They observed how the interviewer reacted to the story and drew conclusions about what was being discussed from this point of view. Time and time again, this exercise had similar results across all levels of the organization. Everyone has a stronger capacity to *listen to respond* versus *listen to understand* capability. In your next meeting, try this test. After someone gives a presentation, wait to see how the audience reacts. Are there more suggestions about changing the presentation pitch, or more questions about trying to understand how the presenter came to their conclusion? This is a quick way to check if the team is listening to respond or listening to understand. The key takeaway is that people need to practice and develop their listening skills. In a discussion between two people trying to resolve a conflict, being able to listen to understand will de-escalate the situation very rapidly. During this stage in conflict resolution, listeners try to uncover what are the needs and motivations of the other person.

Listening to understand gets harder for people when the discussion is between people from different social levels in the organization. Those at the higher level may feel the need to know the answer and provide the solution. The pressure for them to deliver this answer may prevent them from taking time to hear what the other person is saying. What the listener does instead of listening to understand what the other person is saying and is to tell the speaker what they think is the right answer. In situations where I see poor listening or listening to respond, the responding individual has no pause or reflection time from when the speakers stops talking to their own opinion. In almost all situations, the other individual starts immediately after the person stops speaking or interrupts the other person without asking for permission to break into the conversation. Listening to respond indicates that the speaker has challenged an assumption of the listener or the listener's mental model. Listening to respond is generally the listener seeking to defend or rationalize their assumption or way of thinking. If the two in the discussion are from different social levels in the organization or one feels superior to the other for some other reason, then the listen to respond action is an act to reinforce the feeling of superiority one feels over the other. The listener wants to provide their solution to the speaker without first understanding how the speaker came to their current understanding of the situation. When people listen to understand and don't respond to the person, the organization will take on a more collaborative and innovative culture. It will help people within the organization develop stronger relationships among peers and managers and move teams from conflict to tension in most cases.

Diversity Supports Growth and Development

Leveraging the diversity of an organization will promote its ability to design flexible and sustainable solutions for its customers. Diversity creates an environment where people seek out diverse points of view and look to others to make more holistic and impactful decisions about their work. A diverse work environment is more than just having multiple races, genders, nationalities, and experience levels in the organization. Diversity is also about different ideas coming from people who are similar in these categories. Diversity of perspectives and ideas is as essential as diversity in physical characteristics. Let's look at an example from China. Within a design team that is creating a new way of working with the customer, the team members were all Chinese. The group is made up of both male and female, and the experience level for the team varied from senior to newly hired team members. However, in promoting diversity, the team is cross-functional. It is not only marketing and sales people on the team from the same level within the organization but includes team members from human resources, engineering, policy, legal, etc. The team also includes people who work at customer facing, back office, managerial, and technical roles. In a few teams that applied this cross-functionality, even admins from different departments such as quality, legal, or supply chain are included on the teams. The team not only leverages the diversity of physical features but also brings in the different points of views of different departments to help create the best possible solution for the customer.

In conflict resolution, diversity creates conflict within the organization in two ways. Lack of diversity on a team will create conflict within the organization through a lack of transparency and trust. If a team is only composed of a small segment of the organization, then the outcomes from the team are narrowly focused on doing what is best for that function or group of people. In these narrowly focused teams, the MVP process is overshadowed by actions that seek to please the managerial or leader of the department instead of focusing on what the needs are for the customer. As a result, the team delivers a lack luster solution that marginally creates more value for the organization. The team innovates only to the level that is best for the team members, their function, and their leaders. As a result, those reviewing the team's work from outside the department question the effort and outcome. In the end, the marginally MVP may create conflict about the team's performance results and the lack of value the MVP delivered to the customer.

Diversity that is promoted along the lines of physical features of employees can also create a "we" versus "them" environment. Naturally, this will result in conflict within the organization that some people have different rules than others within the work environment. Protecting diversity in the workplace is key to tapping into diversity as a lever to pull for innovation. As stated in Breakthrough Agile, employees across the organization need to be educated and trained on the benefits of diversity, and how it helps the organization to be more holistic and connected to the customer.

Deal with Conflict, Avoid Escalation

Individuals within the organization need the skills and confidence to work through a conflict without the need to escalate it or use an arbitration type of process. In Breakthrough Agile, teams are empowered and work in a self-managed environment. Conflicts will occur and team members need to be aware of when they are in a conflict and how they should act if they are a part of the conflict. The team as a whole needs to take a role when a conflict occurs on the team. In these conflicts, team members can be coaches or mentors to those who are in the conflict. All team members need to practice using appropriate conflict resolution skills during the course of their work. When all team members understand how to manage a conflict on their own, without escalation or a formal arbitration type of process, then team members develop a stronger relationship among each other. This relationship allows them to be vulnerable in all aspects of their work. This openness within the team leads to teams developing a stronger sense of security to speak up and innovate on new ideas or solutions. These new ideas will lead to different actions that result in outcomes for the organization that create better partnerships with customers.

The trap of escalating conflicts to the next layer within the organization for resolution is that the team loses its autonomy. When this becomes the standard practice for the team, the leader of the team continues to be the traditional command and control leader who is seen as the judiciary office for the team's problems. In my experience, when conflicts are escalated, then both parties move from a resolution mindset to a win–lose proposition. Escalation generally ends with the higher authority telling the two people to make amends and work together. Phrases like put aside your differences and work like adults, not children, may be heard in the escalation process. Avoid escalating conflicts to a higher authority for resolution. As we think of the organization's cultural transformation, knowing that teams work around conflict will lead to poor performance. The team will lose its feeling of psychological safety and members will be skeptical of each other's motives for every action. At this point, the team becomes dysfunctional and the traditional command and control way of working comes back as the catalyst to move the team forward on meeting its goals. The team leader approves and disapproves certain behaviors and the whole team works from their individual comfort zone.

Key Points on Conflict Resolution

1. Unresolved conflict will derail the transformation efforts of the organization (Figure 5.5). People within the organization need to have the capabilities to deal with conflict and seek to turn conflict into a business tension.
2. Being able to empathize is key to resolving conflict within the organization. Empathy is a skill that needs to be developed and should not be seen as being nice.
3. Listening is another is an essential skill of Breakthrough Agile. Building up this capability with all people takes practice and a good understanding of what is an is not active listening.
4. Diversity is embraced and sought out for teams and individuals in Breakthrough Agile. Diversity drives innovation and growth within the organization.

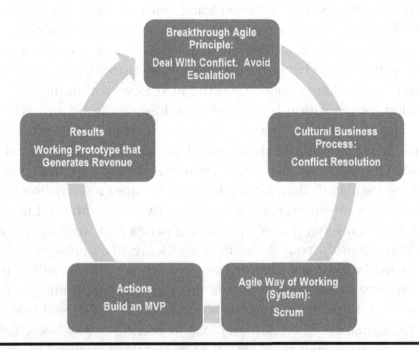

Figure 5.5 Breakthrough Agile's operations model on conflict resolution.

5. Escalating conflicts for resolution should be seen as a last resort for a team. Escalating disempowers teams and their members, and should be avoided.
6. Business tension within the organization isn't conflict but a catalyst to help an organization perform at a higher level. Business tension results from people staying focused on the customer needs and meeting stated objectives that are created for the business.

Example of a sensing guide for conflict resolution.

Conflict Resolution Sensing Guide				
Breakthrough Agile's Principles	Experiencing	Seeing	Hearing	Anti-Pattern
Develop capacity to empathize Listen to understand. Discuss the idea, do not respond to the person Diversity supports growth and development Deal with conflict. Avoid escalation	People engaged in deep conversations discussing why they are in conflict. Team members being more open and vulnerable on topics that trigger conflict. Conflicts being resolved without the intervention or escalation of a leader/manager. Ideas moving forward for value creation from all team members.	Conversations that discuss topics or ideas versus people. Team members showing respect and listening to each other within interruptions or opposition statements. Less conflicts and more people discussion tensions about solutions to meet customer needs.	Conflicts discussed without highly emotional or charged language. Team members seeking to understand through open ended questions like "what" and "how." Suggestions or ideas coming from all team members. Silence across the team after a team member explains an idea or solution.	Highly judgmental language toward new ideas. Discouragement of new ideas that challenge the status quo. Escalation of conflicts for a manager or leader to intervene. Conflicts lasting over time, going unresolved and affecting the team dynamic.

Chapter 6

Strategic Planning

> Strategic – of, relating to, or characterized by the identification of long-term or overall aims and interests and the means of achieving them; designed, planned, or conceived to serve a particular purpose or achieve a particular objective.
>
> **Oxford English Dictionary**

A look inside:

- Setting context of strategic planning
- How traditional financial planning competes with Agile strategic thinking
- OKR framework and its role in an Agile organization

Chapter 6 discusses how strategic planning is a cultural business process and practiced in Breakthrough Agile. Strategic planning is the process of defining the future of the organization using input from financial/geopolitical data, market trends, and business insights to decide what initiatives/products that the business will offer to customers. Strategic planning answers the question of what is the next destination for the organization in the next 3, 5, or 10 years. Defining what the organization will do, how it will strategically maneuver its resources, reshape its operating model, and turn ideas into value provides an overview of strategic planning. Generally starting with a strategic vision followed by a narrowing of scope of action from corporate to division to business unit to department and down to the individual, the strategic planning process will trigger activities that are intended to make the business more competitive, grow its market, and improve its valuation.

DOI: 10.4324/9781003335702-6

Usually, a timed milestone approach illustrates and helps to communicate to employees the vision and the pace of change. At other times, the vision is timeless and remains a permanent driving outcome for the organization. Surprisingly, in many conversations over how to present a strategy, hundreds of hours can be spent on deciding the timeline for the plan. I say surprisingly, because as it turns out, less time is spent on review of the outcomes of the strategic initiatives throughout the course of the year. For whatever time box horizon, you choose, the process of creating the strategic plan is generically the same.

In my opinion, most organizations now experience a more rapid and disruptive business cycle than 30 to 40 years earlier. Prior to the information revolution, barriers to entry kept large stable companies comfortably on top with their portfolio of products and services. However, in the past 10–20 years, the flow and availability of information and creation of startup competitors have disrupted the way strategic planning is executed. Today, companies need to identify and react to changing business trends using shorter time boxed horizons. This compliments the Agile mindset of working in short succinct bursts to produce a prototype. A 3- to 5-year strategic planning horizon serves well for most commercial business organizations. To balance the shorter time boxes in planning, organizations are adopting the "North Star" approach. The "North Star" is the guiding vision for the people within the organization and guides the strategic planning of senior leaders. With a North Start as a guide, the 3- to 5-year strategic plan is able to leverage the current products and services pipeline, while looking at the future business needs of the organization. Tied closely to the "North Star" approach is creating a business purpose for the organization. The purpose complements the "North Star" as a way to describe an overarching principle that needs to be reflected in everyone's behavior within the organization. The two work together to provide the broad guidelines that an organization will use when it decides its strategic plan and outcomes to pursue.

The principles of Breakthrough Agile will strongly shape the North Star and purpose of the organization. As the transformation journey is underway, strategic planning will keep the journey moving forward, as well as shape the products and services the organization will provide to the customer. This planning process will strongly influence the culture of the organization. People's work will focus on delivering the strategic plan. Additionally, the deployment and execution of a strategic plan is a touch point for leaders to role model Agile leadership within the organization. Day to day and over the course of months and years, leaders will support their teams in improving, growing, and developing through coaching and periodic reviews of strategic initiatives.

In Breakthrough Agile, the strategic planning process is an opportunity for senior leaders to bring their experience and knowledge to shaping the future of the business. These leaders are in touch with the business world trends that are currently influencing customers. They are analyzing market intelligence on competitors and the evolution of their products. This information shapes the strategic activities that are part of the strategic plan. Throughout the life cycle of a strategic plan, from conception to execution, leaders are engaging their teams and practicing Agile leadership skills. Leaders will coach their teams on what is the North Star and purpose of the organization. Leaders will connect the team's work to the North Star and high-level strategic initiatives. Leaders will engage teams and develop their ability to solve more complex and challenging problems in a safe and rewarding environment. When leaders perform well in this space, employees feel passionate about their work and are motivated by the higher purpose to perform above expectations. By connecting the employees' work to the future success of the organization beyond the short-term impacts of reducing costs or maintaining market share, the intrinsic feeling of taking ownership and feeling proud becomes part of the culture. When leaders understand the broader landscape of how employees work contributes to achieving greater outcomes and communicates it clearly, the leaders develop a sense of pride and motivation for their teams and individuals. In practical terms, leaders will operationalize the strategic plan through effective Agile leadership.

Strategic Planning in Breakthrough Agile relies upon assimilating various key inputs to the business, both internal and external, to define the future of the organization. In essence, it is keeping an eye on the future needs and motivations of customers, while also designing an organization that will be competitive through the improvement of internal capabilities and process re-engineering of the organization. Depending on the organization's current business foothold, actions are created during the strategic planning process to enhance the organization's current products, develop new market segments, or develop internal resources to generate better value. This applies equally for a company with a legacy reputation and products to those with new to market ideas and services. Look at Apple, Google, and Tesla and how these organizations are consistently delivering new innovations on their current products to the customer. Even less glamorous businesses such as consumer goods organizations such as the Procter & Gamble,

Whirlpool, or Braun are delivering consistent innovations on their products. Take, for example Braun and its electric toothbrush. By including a digital application to monitor brushing, the company has changed the length and duration of how people brush their teeth. The application also includes a quality check on how well each brushing session was performed. Something as commonplace as brushing teeth is changing to keep pace with the way technology influences the market and customer's motivations.

In Breakthrough Agile, "customer centricity," the understanding of the primary customer's needs, wants, and motivations will shape an organization's strategic roadmap and future of the company. Empathizing on the wants of the customer and sensing the direction customers are moving toward require an organization to assess their current products and services and be bold enough to innovate on them to capture the future opportunities. From this analysis, the organization builds a coherent portfolio of initiatives or roadmap to start building those products and capabilities. Breakthrough Agile's principles on strategic planning helps the organizations develop this future roadmap.

In Breakthrough Agile, strategic planning centers on what the company is good at doing. How the organization can leverage the skills, experience, knowledge, and products that it currently has available is a strong force in shaping its strategic plan. Think of the different iterations of the iPhone. Apple, while continuing to look at new services or products like Apple Pay and Apple TV continues to modify and redevelop its already successful products to meet the future needs and unknown needs of its customers. How many people now use their phone's camera instead of a personal camera? How many people drive using their phone's GPS instead of an independent global positioning system (GPS) device? How many people have had video meetings on a phone? Apple's continuous pursuit of innovation on its current products continues to increase demand for this product. It is a lesson for everyone that customers' needs change and products need to have the flexibility to adapt and change to meet those needs.

Companies need a strategic planning process to create their roadmap. Reflect on what happened to personal cameras and GPS OEMs after the iPhone displaced their market. They had to strategically change or end up becoming obsolete. Personal cameras went digital and added features such as video and other special editing functions to retain their customers. GPS OEMs focused on building navigation systems and markets where smart phones weren't viable – watercraft and aviation. Even automakers adapted to the change in customer's habits when personal phones began to dominate their customer's attention. They designed connection ports and Bluetooth capabilities into their vehicles. Lately, even the introduction of a tablet touch screen is common in late generation automobiles. These companies strategically planned to adapt to the customer's needs and wants that were created by the personal phone disruption to consumer's behavior. It is very interesting to see how one innovation led to the change in strategic planning of other businesses. This is in contrast to organizations with a fixed mindset that avoids or minimizes the value of a strategic planning process. Fixed mindset companies usually take a defensive stance to disruptive innovations and look to protect and sustain their current level of business. Most will introduce a like product based on the disruptive technology that was originally introduced. However, whether the automotive makers liked it or not, instead of being defensive to the use of personal phones as navigation or music systems, they strategically decided to make using them easier in their products to appeal to their consumers' wants. This step resulted in an outcome that the customer has a more enhanced user experience when operating their vehicles.

Strategic planning is an exciting and adventurous activity. I've led many workshops for organizations on strategic planning, I am always excited when new ideas or initiatives come into the conversation. Being bold and courageous in the context of being innovative moves the organization toward a higher level of performance. As these ideas develop from a brainstorming idea to more concrete outcomes for the organization, there is a special synergy that is generated between employees and the company. A good strategic plan is a boost of energy and motivation for the organization. People understand that a bold outcome will rally people and get them excited about coming to work each day. In reflecting on the past few years, companies that were directly connected to providing services and products to manage the COVID pandemic experienced this energy. These companies had to set new strategic outcomes that far exceeded anything that they had done in the past. New products had to be developed faster than ever before. Materials and products shipped with much shorter lead times and incrementally across the world. Commercial organizations had to work closely with customers in their regions to ensure that the public had the needed products. Although organizations pre-COVID had these processes in place before, the speed, the consequences of underperforming, and the need of the customer shifted the strategic planning and created a new performance bar for many companies. Now, as the world shifts to endemic thinking and COVID seems to be the new influenza, the challenge for organizations is to continue their learning from the pandemic experience to influence their strategic planning for the future. Let's hope we don't wait for the next pandemic to drive the next change in strategic planning for businesses. Strategic planning permits teams to leverage their experiences from the pandemic to create outcomes that will redesign work processes, eliminate redundant checks, and improve better quality of products.

Strategic planning in many organizations has competing processes when it comes to executing the roadmap. In traditional organizations, the old school principles of operating and running the business will compete, and at times, overshadow a bold strategic plan that has been influenced by Breakthrough Agile principles. In working with these companies over the past 20 years, one process that creates this conflict is the annual financial planning or a company's business/budget planning process. With a fixed annual kick off date, the financial planning process takes anywhere from 3 to 4 months to be completed. The output of this planning process is a detailed plan describing how the organization will spend its next year's budget. At times, the budget itself is called the strategic plan. Usually, the guardrails (limits) for the budget are cascaded down with the focus of achieving financial key performance indicators (KPIs). Publicly traded organizations invariably get more expense and cost challenges coupled with higher sales and revenue targets. These efforts to appease stakeholders and investors overshadow the customer needs and wants, and produce narrowly focused outcomes that increase the company's profitability for the short term. With publicly traded companies providing full disclosure of its spend and revenue, inventors are quick to look for areas that exceed their tolerance for operations. This applies additional pressure on the traditional organization to deliver short-term results. As expected, innovative strategic planning loses out to financial planning when investors have a strong influence on the organization's future direction. Add into the mix, the life cycle to create and commercialize a new product or innovate on current products, and the organization bends and breaks under the extra stress placed on it by financial investors.

As next year's financial KPIs are cascaded, leadership teams throughout the organization mobilize themselves to work out a (strategic) plan to decide what actions they will take to meet the top–down cost and revenue targets. This process continues with further cascading of targets or KPIs throughout each business unit to the level where a department or team leads start to cascade personal objectives to team members and individual contributors. At this point, individuals then create performance objectives that on paper will help the organization achieve its overall financial targets for the year. This reflects the current state of how the financial planning process overshadows an innovative strategic planning process.

Throughout the financial planning process, a reverse reporting event occurs. While actions and initiatives are cascaded downward to the individual level, the budgets are sent up for approval. The final budgets of teams and departments are rolled up into a business unit budget. A team's budget is approved at the director level; the director level's budget (a roll up of all their team's budgets) is approved at the general manager level; the roll up of all the directors' budgets gets added to the GM's budget, and this business unit's budget gets approved at the VP or global level, and then a global business unit's budget gets rolled together with all the other global business units for approval at the president or CEO level. From this description of the process, one can infer the total number of people and hours that are absorbed by these activities. It is a tremendous amount of work by thousands of people for months. At times, I have heard leaders jokingly state that there is little confidence in the process and the numbers are little more than last year's with some minor tweaks. Generally, at each level of review, there is a push downward for more – either reduction of cost or higher revenue.

In practice, the output at each level is little more than a restatement of the previous year's costs and activities. Ironically, less attention is paid to customer needs and more to the accuracy of the rolled up numbers throughout this process. This is a direct reflection of how traditional organizations embrace a cost cutting principle way of working. I recall in one meeting, a global leader made light of the budget process, when they saw the dollar amounts for a small business unit were measured down to the fourth decimal space in a team's presentation. I guess when these smaller budgets are rolled up into the larger ones, the 100,000th of a cent adds up to a make or break year for the business.

As the months of meetings wind down with final preparation, and hours of massaging numbers, the business units/teams get their stamp of approval from the next level up. Once the final budget gets the approval from the top official, then the governance process of monthly and quarterly checks starts. Over the year's budget cycle, a finance officer will track the performance of the organization and provide updates on how well their team's performance is to budget based on what they thought 6 months ago. If the team or organization is over or under spending, then the finance officer steps in to investigate and provide guidance. As we now know, much can change over

6 months and the fortune telling skills of the business plan aren't sharp enough to predict outcomes 6 months into the year. Personnel changes for one would drive inconsistency in how well a financial plan is executed, as well as inflation, exchange rates, raw material costs, and other natural phenomena.

For an organization that is transforming itself with Breakthrough Agile, the principles for strategic planning will guide teams to co-create initiatives that will bring greater value and a higher level of performance within a shorter time frame to the organization. Breakthrough Agile's strategic planning will result in friction with the traditional financial planning process. Since strategic planning asks people to think about the future of the business and the financial business planning process asks people to look to the past, there is an inherent conflict to have both on-going. With Breakthrough Agile, teams will focus on their North Star (Figure 6.1) and align their strategic and tactical outcomes into different rhythms of work. Progress will get measured differently than how the traditional organization approaches it based solely on KPIs. Generally, an Agile organization will create their 3-year outcomes, and then proceed to break these down into smaller packages of work to be completed in a shorter amount of time. In the end, employees will work on a 90-day planning cycle for strategic initiatives. Objectives and key results (OKRs) will provide the framework for the organization to achieve this shift in business planning and execution of its strategic plan for the future.

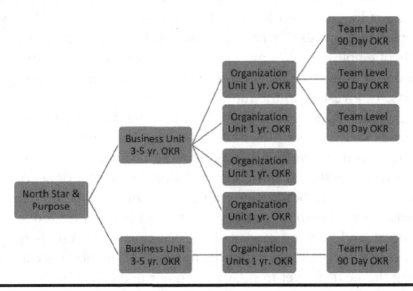

Figure 6.1   Generic strategic thinking alignment from North Star to 90-day OKR.

To understand how Breakthrough Agile impacts strategic planning, let's look a little closer at how a traditional organization creates a strategic plan. Generally, a few months after the announcement of the financial planning/ budgeting process, the senior leaders of separate business units, big and small, cascade the financial goals and objectives for their teams for the upcoming year. This cascading, or target letter event, triggers various types of strategic planning sessions throughout the organization. These sessions may run 2–3 days or more and generally consist of brainstorming ideas around the cascaded goals. In most cases, the cascading goals are the normal KPIs for the business unit. As a result, the brainstorming activities generate a list of on-going routine business practices with an increase in efficiency or productivity, or possibly the introduction of a new product or service in the market. Normally coupled with the activities to support the business KPIs is a set of goals with a human touch – talent development, diversity, and morale type building goals. In the end, the goals are aligned with meeting either the bottom line or top line of the budget.

The output of the brainstorming sessions is a list of activities for the business unit, categorized by various strategic themes. As these activities are cascaded throughout the organization, part of them end up as an individual's personal performance objectives for the year. And since they are routine in nature, the concept that completing one of the activities and delivering a new or additional value to the customer is buried in the variation of all the other routine tasks individuals have to do daily. The intent of this type of strategic planning process is to decide on what actions will meet the annual KPI targets set by the senior level leaders. This is a "protect the business strategic planning process," and I have led and introduced these plans to thousands of employees over my career. The results of these plans are varied and as a *protect the business strategy*, it drives the short-term results at the expense of investing in the future.

Strategic planning that is strongly linked to the financial planning process leads to a number of self-limiting behaviors across the organization. As mentioned, it is a protect the business strategy which minimizes the growth and development of new products or services. In industries that sustain themselves with a consistent flow of new products, in the protect your business strategy, the focus becomes on reducing product price, and keeping market share. Valuable time and energy is spent on reactive strategic initiatives to meet these ends instead of identifying the next market trend, or customer need. When a new or a revised product is ready for commercialization, then the strategic initiatives reflect the focus of the company. There is a strong emphasis on launching fast. Supply chain, quality, manufacturing, and commercial units support the launch with their own strategic initiatives to support launch readiness. This is important to the organization, but most of these organizations have departments or entire business units focused on launching a product successful. At times, it seems as if this routine event is placed on a pedestal since the financial importance to stockholders is so great. To me, it's sort of like an airline that promotes as part of its strategy that it can land a plane safely. Something that should be expected of an airline organization. Shouldn't we expect that we have this capability without creating a strategic initiative around it.

Another trap of the protect the business strategy is that it promotes a system of silo thinking. Each team or organization unit will be focused on meeting its financial target. This prevents the organization from being bold and courageous in its thinking and taking risks to create something new and innovative. The strategy focuses on protecting the current state and avoiding risk or disruptions, that may result in increased costs or lost customers. This traditional mindset leads to limited opportunities for growth, both internally and externally. However, in Breakthrough Agile, the principle-based approach to strategic planning is to look for bold and courageous ideas. The idea is to separate what is needed to run the business successful, from those ideas or innovations that will disrupt the market in the next 3-5 years. Breakthrough Agile's mental model encourages strategic planners to explore an abundance of new opportunities available to the organization. Then, through consultation and deep discussions with people across the organization, prioritizing which ones will deliver more value and growth in the future. In the traditional approach to strategy planning, each function develops its list of strategic initiatives to meet the financial targets. These are generally independent of other functions within the same organization. The output is possible that hundreds of initiatives will be kicked off and communicated to the business unit's personnel. Employees then feel overwhelmed with strategic priorities with a financial context. With Breakthrough Agile, the routine business activities need to happen and a robust system of review needs created to support the execution of them. Ceremonies that support this robust system are daily team stand up meetings, Kanban boards, rhythmical review sessions, and strong Agile leadership. With this system in place, the strategic planning process has selectively chosen the products and services that will meet the customer's future needs and wants. These are the strategic actions that go onto the strategic plan as they make the company more competitive and motivates employees to work toward a higher purpose.

Some of the ideas I mentioned here are in practice today and have some interesting twists to them. For instance, in advanced traditional organizations the idea of a North Star or vision concept has been adopted, and it is used to inspire the organization to a higher level of performance. However, their reliance on it to shape the strategic plan is minimized as the financial KPI approach continues to dominate the strategic planning process. In these organizations, the North Star is more of a "feel good" statement than an outcome that drives decisions and actions of the business. Relying solely on financial KPIs as the strategic direction for the organization results in a short-sightedness plan for the future. In practice, an organization that relies upon the traditional principles of financial controls, conservatism, status quo, and command and control leadership will see their North Star as a *nice to have* slogan. Something to put on posters in their hallways and cafeterias. Generally, these company's North Star lack any external focus and tend to look inward. For instance, organizations state in their North Star that they want to be the best, world class, or most cost effective. The first challenge might be defining the criteria for *world class* or *the best*. In these examples, the North Star statements are inspiring but then the strategic plan mostly focuses on internal processes and how to operate with lower costs with smaller resources. When we think of organizations that have changed our consuming behaviors their strategic plans focused on how to create that change in customer's behavior. How Apple, Facebook, Amazon, and CNN have revolutionized the way we live, seems to be less about the company being the best through reducing costs or operating to a budget and more about exceeding its customers' desires and needs. To be the world's best, can it ever be achieved by focusing the organization's energy and resources on meeting or exceeding a financial KPI? In retrospect, the highly innovative companies mentioned all started with a high-risk approach toward changing the customer's behavior. CNN changed how we watched news from a specific 30-minute time slot to a 24/7 platform. Apple changed how we communicated and spend much of our idle time. Amazon, Facebook, etc. all changed consumer's behaviors in the way people interact, socialize, and practice consumerism. In the end, these companies might be the best in their respective markets, but it started with a vision to change the way customers act and behave.

The reader may be sensing that financial responsibility is absent from Breakthrough Agile's principles or ways of work. This is not the case. Within Breakthrough Agile, there are rules of the game that define the performance of a team or organization unit. High performance of teams is a paramount goal for an Agile organization, and it is through the identification and delivery of value that is the measurement. The leadership within a Breakthrough Agile organization takes an active role in sensing a team's performance and taking action when performance is below expectations. This could include both cost and revenue performance, as well as the dynamics of the team in their execution of working toward a strategic priority. Saying the financial planning process is ineffective is too far a step to take for anyone. The data that is generated by the financial processes such as analyzing costs, sales, inventory, cost of quality, personnel, etc. needs to be maintained by the financial teams of the organization. These measurements provide insight into the health of the organization. In a culture of Breakthrough Agile, balancing these business necessities with the game changing strategic activities defines the business acumen that is needed by leaders.

In the past decade or so, there seems to have been a shift in organizations that all leaders need to have financial planning and monitoring capabilities. At times, I think this might be a result of the financial pressure of organization to reduce their labor costs. As a result, some of the work of the financial offices gets pushed to others, such as the leaders of the organization. There is a value for the leader, as they take on a new role in the Breakthrough Agile organization to have this financial capability. It will benefit the leader to be effective as they monitor their top and bottom lines of the balance sheet. This gives them a pulse check on how the routine business is running and the impact of completed strategic initiatives. This financial analysis is not the priority for all team members to focus their energy on. Following the strategic principles of Breakthrough Agile, different actions will be developed by the company. Leaders and teams with diverse mindsets and perspectives on the future will produce a different set of actions to achieve the future state. These novel customer-centric actions drive the identification of value and its value realization for the organization. Teams need to stay focused on these long-term actions over the short-term routine business activities. Prioritizing the short term over the long term will be a trap for an organization that is transforming itself. Additionally, the leader needs to be aware and an active participant in the strategic planning process for the team and share their experiences when they develop their Objectives and Key Results (OKRs). Through this more dynamic leadership presence, the financial stability and future success of the organization is reaffirmed.

The principles of Breakthrough Agile for strategic planning focus efforts on the long-term vision and how their products and services will change the customer's behaviors. This higher ambition needs to be embedded within the organization to create an energy to achieve results that originally were thought of as impossible. Strategic planning using Breakthrough Agile stretches the organization's capabilities and resources. As mentioned earlier, organizations need to leverage their learning from the pandemic and bring that same focus and internal alignment to setting and meeting their strategic objectives. This is a lesson learned from COVID for businesses. To guide an organization to this new level of performance in strategic thinking, here are the Breakthrough Agile principles:

■ Empathetic outcomes based on customer's needs, wants, and motivations
■ Transparency of work produces high performance
■ Plan for the long-term value, execute for short-term delivery
■ Minimal viable product (MVP) thinking for every solution

Empathetic Outcomes Based on Customer Needs, Wants, and Motivations

Remember the saying, "the customer is always right?" Breakthrough Agile shifts the perspective on this adage, and creates the principle that empathizing and understanding the customers wants, needs, and motivations are key to achieving breakthrough results for the organization. The adage above generally induces a behavior in employees to do whatever it takes to meet a customer's complaint or request, regardless of its draw on resources from the company. This was the traditional way of measuring customer centricity. Spend any time with a sales person or other customer facing individual and they will have numerous stories of outrageous requests that were asked by upset customers. Even today, sitting in meetings with product managers or customer facing individuals, the dings and bells from WhatsApp or text messaging are continuous for these individuals. The evolution of smart technology has given rise to people being reachable at all hours of the day and for a demanding customer this can be a physically draining for an employee. There is a classic story I remember that always helps me frame up why being reactive to every customer's complaint might not be the best for the company. It is a story about a customer complaint at one outdoor consumer goods company.

The story goes that a retail customer service representative received a call from a customer with a complaint that they were shipped a bicycle when they actually ordered a canoe. The customer service representative was trained in the principle that the customer was always right and do whatever it takes to satisfy the customer. So the customer service representative jumped into action to resolve the mis-shipment. In this case, the representative went to the warehouse, acquired a canoe, strapped it to their car, and then drove it to the customer. Complaint solved and the customer is happy. Is this an example of the customer centricity that we want to develop for an Agile organization? Firefighting to correct a poor business process is not customer centric. It is a waste of value/time for everyone and costly. Although getting the customer the canoe was a priority, the mis-shipment is an indication that something far more was going wrong at the company.

For instance, what warehouse and invoicing process would allow for such an error? How are orders staged and then shipped to ensure customers get the right item? A mistake of this magnitude indicates that it wasn't the first time the wrong item was sent to a customer. In the past, what were the corrective and preventive actions taken to eliminate recurrence? Most likely a round of blamestorming went through the warehouse and a warehouse employee was reprimanded/dismissed for not seeing the mistake. As an action, the company would retrain warehouse and planning staff to follow the procedure or even a rewrite of the shipping procedure with more administrative checks would get done. However, was there a true customer-centric approach applied to the critical processes of delivery? Was the organization thinking how it can guarantee the right product gets to the customer that ordered it? For example, did the leaders look to improve their ordering system from a manual process to something automated? Was there an outcome for the warehouse to work with 100% accuracy on all orders picked? What customer-centric outcome was created to build a system with sustainable robustness in picking and shipping products to the customer. This is the customer centricity principle of strategic planning that Breakthrough Agile embraces and moves the organization toward.

Applying Breakthrough Agile's strategic planning principles to this incident, the question that needed to be asked by the leaders and staff should focus on the customer. What do our customers want from our company's on-line or phone order systems? This simple question would drive the organization in a direction to being more customer centric.

Being empathetic to the customer needs, one would conclude that customers want the item they buy online, as it is represented online, in the time frame promised by the company. Using Breakthrough Agile strategic planning principles, the strategic planning team would then create an objective and key results (OKR) goal. The objective might be something like – "develop an online ordering system that prevents any error in product type, quantity, or delivery information." The key results or measure of success:

1. Picking order lead time is less than 24 hours from order entry to truck
2. Original orders and picking orders are electronically cross-checked for 100% accuracy at point of departure
3. Customer order lead time from customer receipt to warehouse picking order is less than 12 hours

Being customer centric indicates that your systems of work are designed to meet the needs of the customer. Above are simple measures of success for the online ordering system. Fast and accurate order execution. When the work systems are customer centric, then the employees become experts at the execution of those systems, delivering true value to the customer and company. Understanding the customer needs, wants, and motivations is essential to developing insights into what type of future systems and products the company will create for capturing higher value. Strategic planning means asking what is that future customer's needs for your organization's products and services. What are customer's seeking and what influences them to purchase your products in the future. If done properly, then your organization's services or products will meet the customer's requirements of the future, not the past. By selectively identifying the strategic objectives through a robust strategic planning exercise, you develop these long-term objectives.

From this point of view, information that builds insights into the future of the market and customer demand becomes important. Taking time to analyze and research trends is needed when developing customer-centric objectives. It takes bold and courageous objectives on the part of visionary leaders to guide the organization into the future. Too often, the objectives that come out of the strategic planning process are conservative and lack inspiration. For example, if one would think back to the mid-1990s when email was first being introduced into the mainstream of our society, how many people envisioned the communication tool would dominate our way of communicating in the early 2000s and beyond.

How many business leaders envisioned the effect of instantaneous communication across the world? It took exceptional visionary leaders to connect the dots between the technology that was emerging at the time and the future needs of its customers to see the potential value in this means of communication. By envisioning this new need, the world was revolutionized on how it communicates. Over the years since its first introduction, email has developed and grown with innovations creating new features that allow email users to manage everything from appointments in calendars, contacts, photos, and send videos. Taking it a step further, the 2020's email is becoming obsolete as chats, instant messaging are becoming the norm for communicating and sharing information. All of these advancements were achieved by developing customer-centric objectives and using an OKR framework to develop or innovate on their products. Email turned out to displace a traditional system of communication tool that many of us used at the start of our business career. Good bye to the Rolodex!

Transparency of Work Produces High Performance

The strategic plan needs to communicate to everyone the future direction of the organization. The plan should be transparent in order to provide guidance on outcomes for alignment and transparency. This enables the business units to align and focus resources on the critical initiatives that will generate breakthrough value. This is a key to being competitive and striving for a higher level of performance. Transparency in the strategic planning process is twofold: First – everyone knows what are the prioritized strategic work initiatives that have to be completed and; secondly transparency enables greater alignment vertically (up and down) as well as horizontally (across teams or departments). Through a clear communicated message and a rhythm of work to review progress toward the strategic goals, the organization is able to link a team or individual's work to a strategic goal. This rhythm of work also creates a collaborative environment where different functions can support each other in the achievement of the company's strategic plan. The review process is called the 90-day planning cycle review in Breakthrough Agile and will be discussed in Chapter 7. Being transparent about the strategic initiatives, and executing to the shorter term OKRs create the flexibility needed for the Agile strategic planning process.

Today, there are a number of strategic planning models in use. Business schools are enticing prospective students to their classrooms with chic and novel strategic thinking processes such as Blue Ocean thinking, Porter's Five Forces, SWOT, or the Balanced Scorecard. Across all of these models, communicating the output or strategic plan is the first step to being successful. An organization that has a clear strategic aim with clear outcomes connects employees and their work to the vision of the organization. This clarity promotes a higher level of engagement from teams and focuses their energies the high-level outcomes of the organization. In my experience, I have often used a simple slide (Figure 6.2) as a training aid that many readers to communicate the output of the strategic planning process.

It is a photo of a cleaner in a Tyvek suit vacuuming a lab for NASA. The story goes that a group of visitors saw this person and asked the employee what they were doing. The response was "helping launch the space shuttle." Although anecdotal, the intent of the story is relative to the principle of *transparency leads to high performance*. Think of how proud this worker felt about their job, and the importance of completing it well and with high quality. Our human emotions drive high performance when we understand and can interpret how our work links to moving the organization closer to its strategic goals.

All employees need to be aware of how they contribute to the success of the organization. Whether the transparency is through electronic and

Figure 6.2   Visual aid to explain how strategy is everyone's job.

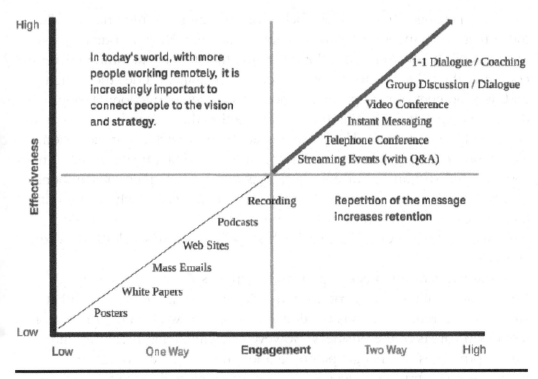

High

Effectiveness

In today's world, with more people working remotely, it is increasingly important to connect people to the vision and strategy.

1-1 Dialogue / Coaching

Group Discussion / Dialogue

Video Conference

Instant Messaging

Telephone Conference

Streaming Events (with Q&A)

Recording

Podcasts

Web Sites

Mass Emails

White Papers

Posters

Repetition of the message increases retention

Low

Low   One Way   **Engagement**   Two Way   High

Figure 6.3   Visual aid to support physical interaction with communication change and transformation.

visual communication methods, leader storytelling, or inclusion in the strategic planning process itself, the power of transparency will lead an organization to higher performance of individuals and teams. The Balanced Scorecard approach to strategic thinking offers some insightful tips on how to make an organization's strategy transparent. Within the approach (Figure 6.3), one can frame a communication plan to help make the organization's strategic priorities transparent.

When practicing the principle of transparency for strategic planning 2-way communication with repetition will help the organization with strategic alignment.

Plan for the Long Term, Execute for the Short Term

When engaged in developing a strategic roadmap, how fast you deliver on your objectives is critical to your business' competitiveness. One cannot be the last competitor to the market with an innovation and expect great results.

Innovation change the customer's behavior through something new, while those that re-engineer a proven concept are lagging. How an organization executes on the outcomes developed during the strategic planning process correlates the value received from the customer. This includes the design and development of new products and services, self-corrections during design and launch, launching them, and meeting the demand once the item is available to customers. The balancing act between achieving the visionary aspiration of the organization, designing and developing new products and services, and sustaining current operations requires a tremendous amount of effort. Usually, companies only do one of these well, which is sustaining current operations. In order to get good at the other two, the strategic planning process as described in this book will support developing those capabilities.

Today's organization is complex and change is risky and takes time. Complexity inhibits innovation for most. Why? Organizations are good at sustaining current operations by allowing people to work in the known or less risking areas of the business. However, by embracing Breakthrough Agile's principles of strategic planning and embracing a customer-centric perspective on strategic outcomes, the organization will move forward on projects that have an element of the unknown. In these cases, the risky outcomes are generally worded as long-term outcomes; those that take 3–5 years for the company to fully benefit. It is unfortunate, but for most companies, these long-term outcomes never get resourced fully or the outcomes aren't linked to the short-term outcomes. Generally, strategic initiatives that are planned three years out are just independent activities the organization thinks it will do 3 years from today. There are no links from the 3 year outcomes to the outcomes for the current year, or piloting process for the long term outcomes. This is a blind spot in strategic planning. This is where the routine business activities are described as being strategic outcomes for the current year. People in the organization question long-term outcomes because most likely something will change between now and the 3–5 years that will make the goal obsolete. The change could be from the business environment, CEO, interest rates, or acquisitions, or another force that shapes a perception of risk in the minds of people. This is why the routine business is commonly listed as a strategic initiative in most strategic plans. As most leaders know, time can derail long-term strategic outcomes. After all, most organizations are good at firefighting and short-term wins. Long-term goals need more time to be realized than the organization has patience for.

Generally accepted today is that we work in a business world with a desire to see quick results from strategic initiatives and roadmaps. The idea is that people within the organization receive gratification for these quick wins. Being good at firefighting is a sign of a good leader or team. We rarely recognize or reword a team that takes 5 years to achieve a significant outcome. As a result, planning for a 5-year horizon is a skill that is lacking. When an organization feels the pressure to sacrifice its long-term goals to meet short-term results, this creates a culture with a lack of focus on the future. When stuck in this strategic tar pit of short-term activities over long-term outcomes, short term wins out. There may be time spent discussing the long-term vision and goals, but it is usually at such a high level that any value is rarely achieved. On the other hand, by focusing on the short-term gains, quick wins and small gains are achieved. The short-term approach also reinforces the use of the annual financial planning session to create new initiatives. As a result, most strategic outcomes are focused on financial KPIs. In Breakthrough Agile, balancing between these two, the short and long terms is critical to developing a rhythm or pattern of work internally for the organization. Developing the capability to align short-term initiatives to the long-term goals creates a culture that consistently harvests new value from the market both quicker and over time. When done well, the results of short-term goals are building blocks for the long-term goals and results. Within a Breakthrough Agile organization, the Objective and Key Results (OKR) Framework is an integral part of achieving breakthrough results.

Using an OKR framework to plan for the long term and execute on the short is the way forward in Agile strategic planning. First, defining the time box to realize the future state has to be clear. Then deciding on the strategic outcomes that are needed to reach that state. From these long-term outcomes, a process of outcome simplification produces a set of shorter term OKRs that guide the employees on what to work on now. These shorter term OKRs have a time box of 1 year, and then these are simplified to 90 days. By executing on the 90-day OKRs, the organization realizes value from the future state quicker. In the prioritization of the short-term outcomes, the question that needs to be asked is, "What can an organization start today to meet its long-term aspirations/objectives?" By managing this relationship between long-term and short-term OKRs and keeping focus on what is important to start today, the business gains the value it is seeking to achieve in its true north or vision. The next step in this logic train is the question, "how do we know we are on track or working on the right activities?" How do we know if we are moving toward our north star and vision? Through a robust OKR framework, a Breakthrough Agile's company will manage the long-term and short-term objectives through a governance process called a 90-day planning cycle review. Both of these systems, OKRs and 90-day review, ensures the right activities are being worked on and that the activities are moving the organization forward.

The OKR framework includes a number of features including a governance process, roles and responsibilities, and structure for drafting OKRs.

Let's take a closer look at how an OKR framework helps organizations achieve their long-term and short-term objectives. In this section, we focus on the structure of how a long-term OKR is simplified to the point that a team or individual can execute on it within the 90-day time box.

A common understanding of OKRs is that there is a simple formula to use to write an OKR. The formula looks like this:

We will _____ as measured by _____ so that we can _____.

Let's put this into practice. In this example, we will use an industrial manufacturer that produces values and pipes used in refineries or chemical processing plants. When this company set its vision as being the #1 supplier for the world's leading oil companies, they established a long-term OKR:

> *Objective & Key Results: We will become the leading infrastructure supplier to oil companies by providing products to our customer faster than our competitors as measured by: 1) Greater than 95% of orders are filled within 24hrs, 2) Greater than 30% of new customers reorder within 3 months, 3) 35% increase in organic sales growth, and 4) Greater than 50% increase in revenues from new products, so that we can sustain our organization and grow into new markets for our company.*

This was one of the few OKRs the company had for its 5-year vision. Once the senior leaders aligned on this OKR for the operation, the divisions then simplified it. By simplifying the long-term OKR, the business units could develop more discreet actions to execute on with their resources. By aligning on each key result of the long-term OKRs (Figure 6.4) and creating a shorter time box OKR for the business unit, the operational teams at the manufacturing plant are able to take action.

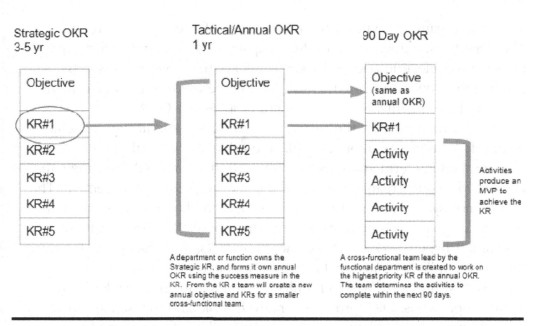

Figure 6.4 OKR explicit alignment from strategic to 90-day OKR.

In this case study, the teflon-lined value stream focused on the first key result from the 5-year OKR and formed its own annual OKR to align with the long-term OKR. Here is what the value stream developed as its annual OKR for the team:

> *Objective & Key Result: We will become a champion of meeting and exceeding our customer's expectation for delivery and quality as measured by: 1) Greater than 90% of the products produced are on a Kanban 2) Inventory turns within the machining operations go from 26 to 100 3) Lead time reduction from 3 to 1 day 4) increase in productivity of 20%–30% within each MFG cell, so that customer orders can be filled as within 1 day.*

This became the annual, shorter term OKR for this business unit within the organization. As it happened, once the team established the annual OKR, it then created a monthly plan of smaller activities to achieve the annual OKR. Using a future state value stream map as a guide, the team identified multiple kaizen events that would help the value stream achieve its annual OKR. By prioritizing these events and activities by impact and effort, the department was able to achieve the annual OKR. Within a year, the value stream had met the criteria of the annual OKR and as result saw a top-line organic growth for the product line of over 10% in revenue. The department added value to the company by focusing its efforts and resources on meeting one of the key results of the long-term OKR. By aligning their own annual OKR with the long-term OKR, the department supported the organization achievement of its 5-year OKR.

An OKR framework is the secret weapon for an organization to achieve its transformation aspiration. It fulfills the principle of Breakthrough Agile – plan for the long term and execute on the short term. OKRs also meet the needs of an Agile organization when it comes to project management. The governance system around OKRs allows for flexibility and self-correction of strategic goals on a monthly and quarterly basis. We discuss this Agile system in Chapter 7. One last comment on OKRs. Many people will say this looks similar to traditional methods of goal setting. On the surface, there is this similarity; however, unlike most top–down, cascaded goal setting approaches, OKR provides a more flexible and focused approach to goal setting. The structure of a good OKR allows for explicit alignment between long- and short-term outcomes (Figure 6.5). The rhythm of work around the OKR framework sets it apart from other traditional goal-setting methodologies. Be aware, however, there are many traps of inefficiency and superficiality around goal setting that companies fall into. To make OKRs' work for the company and deliver the value it seeks through its resources takes practice and patience. For an organization to be successful at planning for the long term and executing on the short term, discipline is required to follow the structure of the OKR framework.

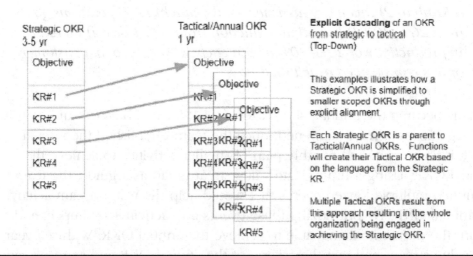

Figure 6.5   OKR explicit alignment – showing multiple annual OKRs.

MVP Thinking for Every Solution

Strategic planning delivers outcomes that change a customer behavior in the utilization of the organization's products and services. Weighing the significance of this statement then at any one time, only a few key strategic objectives are being resourced in the strategic planning window. When acted on, these strategic OKRs will generate work for the entire organization (Figure 6.6). To be effective, the execution needs these three elements to them: Speed, execution, and delivery. In traditional organizations, the flexible factor for most strategic goals is time. Meaning, the time to complete a goal changes randomly and without any consequences. In Breakthrough Agile, work is scoped down in 90-day increments and time is non-negotiable for OKRs. Teams and individuals will work to this rhythm of work to complete the 90-day OKR. Breakthrough Agile framework defines what it wants to do in the long term to meet its visionary objectives. The principle-based cultural business processes then simplifies the long-term objectives into short-term activities to a 90-day time box. Figure 6.6 helps one visualize the process of unpacking a long term OKR down to a short 90 day OKR.

By taking action within 90 days, the organization speedily produces an minimal viable product (MVP). Using MVPs to help the organization

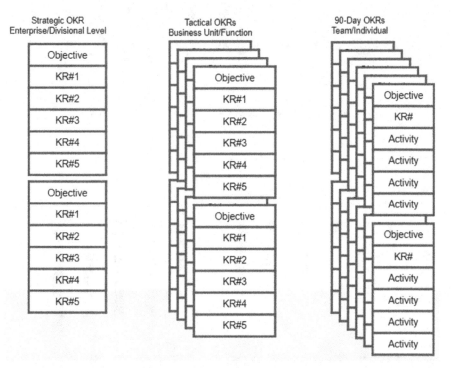

Figure 6.6   Fully deployed OKR framework with explicit alignment.

achieve its short- and long-term goals will increase the speed and delivery of value to the customer and organization. Using an MVP approach generates value sooner than an organization that uses traditional waterfall project management approach to strategic initiative (Figure 6.7). MVPs are pilot or small-scale replicas of the innovation. The smaller scale model allows for experimentation, learning, and self-correction prior to scaling up to a broad commercial level. The MVP allows for iteration and revisions of the original MVP to create the most value for the customer and organization. Apple has become an expert at self-correction and revision on its products – think of the different versions of the iPhone, iPad, and operating systems. Apple typifies how MVP thinking can generate more value for the company. For Apple, the journey will continue with their products. They will revise and iterate on the current versions of their product to meet the needs of the customer. MVP thinking can be applied to products, services, as well as internal business processes.

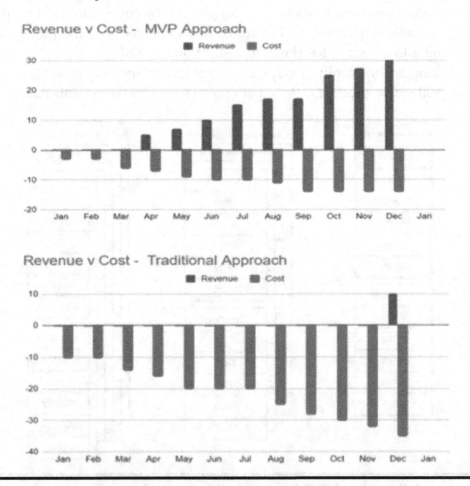

Figure 6.7   Examples of impact of MVP thinking on generating revenue.

Take, for example, a company that has one of its long-term OKRs, an objective to develop an innovative culture by recruiting and retaining the best engineering talent from A+ schools within its geographic region. The HR function that owns this OKR has as one of its key results to increase the number of talents by x% from all the universities within the region. When Breakthrough Agile is applied, the long-term OKR is unpacked into shorter term OKRs for the organization. The shorter term OKRs allow for a team to develop an MVP that will increase the retention of these talents. In this case, the team may focus its activities on creating a new recruiting tool to be tested at only one or two specific schools. From this testing, the design team for the OKR can receive feedback on the MVP and refine it before scaling it up to all the schools within the region. As the MVP is tested with its customers, the desirability and needs of the customer for the product or service are analyzed. This is a learning step that enables better understanding of the customer and what motivates them. This learning process continues from iteration to iteration of the MVP until the desired objective/outcome is met.

As the design team iterates on its original MVP, the learnings from the customer helps the design team identify what to stop, start, or enhance on the previous MVP. With the second iteration, a new cycle is started with the MVP and it continues until it meets the needs of the customer and the company can scale it sustainably. Another possibility is that the OKR owner stops and disbands the design team. Maybe the learning from the customer was that the MVP didn't add value or meet any need. Maybe recruiting didn't improve as a result or the customer expressed dissatisfaction with the tool. MVP thinking will increase the value realized through an early introduction of a product or service to the customer (Figure 6.7). Compared to traditional product development project with yearly lead times, MVPs give the organization feedback in the introduction phases of commercialization. As well, MVP thinking allows the organization to refine and re-create a product or service that is more appealing to customer's needs. This cycle of learning and iteration leads the organization to design a product that in the end, changes the behavior of the customer for the company's products. Customers see the value and want to own the product or use it.

MVP thinking is another key element of Breakthrough Agile and requires changes in mindset by everyone. Organizations that seek and expect perfection in detailed long-term plans or practices, struggle with adopting an MVP approach to strategic initiatives. Organizations that are very hierarchical thinking when it comes to decision making will be challenged to adopt this principle of Breakthrough Agile and the OKR framework. MVP thinking requires leaders to let go of control on decisions related to strategic activities. The teams are accountable for the delivery of the MVP and make the decision on *the what and how* of work as it relates to the completion of OKRs. MVP thinking will challenge employees to take on more accountability and ownership for their work then they have experienced in a traditional organization. It is no longer completing an assignment on time for employees; it now becomes a task of deciding what is the content and context of the assignment, how to accomplish it, and what is the rhythm of work that will be used to create the MVP. These changes in work sound subtle; however, they are not easy to adopt. MVP thinking is a major shift in mindset for most brownfield types of organizations. Shifting the mindset toward an Agile organization is the crux of the cultural transformation and one that takes hard work to see the results of Breakthrough Agile.

Summary

1. Strategic thinking aligns organizations to fulfill its visionary aspiration of how they will show up in tomorrow's business world.
2. Having a vision commits the organization to taking action to achieve that aspiration.
3. Organizations need to adopt the mindset that they plan and execute for both the long term and short term. Developing early MVPs leads to higher value generation for the organization in the long term.
4. Change in mindset for all employees is needed for organizations to achieve the potential of strategic planning, and how it impacts the work of employees.

Strategic Thinking Sensing Guide			
	Experiencing	Seeing	Hearing	Anti-Pattern
All Employees	Reduction in the number of strategic priorities launched at one time. More emphasis on customer centricity in actions. Clearer details about what is expected of teams with regard to strategic outcomes. Strategic alignment from bottom to top and across the organization in achieving key results of annual and long-term OKRs.	Simpler outcomes that have clear definitions of success. Leaders embracing customer centric over financial driven outcomes. Fewer initiatives that follow a financial outcome for internal operations. Teams are developing OKRs that focus on customer outcomes. Quicker value realized from faster completion of MVPs.	Leaders are asking open-ended questions like "what" and "how." Less conversations within teams on meeting financial targets and goals. More discussions on prototyping, MVPs, and piloting solutions.	Leaders judge employees' work and performance in front of others. Leaders create an environment of fear of failure. Cost and financial KPIs are used to drive strategic decisions and outcomes. Processes still reflect the financial business planning process as before the introduction of Breakthrough Agile.

Chapter 7

Project Management

There is no disgrace in honest failure; there is disgrace in fearing to fail. What is past is useful only as it suggests ways and means for progress.

Henry Ford, My Life and Work

A look inside:

- Agile and a brief history
- Gaps to current project management
- Agile project management – scrum methodology
- Traps of traditional project management

Project management as a cultural business process is the center of discussion for Chapter 7. Project management finds its way into the fabric of every organization regardless of the business. Projects can range from small-scale do-it-yourself (DYI) type of projects, to those that are in the hundreds of millions of dollars, requiring hundreds of people to complete. Every organizational function will have projects: Sales, marketing, quality, manufacturing, supply chain, finance, HR, etc... Ironically, the size and impact of a project are positively correlated between time and attention. The longer the project's time line and cost, the more attention it receives from the senior leaders. Smaller DYI type of projects usually escape the micromanagement of senior leaders since they don't have any financial risks.

Project management has a home in an Agile organization. One would technically be correct if they stated Agile had its genesis in traditional

DOI: 10.4324/9781003335702-7

project management functions. Agile was developed due to the performance gap inherent in waterfall project management methods. This gap is what triggered the pioneers of Agile to create a more flexible, robust way of executing and finishing projects. This gap was experienced when developers and designers were challenged to complete projects of high quality, quickly, and to plan. Teams that followed the traditional waterfall method lacked a sense of cohesiveness, and purpose as they followed the highly detailed Gantt chart. In the end, projects were either completed with features that the customer didn't want to pay for, or not at all. Two business leaders in the software industry at the time, Jeff Sutherland and Ken Schwaber recognized this gap of using the waterfall method of project management for managing complex and sophisticated software projects.

Dissatisfied with the current results, they innovated on the approach. After a few years of experimenting and retrospection, in early 1994 Scrum was officially being used by software companies as their project management system to design and launch new products. Today, when people think of Agile or Agile organization, most think of the Scrum Framework designed by Jeff and Ken's work in the 1990s. The other feature of Agile most people are aware of is the Agile Manifesto. As you unpack the contents of the Agile Manifesto, it is easy to conclude that this document is used by Agile Organizations to address the drawback of traditional project management. The original founders of the Agile Manifesto understood this and produced the Agile Manifesto with its 12 principles and 4 values to guide organizations to overcome the constraints of traditional project management bureaucracy. Today, all principle-based organizations will discover additional value when actions are driven by Agile principles such as those found in Breakthrough Agile or the Agile Manifesto. On this journey of value identification to value creation, Agile organizations will utilize Agile systems or ways of working to harvest the value.

In the past, the Agile Manifesto reinforced how Scrum was to be practiced by an organization. In today's networked business world, additional principles around the cultural business processes of decision making, conflict resolution, strategic planning, project management, and performance management will speed execution, iteration of MVPs, and delivery of value to the customer and organization. In Breakthrough Agile, the principles of this approach are designed to do the same as the Agile Manifesto did for projects in the early 2000s.

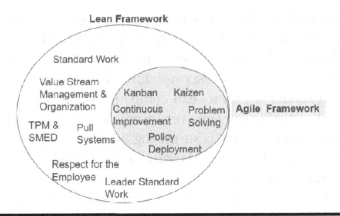

Figure 7.1   Agile's adoption of Lean systems.

One interesting note on Agile's history from the 1990s, the designers for Scrum and other Agile systems, borrowed best practices from the other transformation methodologies. In its current state, Agile adopted into its way of working Lean systems (Figure 7.1) and tools that complimented the intent behind Scrum and the Agile Manifesto. For instance, the Kanban was a concept that Agile adopted from Lean Manufacturing. Both a Lean and an Agile company use it for the same purpose: To improve the planning of work, and reduce work in process (WIP). Kanban in a Lean system controls the flow of production and WIP. In a Scrum event, teams use a Kanban to prioritize their Sprint planning and create a backlog of actions. The team uses the Kanban board as a way to make their work visible, and control how much work the team starts, what work is in process, and deviations that are delaying the completion of tasks. Additionally, Agile teams may use a Kanban approach for routine work within their department for the same purpose: To level the flow of work, and control the WIP. In both frameworks, there is a capacity formula that produces a rule for how much WIP can be in the process. Another overlap between Lean and Agile is the Sprint. This is Agile's adaptation of a Lean kaizen event that is used for problem-solving and continuous improvement. Both are time-boxed events with an intense focus on delivering a better way to meet the customer needs. Design thinking sprints develop an MVP through problem-solving and seeking to improve current products or services. Within Lean, solving the problem and making process improvements is a central principle to the transformation framework. Another crossover between Agile, Lean, and Six Sigma, are the unique roles to Agile. Think of the roles within Scrum methodology: Scrum Masters,

Product Owners, and Design Teams each can be traced back to practices in Lean and Six Sigma. Reflect back on how Six Sigma practitioners adopt different level belts to identify skill and knowledge with the methodology. The Product Owner has similar responsibilities to that of a Value Stream Manager or Lean Leader within a Lean company. As one examines deeper the activities within an Agile organization and those practicing Lean, the number of similarities is surprising. Just focusing in on role and responsibilities, think of how important this is for all three of the main transformation frameworks. In an Agile organization, these clear roles and responsibilities reinforce the new organization model and help to embed the Agile ways of working within the organizations. By having people within the Agile organization adopt new roles such as Product Owner, Scrum Master, Agile Coaches, release train engineer, and user story owners, their experiences will change the mindset and behaviors of teams across the organization. This shift in mindset and behaviors is the cultural shift that represents the impact of the transformation.

As the discussion on transformation moves into the space of discussing what to do, or more importantly, what to do differently than before, the concept of the "North Star" or "purpose" statements emerges. For most organization's embarking on the Agile way of working, being visionary, or purposeful, is a repeating value. People want to belong to an organization with a higher purpose other than generating revenue. Employees are more motivated and inspired when they connect what they do to a purpose that generates a value for society, and improves the ecosystem around it. With this pretext of what is motivating employees to work harder, and commit more to the organization, the strategic initiatives that are developed need to reflect this mindset. This is what the "North Star" is designed to do. It is the guiding principle for the organization on its journey to transform itself from its current to future state. Organizations are using a variety of "North Star" approaches. At times the vision or mission statement serves the same purpose. Some organizations have all three: North Star, Vision, and Mission. There isn't a right or wrong, only the intent that the organization needs to articulate its future end state. From this standpoint, then the strategic initiatives are aligned up and down and across the organization toward that higher purpose. It is important to note that Agile is unique in a few ways and these unique features to its transformation methodology make Agile appealing to many.

How organizations apply project management to strategic outcomes changes in a Breakthrough Agile organization. Traditionally, project management is a formal office with dedicated people to manage and support initiatives of all types of scope and investment. It is also a skill that is utilized by functional personnel to coordinate resources to complete an initiative. Project management exists on every level from the C-room down to the smallest of teams, and individual level. In organizations that have a traditional hierarchical structure, project management becomes the strategic arm of the organization and is responsible for the implementation of those strategic initiatives that the organization senses are needed to help it survive and be competitive in the future. Traditional project management survives when the strategic model is one of protecting the business. In this case, projects are usually long and drawn out, with little unknown about the solution. Most of the projects in this space are implementation solutions with a cost saving or efficiency theme. When a cultural transformation effort is started, it is usually the project management team that creates the implementation plan. This maintains and reinforces the command and control culture of the organization as it implies there is someone responsible for the transformation. In these situations a new role is developed for this purpose called the transformation lead or transformation manager. Applying the same principles from their past experience in project management, the new leader creates a project plan to illustrate the different phases of the transformation and how it will be deployed. Usually, the plan is linear with timelines and an end date.

As the transformation begins to take shape, personnel from the project management team may end up as the first champions of the transformation methodology and conduct the initial training for the organization. I have met many people with a project management office (PMO) background who are either Six Sigma trained or Lean subject matter experts. Since the transformation is usually viewed as a project (having a start and end date), the PMO function and its resources are assigned the task. There are talented people in the PMO and many will seek out additional education and certifications to help build up their credibility at the beginning. For instance, these individuals seek out Product Owner, Scrum Master, or other Agile training or certifications to gain a better understanding of the transformation framework. As the new subject matter experts on the transformation platform, and their background in project management, it logically flows that here are the individuals to create the roadmap or project plan for the overall transformation.

It is at this point, where organizations first get derailed in their transformation efforts. Since the transformation is viewed as a project with start and end dates, the roadmap assumes that a waterfall type of approach to the deployment is the best way forward. The roadmap (project plan), then details by week, month, and year how the tools of the transformation are deployed in periodic waves. The plan gives the high-level overview of how every organization unit is included in the rollout. At least the ones people think will benefit the most from it. Since the plan focuses on tool usage, then the more process-oriented business units are covered first. In Lean, these are usually the manufacturing areas, supply chain, and maintenance. Since the organization's principle of cost-benefit drives the thinking behind the roll out, the PMO recommends areas where quick wins will be generated. Then depending on the size of the organization, the administrative areas, such as HR, finance, quality, R&D, Engineering, communications, etc. are left untouched by the transformation for months, potentially years. As mentioned, this is the start of the derailment for most transformation, and why Breakthrough Agile advocates focusing on principles and cultural business processes first. More robust roadmaps will include a leadership training at the beginning, which includes all leaders from all functions, but then the diligence to ensure leaders practice the new behaviors is absent. In Breakthrough Agile, establishing an Agile rhythm of work, commonly called the 90-day planning review cycle, will help embed these new leadership behaviors in the organization, as well as redefine how projects are tracked for business units.

One last point on the traditional PMO waterfall transformation project plan. The question that doesn't get asked, is "how far is the organization willing to go" with the transformation. The answer to this question, needs answered by the organization's senior leaders, and will impact any deployment plan. It is also key to an effective change management plan with employees. Being clear on the pace of change, and what is changing to all employees, prevents unrealistic expectations and fears from developing at the start. It is also interesting to note, that whoever becomes the lead in defining the transformation roadmap, their personality will influence the speed, direction, and pace of change. A traditional, conservative PM who takes over a transformation effort, will apply their experience in waterfall project management approach to the deployment plan, leading to a slower pace at which value is generated. Someone with a history of leading transformations, and knowing the traps, will create a roadmap with different context, speed, and rate of change. In either case, the need to have knowledgeable people who know the systems and ways of working for the transformation are critical to the successful deployment in the beginning. The focus will be different depending on how leaders answer the questions of , "How far do we go?" with the changes. A seasoned transformation leader will identify the transformation as a learning journey, one that starts but never concludes as the organization continuously learns from its transformational experiences to shape its future.

Rhythm of work is a key feature of Breakthrough Agile's approach to project management. In both types of businesses, traditional and an Agile organization, initiatives come in all sizes. Some have scopes that require a high level of resources from the organization. For instance, building a new facility, bringing online a new material/enterprise requirement planning (MRP/ERP) system, closing down facilities, or transferring products overseas are examples of these types of projects. These multi-million dollar projects are part of the organization's strategic planning process and with the amount of cash invested, there is a sense of "right first time" in terms of execution of the project. Usually, these multi-year projects with hundreds of hours of planning and proscriptive outcomes based on the plan absorb the time, energy, and resources of many of the PMO individuals and teams within the organization. Watching these large-scale projects work their way through a corporation at a slow pace has been a lesson for many on how speed impacts results. The downside is that this same approach is applied to smaller projects. Breakthrough Agile changes the model of project management by focusing on a rhythm of work combined with an MVP mindset. Seeing personnel spend years as a project's steward, without growing or developing their skills and abilities, has left me to believe that a better way exists. How project management is positioned within the organization and the portfolio of projects, influences how people work and what is viewed as being important to the business. This is a direct influence of the organization's culture.

Let's dig a little deeper into the concept of rhythm of work and how it plays a role in an Agile organization. One aspect of Agile that is different to Lean is its application of Scrum. As mentioned in the preceding paragraph, a Scrum event is similar to a Kaizen event, however, Scrum provides a more robust system of execution. With a Scrum event, the output is to build on the long-term goals of the company through short bursts of work. The Sprint cycle is an iterative rhythm of work to develop a minimum viable product (MVP). This sets it apart from a kaizen team's approach to developing a finalized set of standardized work instructions for a process. The MVP leaves open the flexibility to change quickly and redefine the customer needs based on customer feedback. A sprint will focus on the external stakeholder, and seek to meet those needs. In a Kaizen event, there is normally a focus on an internal KPI that needs to be improved. Lean assumes that if we deliver a product faster to the customer, then our business will be more successful. Agile looks at delivering a product to a customer faster by focusing on only the minimum needs of the customer. Building the customer's basic wants and needs, and then testing the MVP with the customer to gain feedback is a fundamental concept of Scrum. Agile's approach relies on the feedback loop from users to re-work the MVP to grow and scale up. This feedback loop builds in a system of self-correction and differentiates Scrum from Lean's kaizen approach (Figure 7.2). Many times in a Lean organization, Kaizen events are planned with a desired outcome, and this what the team works to accomplish. If the desired outcome generates a cost-saving for the company then it is considered successful or good.

Cost efficiency, a key principle for Lean organizations, starts with an inside-to-outside view of the customer needs. Agile takes the point of view from outside to inside on delivering products to the customer. In a sprint, the minimum viable product (MVP) allows the design team a chance to iterate and co-create with the customer as the customer uses the MVP. Then the design team co-creates with the customer on enhancing the product features to maximize the impact for the customer. During this time the MVP may be generating revenue or value for the company. This iterative process increases the value of the company, creates a more robust product, and changes the customer behavior toward the company. This desired result is an increased use of the organization's products and services. Agile creates value for the organization by engaging with customers earlier than in a traditional project-managed initiative. MVP thinking allows the design team to drop features that do not work, or modify experimental features the customer liked but thought could be better. This feature gives the organization an competitive flexibility to meet the customers' needs and wants.

Scrums are designed for speed and results. The mindset of the scrum team isn't to create a right first-time product but to develop a product that meets the customer's minimum requirements. The advantage of the MVP approach is that the scrum team can change the design of its product based on actual usage and feedback from the customer. This iteration concept also promotes a more prototype mentality within the organization. In the past, when it was required to have a "capital approval request" with a detailed 3- to 5-year plan that resulted in a perfect product, now an Agile

Features	Scrum	Lean
Opportunity or problem statement	User stories & tasks	A3 (eg. 7 Block A3 or 9 Block A3)
Roles	Product Owner, Scrum Master, Agile Coach, Design Team	Value Stream Leader, Kaizen Lead, CI manager/practitioner, Kaizen team

Chapter 7 – Project Management

	Scrum	Lean
Tools used during event	Brainstorming, customer journey mapping, Design thinking, prototyping, iteration	Standardized Work Instructions(Layouts, time studies, Work Combination sheets, Capacity Charts), Value Stream Mapping
Focus of team's efforts	Unknown solution	Reworking a given process(SMED, WorkFlow, etc.)
Governance	Ceremonies & Rituals(daily stand up, reviews, Burn off Chart, sprint planning, point allocation, retrospective, time boxed, Kanban for work prioritization	Kaizen report out
Team's Character	Self organized team that defines the what and how of the team's work. Focus on achieving the outcome of the user story.	Improvement team by Kaizen lead or CI personnel. KPIs drive the work content. Efficiency and cost saving are generally the outputs of the kaizen team.
Process	MVP - Iterative & Feedback driven – Can change after customer and stakeholder feedback	Standardized – will train everyone on the new process and make them follow it. Resistance to changing SW once completed.

Figure 7.2   Table comparing systems within Agile and Lean.

organization can seek a minimal budget to design and implement on a smaller scale first. Then through product iterations based on user feedback, the team continually creates value for the customer and organization. With an MVP mindset, there is built-in flexibility on making changes to meet the customer's needs. The idea of speed, flexibility and customer centricity gives the team working on the product flexibility to design a product that works with minimal features. This eliminates the time and resources of creating a perfect product at the end of a multiyear waterfall Gantt project. An Agile organization also builds upon its existing products to create more value for the company. The principle of customer centricity, and designing products to meet the customer needs, wants and motivations, through scrum action, is a key cultural feature of Agile Organizations. To get to the point of realizing the value of scrum activities, an organization needs to prioritize and select what initiatives to complete. This is why project management becomes a principle-based cultural business process in Breakthrough Agile and the scrum methodology a system that reinforces the new way of working.

Waterfall project management techniques follow a logic of developing perfect new products or services right the first time. Or even worse, in a traditional organization, Waterfall Project Management is more about following the plan than understanding and verifying that value will be created from the work. Having spent thousands of hours in PMO report out meetings, meetings, I have seen hundreds of projects that get carried over year after year. Rarely, if at all, does the question get asked if this project will deliver the intended value it was assumed to deliver. But, since the project went through the approval hoops at the start, and was endorsed by a committee of senior leaders, it continues to stay on the business unit's initiative radar. The hidden cost for all companies are these projects that still require millions of dollars and thousands of man hours to prop up as viable projects. It is ironic that projects that were vetted years past, keep going through multiple committee sign-offs, and often end up providing little to no value for the company. This typifies the traditional, conservative risk-averse organization.

In this context, teams spend hundreds of hours creating a multiyear plan, drafting proposals and updates for committees, and working tirelessly to get people on board with the project. Since pushing out timelines is the standard, then performance is of secondary importance. The waterfall method of project management increase complexity in decision making by requiring multi-level decision-making bodies to endorse and resource projects year after year. Since these decision making bodies use a team based consensus method for decisions, progress is slow and innovation is limited to ideas with the least risk. When any new or bold idea surfaces in the project plan, it will usually get water-downed to get the consensus agreement. Traditional organizations value this approach. It follows their conservative approach of controlling the outcome of the project. The highly detailed plan, risk-averse activities, control over the team and project leader all guarantee a stable and minimally disruptive outcome for employees, and ultimately the customer. The more detail and perfect planned timing, then the better chance that a senior-level committee will endorse the project even if the outcome doesn't meet a customer need or a business need. These layers of committees to endorse projects moving forward through consensus decision making is a strong contrast to an Agile organization of using a 90-day planning cycle as its rhythm of work for strategic initiatives.

With the waterfall project management technique, the idea of completing a prototype within the first 90 days after idea generation seems impossible. Usually the first 90 days is spent on getting a team together, writing a charter, deciding on who will pay for the project, detailing the year-over-year timeline, and setting up a meeting structure. For an Agile organization, once the decision has been made to move forward with the idea, the scrum or design team starts its first time-boxed event to produce a prototype. The power of the Scrum Methodology and using it as the organization's rhythm (pattern) of work for strategic priorities is a defining transition from a traditional project management approach to Breakthrough Agile's approach. For non-software companies, Scrum is applied to both software applications and common business processes that are offered by the company. This change in the rhythm of work from the traditional yearly or multiyear project plan to a short 90-day cycle of sprint bursts delivers value sooner to the organization. Having the rhythm of 90 days creates a drumbeat for the organization to deliver on prototypes or MVPs consistently.

Many software companies have articulated the MVP drumbeat as a train leaving the station. On a certain day of the calendar, the train leaves the station (e.g., The product goes to the customer). On this train are the new features of the product that the scrum teams have been working on for the past 90 days. In practice, at the end of 90 days, all features that were planned for the previous 90 days completion are on the train, whether or not they are completed. As the train leaves the station (goes to the customer) the features that are completed get used by the customer, while those that are still in progress are delayed while the team responsible for them works to complete them. As a result, customers experience new features of the MVP, and can provide feedback to the organization. This cycle continues as all the features get completed for the cycle. In the next cycle, there is a new train, with new features based upon feedback that was received from the customer. A self-correcting and perpetuating rhythm of work for the organization.

When a brown field organization starts to practice this approach with projects, it disrupts a very entrenched way of working for many individuals. The traditional way of working is turned upside down with this new rhythm of work. In a traditional organization, strategic priorities imply that a multiyear project team is needed to deliver the final output or product. In a brownfield organization, legacy or carry over projects will continue to appear in the strategic plan. In the first round of executing an Agile project management approach, the team will potentially have to deal with 50 or more strategic projects. These projects are the result of how the brownfield organization conducted its strategic planning which is generally using key performance indicators (KPIs) to drive strategic goals. With Breakthrough Agile, an organization will start to see the benefits of a strategic priority within a much shorter timeframe. By scoping down the work to a 90-day cycle, the design team will develop a prototype through a Scrum on the strategic priority. The design team members may change over time, and as different needs are identified by the customer. With this approach, a pilot MVP can be developed within 90 days using a scrum approach.

This change in rhythm of work creates a number of benefits for the organization. Introducing prototypes in the market earlier has the potential to create a new revenue stream. Through Scrum, employees develop stronger problem-solving and creative thinking skills as it is applied to the current products and services of the company. This change focus' leaders on creating business transformation initiatives that delivers value quicker than it has ever done before. In practice, there are few barriers for Scrum in today's organizations. Outside the obvious of creating or modifying software applications, Scrum is an effective system for continuous improvement in other business processes. From redesigning an invoice processes system, or an employee onboarding system, or how sales contracts are designed, all can be influenced by a design team in a scrum. In each of these examples, using some type of digital prototype as a solution needs to be explored. Over the years, I have seen applications developed that included a bar-coded Kanban system for service materials, an internal customer portal, digital visual boards, and many more. The customer portal application was one I saw a few times. In this application, anyone that was planning to visit a particular customer could log into the portal, and see notes from the last person that visited this customer. This would create a cross-sharing of information that detailed the customer's latest concerns, purchases, complaints, and future aspirations. Now, any person visiting this customer would have more information about the customer's needs, wants, pain points, and motivations. This information always led to having a more informed employee talking to the customer, resulting in a more value-adding visit for the customer by the company. A prototype for this application was completed in less than 90 days using a scrum approach.

Scrum is introduced in this chapter, as it is a way execute projects. Project management and strategic planning are closely linked, much like all the cultural business processes are interrelated. Project management becomes the execution arm of the strategic planning process. How the organization executes on those initiatives directly correlates with the value it creates for the customer and company. Being fast and flexible or slow and rigid may be a conclusion a customer has as a result of how new products and services are delivered to the public. Breakthrough Agile accelerates the rate of change that occurs with a company's products and services. Stepping back and looking at the model for Breakthrough Agile, the picture of why the five cultural business processes define an organization's culture becomes clearer (Figure 7.3). There is a strong interconnection from one to the other. With Strategic Planning and Project Management, the output of the first is an input to the latter.

Agile project management is a different experience. In the traditional organization, the process relies upon a PMO function to document and track projects using waterfall project management techniques such as Gantt charts,

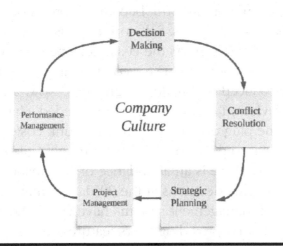

Figure 7.3   The five cultural business processes interconnect between and across each other, this fabric of how an organization works shapes the culture of the organization.

excel sheets, project charters and capacity analysis. Within the traditional approach, a large amount of time is spent on developing a multiyear plan, getting funding approval, lobbying for resources, and aligning on a "go-live" date. At times, this is followed up by a change management "road show" were members of the project team travel the globe and share the plan, budget, resources, and ask for everyone's support in the upcoming changes. As the project kicks off with a wave of energy and enthusiasm, the reality of how inefficient this approach actually is surfaces. Soon after kick-off, due dates are being missed, personnel changes on the team, rebranding, and restarting of the project occurs. Many times these set backs are written off as the complexity of the project. Most of the time, it is self-inflected by the organization due to their approach to projects, and how they make decisions. Within my career, the number of high-level projects that were meant to change a business process that ended up fizzing out or "DOA," *dead on arrival*, is a strong motivator for organization to embrace a new way to execute on its strategic priorities.

I remember being told once that a foreseen DOA project was still ongoing because the organization had already sunk so many millions of dollars into it, that they didn't want to be embarrassed by stopping it and admitting it was a mistake. These are risks associated with taking on new initiatives. In an Agile organization, the 90-day planning cycle is a system that can stop a project early in its development stage, if the project doesn't deliver on its intended outcome. Or better yet, there is an opportunity to self-correct an initiative, once the team working on it becomes more knowledgeable about the customer needs through MVPs. Self-correction is a step to redefine the product or solution so that it meets the customer's needs in the next 90 day iteration. Making the decision to stop, or continue a project fits into the new rhythm of work introduced by Breakthrough Agile. Now, on a cadence of 90 days, projects are reviewed rhythmically and if needed, changed or stopped. Being able to pull the plug on a project that has sunk costs or doesn't deliver value is a key behavior to develop in a Breakthrough Agile organization. With most PMO teams, there is an abundance of information on key projects that can help with making decisions at the 90-day planning review.

Automated project management systems have eased the manual burden of project management by providing users features such as flagging overdue projects, capacity constraints, and KPI-like metrics such as actual v. planned percentages, budget and hours forecasting. Additionally, information technology is automating these processes and at times linking them with other platforms within the organization. I remember early in my career using

Microsoft Project for the first time, and thinking it was the next great thing to increase efficiency of work. Here was a software system that would give me administrative control over the assignment of tasks, timelines, and dedicated milestones. I thought this would be a great way to motivate others to complete their project tasks on time, have effective team meetings, and complete important projects. I spent hours learning how to link task items, create a project hierarchy, run reports, and assign capacity to project books. As can be expected, my hours of detailed and perfect planning seemed uninteresting to the project team members. We still had delays, changed due dates, and projects that got started, but didn't move from the initiation planning phase. This is a lesson learned early in my career on how people work and the limits of traditional project management.

In today's work environment, project management software is managing projects with detailed-oriented features such as planned versus actual capacity of teams, measuring completion rates, and calculating return on investment (ROI) for the project management office (PMO). On the surface, software automation is the one-stop shop for all the information on the project and this is what has been developed for the modern traditional organization. The measure of success for the PMO is how well they manage this static data and provide reports on project KPIs such as planned versus actual, adherence to milestones, capacity calculations and potential risks to projects. In reality, this becomes a task for the PMO: Changing due dates to make a project's status green, and conducting "death by PowerPoint" presentations for a committee of senior leaders. If you have sat through these committee meetings, then you felt the pain of how the organization seems to be slow and delayed on the execution of projects.

Another trap for companies utilizing a software system is to track and monitor all of the organization's projects, regardless if the project is strategic or routine. As expected this increases the work scope of the PMO, and it also creates a blurred line as to what is important for the organization. As a leader, having a list of hundreds of projects of all size and scope results in lack of focus on those projects that will shape the future of the organization. Trying to focus on too many initiatives leads to a chaotic attempt to deliver on strategic projects and limits progress on the transformation of the organization. For organization's with an activity-based culture, the listing of every project is common. After all, doing something, anything, appears to give people a sense that they are busy and creating value for the organization. Most software systems include a module for forecasting and capacity planning. This model helps detail the forecasted hours of work for the list of projects. This module fits nicely into a traditional organization's principle of close fiscal control and budget management. Unfortunately, these forecasts are usually inflated and lack a reasonable clue as to the work needed to complete the project. One experience I had with an organization using an automated system demonstrates how a good software system can lead a team to poor decisions. At a monthly PMO meeting, the PMO manager stated we had 53 full-time employees working 40 hours a week for the year on strategic projects. This was a brownfield manufacturing site with 500+ full-time employees, including 250 production personnel that ran 24/7 manufacturing operations. There was no new building construction, new products, or equipment purchases happening during the year. The stated number reflected over 10% of the plant's personnel committed to mystery projects within the plant.

As with all software systems the output is as good as the data that is entered into the system. After hearing the statement above, a few questions were asked about the hours total. The system crumbled under the inspection of a few "what" and "how" questions. It turned out that project leaders were reporting planned hours for many projects that hadn't even been started. The list of projects was more a wish list for the site. Additionally, the dedicated hours included regularly scheduled maintenance projects that fell under the scope of work for full-time maintenance employees. As the coaching session continued, it was brought to light that many of the projects were considered daily work for engineers or other technical people within the plant. This example illustrates how the data that goes into the software system is as good as the output. Imagine a committee making a decision on future plant operations using the data that was introduced in the above paragraph. This example provides insights as to how traditional project management has drawbacks and potentially drives an organization to rely on poor data to make decisions.

Forward-thinking organizations are moving toward dashboard and roadmaps to help with managing the strategic direction of their business. Making business or strategic review meetings more efficient and meaningful is the driving force behind these types of changes. Organizations are learning to limit their business reviews to key initiatives that are implemented to drive transformational change within the organization. Only discussing items that are off-track, or KPIs that are in the "red" is a new rule that teams put in place to promote efficiency in this type of business review. This is a step in the right direction and indicates that organizations are welcoming change, however, still groups of people in the background are continuing the efforts of the PMO to be a one-stop shop for a project in terms of details. These PMO teams are still speeding their time on creating presentations that will "wow" and "entertain" senior leaders. Agile organizations are stepping away from this approach and seeking to find a better utilization of the project manager's talents and project teams. Whatever the method used to gather data, this information is beneficial to making decisions during the 90-day planning cycle review.

Over the course of my career, I have seen a variety of approaches from massive Excel sheets with numerous tabs for a project that include project charter, team participants, stakeholder management, Gantt charts, budget information, etc. to sophisticated software systems that allowed web-based access, updating, and virtual capabilities. For a traditional organization, resources are actually needed to maintain these systems, in order to execute on its project. IT resources, project manager resources, administrative, communication, and more, are add-on features to a project management office that practices using the traditional approach to project execution. Ironically, the value of the PMO starts to become more of a data and information manager than one that facilitates the completion of projects or initiatives. In many cases, the organization misses out on leveraging the experience of the project management team. PMO's stop facilitating and removing barriers for teams, and begin to focus more on how information is presented. The PMO performance is evaluated on how well they make a presentation, versus their impact on getting results for a strategic initiative. Agile project management streamlines this approach and minimizes the need for extensive data collection by a PMO. In Breakthrough Agile, project management is defined through a system called the 90-day planning cycle. People within your organization will have to relearn project management based upon the principles of Breakthrough Agile, and the Agile Project Management methodology.

For organizations with a legacy of managing projects through a PMO making the change to Agile ways of working is challenging. The time to cut over to an Agile Project Management approach will correlate with the number of large-scale, capital, and asset-intensive projects ongoing. The challenge to cut over is augmented with the addition of projects that are ongoing and contain "sunk" costs. Legacy and right to operate projects will creep on the strategic plan. In the first round of practicing Agile project management, for an organization with over 100 people expect to see at least 30 to 40 strategic initiatives. For those that are larger, over 500, the number will balloon to 70–100. The lessons discussed in this chapter are the cause of the high number of seemingly strategic priorities. Additionally, the politics involved, and the inertia these projects have on maintaining the old traditional PMO function will be a barrier to switching to the more flexible Agile project management approach. These carry-over projects have legacy sponsors, and teams with members that have roles and current career aspirations linked to the projects.

To help start the transition to an Agile organization, there are ways to jump start the Agile approach. For one, any new initiative, needs to adopt Agile methodologies as an operational element. Additionally, the legacy projects need to be scrubbed. Hard decisions need to be made on projects that have lingered on the strategic priority radar. Leaders need to ask, is this something we need to stop. Or if self-correction on the project is required, then the new direction adopts the Agile approaches. Another approach is to separate the legacy projects from new projects that are identified going forward for the company. The risk of changing to a different approach mid-stream for brownfield organizations sometimes is too great. Legacy project management with links to using the company's capital and at times, large investments, will keep groups like finance and engineering occupied and resistant to changing to a new way of managing projects. This is a strong reason why project management is one of the five cultural business processes. Large-scale projects with millions invested and entire functions focused on the execution of a project will continue to shape an organization's culture. However, taking the first step with smaller, less capital-intensive projects, and adopting the principles of Breakthrough Agile, the organization will see a change. Over time, the legacy projects will become fewer, and more initiatives are categorized as routine or part of the team's purpose, and the 90-day planning cycle will become the norm (Figure 7.4). As this happens the organization will start to reshape its culture to become more Agile with regard to speed, flexibility, and meeting customer needs.

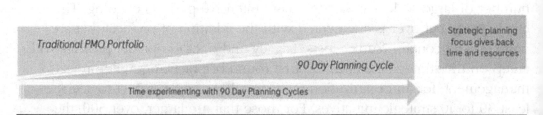

Figure 7.4   Maturity of the organization as it practices 90-Day Planning Cycle and scrums.

For all organizations, the premise of a principle-based organization remains the same. When applying the principles of Breakthrough Agile to cultural business processes, the outcomes of these processes will reflect greater speed, customer centricity, and deliver of better results. Going back to the Agile Manifesto, its authors realized that an organization's culture is shaped by its principles. Principle #3 of the manifesto states that Agile organizations should "deliver working software frequently." This principle guides the organization toward short iterations on projects that deliver MVPs. The designers of the Agile Manifesto realized that project management shapes the rhythm of work of a team and organization. Additionally, a self-organized team will deliver a higher quality solution for its customers. With Breakthrough Agile we look at project management, and the other 4 cultural business processes and articulate principles to follow to change the culture of the organization. Let's review the principles of Breakthrough Agile for Project Management:

- Less is more, Prioritize
- Speed of design, development, production, and delivery is key
- Change is welcomed and wanted
- People contribute through scope of work, not positional hierarchy

Less is More, Prioritize

Organizations with a mature strategic planning process that delivers initiatives with the right focus is the intent behind "Less is more, Prioritize." Naturally, organizations need to provide both internal and external stakeholders with a vision as to who they are, why they are in business, what they want to do, and how they will do it. In a traditional organization, this is articulated in the organization's vision, mission or purpose statements. Having committed themselves to this future state, the next step is to identify what are the key initiatives/projects that will move them toward this future vision. What system or products will they provide the customer in the future? What is the highest priority initiative to work on first? Once the organization is aligned around an initiative, and resources are assigned, the next step is to create a system to monitor how the organization knows it is making progress toward the higher aspirations. It is at this point that traditional project management becomes a function within the organization. Once the initiatives are identified, then time, personnel, and other resources are committed to make it happen. These initiatives are the eggs in the basket the company is betting on to help it succeed in the future. Imagine the stakes for these initiatives.

In Breakthrough Agile, the organization's vision drives innovation that is realized by teams. Teams within the organization define the outcomes that will move the organization closer to realizing its vision & purpose through smaller-scale events. Take Amazon's purpose/vision statement: *Amazon strives to be Earth's most customer centric company, Earth's best employer, and Earth's safest place to work.* Very aspirational, yet if cascaded alone divisions, functions, teams, and individuals would struggle to align their actions to meet the outcome that Amazon is striving to achieve. Amazon then introduces its 4 operating principles to help achieve this future state: *Customer obsession rather than competitor focus, passion for invention, commitment to operational excellence, and long-term thinking.* From here, organization units and individuals can develop outcomes that are focused on the organization's operating principles, and help it achieve its purpose. Breakthrough Agile's principle of *Less is more. Prioritize.* compliments this equation when the organization's teams start to align their outcomes to the higher level principle of the organization.

An organization's leaders realize that they need to provide direction to create an environment that leads to a higher level of performance by its teams. The key to Breakthrough Agile is that working on the top two or three initiatives helps the organization achieve this faster than working on 60–70 different initiatives at a time. In the space of project management, these 2 or 3 key outcomes need to be supported and reviewed by teams throughout the organization. Simplifying the strategic portfolio to 2 or 3 key initiatives is counter intuitive to business culture that is activity based. With all the market & business intelligence the organization has at its disposal, it is hard to decide on what three initiatives to take a chance on. As many colleagues have stated to me in strategic planning sessions, all the initiatives are the right thing to do. However, being focused on those 2 or 3 outcomes that will lead to better performance for the company is key to growing and developing the company. As the organization moves closer to achieving these outcomes, the business becomes more competitive in the market. The key understanding with Breakthrough Agile is that at all times, the organization needs to have two to three high-level outcomes active at all times, which come from a strategic backlog developed by the strategic planning process. When one high-level outcome is completed, then the next most important outcome is pulled from the backlog and put into play at any time during the year. The calendar year, or budget cycle, doesn't affect when a key priority is started within Breakthrough Agile.

To keep this backlog of initiatives current, all organizations will identify more than two to three key long term outcomes during the strategic planning process that are important to move it forward. In Breakthrough Agile, all of these projects are prioritized and those two to three that are determined to have the greatest impact for the future of the organization are triggered, requiring the entire organization to align on them for completion. The remainder of projects are moved onto the strategic backlog. Once prioritization of the backlog identifies the most significant projects, then all business units align strategically to them, and work to complete them in the stated timeframe or earlier. Once the outcome is achieved, then the leaders of the organization go back to the backlog, and take the next highest priority long term outcome. As this is a dynamic process, the backlog is groomed and at times reprioritized once or twice a year. This enables the organization to stay current with the changes in the market, and socio-economic ecosystem that it engages customers in. This self-correcting step with the top key projects, enables an organization to keep flexible and make changes based on the customer's needs and wants.

In Breakthrough Agile, the key to project management is to clearly define the initiatives that are truly strategic from the tactical work. Organizations hire people for tactical/routine work and this work needs to be left off the scope of strategic project management. Building the strategic acumen to synthesize the strategy from the tactical or routine work is challenging for people. An Agile project management process should result in a steady cadence of key projects being completed each year. Whether new products being launched, revised products, or new solutions, the organization's project management efforts will see these projects closed at a steady pace.

Speed of Design, Development, Production, and Delivery Impacts the Business

Execution of the organization's two to three priorities separates itself from the competition. Speed of design, development, production and delivery is the element that will create enormous value for the customer. Faster decisions, commitment, allocation of resources, and getting a working product into the hands of a customer results in value being generated for the organization. In Breakthrough Agile, applying this principle to the execution of the prioritized initiatives is the superpower. By enabling the organization to introduce to the market its innovations of new products, revised products, and novel services, growth and competitive advantage will follow. The enabling framework used in Agile organization is called the 90-day planning cycle. In Agile organizations, this system provides the platform for meeting customer demands faster than the traditional waterfall method of project management. Applying the framework to project management, the 90-day planning cycle embraces faster decision making, MVP mindset, and stronger accountability. The system enables faster speed of design, development, production, and delivery that impacts the business environment. With this approach, teams are focused on the content of the objective, and plan their activities to achieve results in 90-day cycles. For smaller, less complex organizations, adopting this principle is quite easy. However, a large multinational will find it challenging to redirect their current way of working with projects or initiatives to achieve what is being described here. What has to happen in these organizations with broad geographic and massive organization units, is that larger projects or initiatives need to be simplified into smaller, more discreet working initiatives. For example, if an organization has a moonshot strategic outcome of being the digital leader in its market, then business units within the organization may pick a specific product line to work on first, or even a specific model of a product line. By focusing on this one product to start with, the organization experiments with the digital platform, learns how it works with the company's products, how the customer responds to the change, and using this learning cycle to get better with the next product it plans to digitalize. If unable to scope down the scale of these initiatives, then the organization needs to consider a separate way to manage its Agile strategic priorities without combining them with large scale capital or other types of asset-building projects. Reducing a large-scale project down to smaller increments, and achieving an MVP from that effort will lead the organization to achieving breakthrough results. To help the organization achieve this process, OKRs and the 90-day planning cycle will maintain the focus and direction of the organization.

Change Is Welcomed and Wanted

Change is welcomed and wanted shows that the organization is sensing the customer needs during a 90 day review cycle. The greatest challenge for an organization begins when it starts a huge investment project, based upon the knowledge at the time, only to find out a year or two later that the customer needs, or conditions of the business world have changed. At this point, time, money, and resources, sometimes to the tune of millions of dollars have been invested in the initiative. At times, a mini ecosystem has developed around the project internally, giving support to employee's career progression and personal development. However, if there isn't a need or a motivation on the part of the customer to buy the product or service, then is there a rationale for the project to continue? Some organizations continue to source these projects, even if it's known that the customer is not willing to buy the end product or service. At times, leaders at the higher levels of the organization have staked their reputation on the initiative. For these leaders, losing face in the light of a failure is too great for them, and they will continue with a project that might be DOA from the customer's point of view.

Change is welcomed and wanted, and is applied to both the large- and small-scale initiatives that the organization is focused on completing in any given timeframe. On a smaller scale, change is welcomed and wanted implying the feedback rituals (Test & Review) of the scrum event. Employees need to have an MVP mindset on the products and work that they are doing. This mindset includes flexibility with solutions or MVPs to change a feature to better meet the customer's needs and wants. Having an MVP mindset requires that teams are able to stop initiatives that are not meeting the needs of the customers. This ability to say no, or stop work is challenging. Too often, projects that are started may never end as they stay on the radar of a project manager. If a team decides to stop an initiative mid-stream of completion, this reflects courage and system awareness based on customer feedback.

People Contribute through Scope of Work, Not Positional Hierarchy

In many discussions about project management with colleagues, there is always a reference to a project committee that is the decision makers for the work of the project team. This committee assesses the work, judges the quality of the work, and approves the forward movement of the project (value deliver). In some cases, this translates into a committee or sounding board as a feature to each project team. This feature echoes the traditional ways of working with a controlling body over a team's work. Although at the start the committee has a dedication to delivering value to the customer, over time the committee turns into a bureaucratic nexus for committee members. The committee meetings should be designed to provide the project team a chance to obtain coaching or support to overcome obstacles, however, over time, the committee meetings give senior leaders a chance to grandstand or preach. Egos, internal conflicts, silo thinking, and narcissism show up in the place of coaching. Senior leaders may want to get their solution into the project team's work. At times, this means that these committee members give direction or infuse their solutions into the team's work. And what if a project team ignores or doesn't act on the committee members advice or suggestions? The fear of retaliation, conflict, or other disparaging action comes to mind. As the committee approach offers senior leaders a place to become self-important and exercise their positional authority over a team's work, it also reinforces consensus decision making and conservative thinking. At this point, a project's scope or focus becomes less bold and innovative. The influence of these committees is to keep reins on a team, and make sure it doesn't go off track, or in other words do something too innovative. Another intent of the committee is to be more efficient, however, I have rarely met a senior leader who feels the time spent in these committees is productive. In my experience, committees that meet monthly tend to see the same project decks, with limited progress, and outputs that meet internal stakeholders needs more than those of the customer. Smart project leaders will plant of few softball questions to ask the committee members to make them feel good about themselves. A little politic playing in a committee meeting, can carry a person's career through a few organizational layers in terms of promotions. It is important to note in Breakthrough Agile's project management approach, the 90-day planning cycle provides a platform for leaders to engage with project teams on a more interactive basis. Breakthrough Agile will need leaders to become more of a coach to project teams, rather than the solution person.

As Breakthrough Agile framework matures, leaders and those with higher-level positions, will sense they need to let go of knowing everything and making all decisions for their teams. Project teams need to embrace the nature of a self-managed team. By following all of the principles in Breakthrough Agile, one output is that teams have the freedom to determine what they want to do, and how they want to do it. Self-management emerges in an Agile organization as the systems of Agile take root. Empowered decision making, conflicts solved by individuals, small-scale pilot projects, Scrums, 90-day planning cycles, and team-based performance management will generate an internal energy and passion that impacts the delivery of products and services to the customer. In most cases, the customer will experience this through value-adding solutions and empathic conversations about their business. In this ecosystem, the top–down directive leader, or senior subject matter expert, changes. There is no longer a sense that endorsement from above, or alignment of peers to get consensus support is how progress is made. This change affects everyone and by viewing the output of the transformation as a shift from top–down and directive; to equality, advice giving, and self-management, creates a more dynamic and robust organization. Embracing the elements of self-management will accelerate the transformation and generate more value with fewer resources for the organization.

As self-management relates to project management, the team will decide on its strategic projects/initiatives. The team will decide what to prioritize and green-light initiatives. The team chooses and decides on who is assigned to the project, and what other resources it needs to achieve the measure of success to the outcome. The team will solve its own conflicts, and manage its business performance through a 90-day review cycle. Finally, the team will use a team-based performance management system to manage team member's performance. A culture of self-management will only increase the success rate of achieving breakthrough results when applying the principles of Breakthrough Agile's framework.

Summary and Key Takeaways

- The Agile framework has multiple overlaps with other transformational frameworks. Agile borrowed from Lean on a number of concepts that improve the speed and time to make decisions or execute work.
- Project management has strong roots within traditional organizations. Due to the lengthy timelines with large-scale projects, the transition to an Agile project management process can be challenging. Using a 90 Day Review Cycle and Scrum are two ways to speed the transition from the traditional approach to a more Agile approach.

■ Project management is the business process that helps an organization achieve its strategic vision and objectives. This process aligns the investment of the company, its resources, and time toward achieving that strategic outcome.

Project Management Sensing Guide				
Principles of Breakthrough Agile	Experiencing	Seeing	Hearing	Anti-Pattern
Less is more. Prioritize	More focus on fewer initiatives. Initiatives defined by outcomes versus activities.	Smaller scale and faster execution on strategic initiatives. Scope of work for initiatives are clearer and more concise.	Phrases such as what did we learn, what does success look like, what is the customer's needs, wants and motivations.	Long lists of projects. Routine activities listed as strategic efforts. Multiple layers of committees to endorse or approve team's work.
Speed of design, development, production and delivery is key	MVP thinking. Teams working on pilots and prototypes to gain a better understanding of the customer's needs and motivations. Less concern over detailed plans, and more focus on outcomes.	Projects being completed quicker. Higher rates of project/initiatives being changed or stopped. More team's experimenting with new products or services.	Leaders rewarding teams that learn from doing. Team's change their outcomes based on testing of MVPs.	Delays or consensus decision making through committees. Carry over, or legacy projects dominating the strategic landscape. Lack of new or bold initiatives on the strategic horizon.
Change is welcomed and wanted	Outcomes and guardrails being modified. Projects stopped due to lack of value contribution.	Teams seeking feedback and testing their MVPs with the customer. Leaders letting go of "pet" projects that lack value for the customer.	Phrases such as What is working, What do we need to stop, what do we need to modify?	Leaders requesting more detail to plans. Waterfall Gantt charts describing the timeline for multi-year projects.
People contribute through scope of work not positional hierarchy	Clearer direction through focused strategic and tactical key results. Employees feel they own the outcomes of their work. Leaders provide appropriate level of resources (time and FTE) to accomplish objectives.	Meetings include only team members and minimal senior leaders. In team meetings, all people contribute to the final output or solutions. OKR teams prioritize their time to complete activities to achieve the strategic OKR.	Teams working using approaches such as, How might we,...? What if...? Teams talking about failures, and lesson's learned from past experiments. Team members supporting each other and building on ideas.	Team members judging others ideas without testing. Leaders showing up in meetings and directing team members on actions. Team members using higher authorities name to persuade others to go along with their ideas.

Chapter 8

Performance Management

> We must recognize that we are imperfect and will make mistakes.
> Both coaches and players must learn this.
>
> **John Wooden**

A look inside:

- How performance management has become a critical factor in defining an organization's culture
- Purpose of performance management – our we clear on what the outcome is for this system
- Pitfalls of current performance management practices
- Breakthrough Agile principles on performance management

When the topic of transformation makes its way into the board room and senior leaders meetings, there is one topic that always gets raised, yet is rarely acted on. This elephant in the room is how the current performance management system will change or be used fairly and objectively by all employees during the transition from the old to new organization. Performance Management is a key piece of the company's culture and due to its impact on each and every employee usually stays in the shadows when transformation or change is discussed. When knowing that performance management gets to a personal level with each employee, it seems like an overwhelming task to overhaul it at the same time as kicking off a transformation. However, in Breakthrough Agile, it is necessary to

DOI: 10.4324/9781003335702-8

shine the light on this cultural business process, and take steps to modify the process to support the successful transition of the culture.

Performance management theory is divided into two outcomes for the organizations. The first outcome is a business process to develop talent and groom people to increase their performance and contribution to the organization; the second outcome is a business process that measures an individual's performance in the context of its impact and contribution to the organization over a defined period of time. These two subsystems of performance management shape the mindset and behaviors of employees at all levels. How people connect, collaborate, prioritize, and complete their work assignments consciously or subconsciously are influenced by performance management. Performance management has the best of intentions. It is a process to motivate and encourage employees to grow and develop their skills to help the organization achieve greater success. It is a business system that has a meaningful outcome. However, there is still uncertainty about the objectiveness and fairness in practice. In some cases, people view the performance management system as an exercise that has minimal impact on an employee's growth and development, and see it more as a "check the box" activity between a manager and their team members. As one manager told me in a performance management conversation, they were *just doing their job* to have the discussion with me. In this chapter, we will dig deeper into the gaps and drawbacks of how current performance management systems operate, and then how Breakthrough Agile offers a different path forward.

Performance management reviews are traditionally an annual event that falls on every employee's calendar. The announcement and then cycle of performance management creates unneeded tension and anxiety for employees who are in the midst of working on new products or services for customers. Typically, performance management starts its cycle in the final few months of the budget year. Once the cycle starts, employees alter their mindset until the cycle ends. From the start of the performance management cycle, employees start a campaign of self-promotion and personal marketing activities to ensure their manager knows all the hard work that they did over the year. Employees resort to inflating accomplishment at the expense of their peers, highlighting routine activities as being breakthrough achievements, all to ensure that they receive a good performance review from their direct manager. The role of the manager during this time is to assess and develop a written narrative of the employee's impact and contribution. Included in the narrative might be statements regarding the potential and future growth opportunities for the individual. There might be a few sentences on the employee and how well they performed compared to all the other team members. In my experience, managers spend hours preparing written statements that are filled with buzz words and performance cliques that read more like a LinkedIn biography. The idea that this conversation or narrative provides growth opportunities and development feedback to the employee falls short.

In cases where managers are too conservative the "sandwich" method of feedback is used during the annual performance meeting between manager and employee. "Sandwich" appraisals start off with praise for the employee, followed by some general statements about improving a basic skill, topped off with more praise for the employee. The sandwich method ends up giving a confusing message to the employee that they are doing everything great, and if they have time, they might want to consider improving on one or two skills. In most cases, the sandwich method leaves employees feeling appreciated, and lost when trying to move on to new skills or better themselves within the organization. At the end of the cycle, a monetary statement is given to the employee that shows the value of their skills and abilities in terms of a merit increase or bonus. Ironically, companies will sacrifice this step, if their business conditions were less than expected for the given year. In the end, if the enterprise-wide business plan for the organization didn't meet the revenue and cost targets, then regardless of how well an employee performed, they still end up with little payback from the organization. This unfortunately plants in the performance management system an element of mistrust that the system is fair and practiced with the focus of the employee's interests in mind.

In many discussions I have had with peers and through group feedback sessions, employees see their current performance management as being arbitrary and capricious. At times, it is a way for a manager to show favoritism to team members. Within a team, the politics among personalities can play through in the performance management cycle. Other times, the process seems to reward those who took the least challenging and most conservative scoped projects that contributed little to organization's strategic focus. The dissatisfaction with the process isn't limited to those who are being rated, but to the managers who also see the process as being broken. Managers view the annual individual's summary report as a burden to draft. A lengthy narrative with buzz words and clique's that keep the relationship safe with the employee and possibly motivate them to work harder the following year. A typical template for a manager is to not make the employee think they are too good as this might inspire them to question their merit increases, or possibly leave the company for a better role.

Generally, an annual performance management summary for an employee follows this design: Examples of how the employee meets their requirements of their job scope, what the employee did well, and minor points for improvement. In the improvement area, these are usually given to each employee and follow a simple rule. Nice and not too disruptive. For example, "collaborate more across teams," "speak up more," or "be a better listener." Behaviors that all of us work on every day throughout the year to get better at. In the end, the only point of interest for the employee may be their increase in salary, bonus, and maybe a potential promotion. What follows after the summary review is the grading or ranking of the individual into a box. The grading or ranking within performance management has evolved over years and most traditional organizations practice some version of it.

Once an employee is ranked by their direct manager, then the final step is to calibrate all the employees within the business unit. After all, can leaders trust other leaders to use the system objectively and fair? The intent of this step is to ensure a consistency with rankings, and that one leader didn't go rogue and rank his team members disproportionately to how the leaders view the individual. Although the calibration step sounds like a way to gather additional feedback on each employee it is usually a check and balance step to ensure the company doesn't spend more than it budgeted for the performance management cycle. In practice, staying within the budget of one's function or department can determine if the work performed was exceptional or meets expectations. As practiced, the calibration process undermines the value of a performance management system by introducing a cost principle into the process. At this point, accomplishments are downplayed or overinflated by managers. In the end, the impact of the ranking of an employee may set the tone of their motivation in the following year. At times the employee may play the game of "working hard enough not to get fired." Or the infamous "vest and rest" phrase for employees with a long tenure with a company.

Over the years, I have seen different approaches to performance management. In reflection, I had one manager taking the less interesting way by giving me a sticky note with my year-end ranking, increment percent, and bonus; to another who wrote over four pages of narrative just to let me know that I met expectations. If your organization is still using some type of ranking, rating, or grading system to measure annual performance, whether you are embracing Breakthrough Agile or not, then I strongly recommend that you improve this system quickly. The self-limiting aspects of an annual performance management system based on a single manager's evaluation, deadens an employee's innovation, creativeness, and efficiency. Organizations that are authentic in their efforts to transform their organization to an Agile organization will find the traditional performance management system is a barrier and anchor that slows down the best of transformation efforts.

Performance Management has a great purpose. It is designed to provide employees with recognition of their achievements, motivate employees to develop their skills, and help the organization discover talent that will grow the organization in the future. Most agree that this purpose of performance management rings true and is a system that brings value to the organization. Within the organization, let's find the employees that are creating the highest contribution and impact with customers, and develop their potential in the years to come. These employees should receive an annual performance rating that correlates with their actions. The greater your impact and the more you contribute toward creating value, then the greater your reward. On paper it sounds like it should work well. In practice, it is a different story.

The issue isn't that performance management allows low performers to get by, or minimizes the accomplishments of employees not in management's favor, but as currently designed, it relies upon the judgment of one person to decide a ranking for an individual. In general, this judgment is based on the interactions between the manager and employee over the course of the review period. Managers may use different tactics to draw a conclusion on the employee's performance. A manager may observe the employee interacting with others, the reliability of the employee to complete assignments, their ability to handle multiple tasks, and quality of their work. Unfortunately, managers have a bias that influences their judgment with performance management. One strong bias that comes out is halo bias. At times a manager may think that an employee is exceptional based on facts unrelated to the quality of their work, or how they get along with others. Maybe the manager and employee went to the same university creates this halo, or alumni from previous employers, or have the same internal network to each other instills a favorable bias in the manager's mind about the employee. One incident I remember is that a senior level leader was given a role in a business unit because they were good friends with the global business unit leader. The person had good skills, and was competent in their field, but again the interview process was set up with a halo bias from the start because of this relationship. During the tenure of this senior leader in the new role, he constantly reached out to the global leader on all decisions. This backfired on the newly hired leader, when they were sharply criticized by the global leader to take ownership over the sites activities. After-all, that is what they were hired for in the first place. It left me with the impression that the relationship link started to strain at that point. Another strong bias in performance management is confirmation bias. Whether a manager's first impression is good or bad, from that point forward, they may only be looking for information that confirms their initial judgment of the individual. The manager may only look at things as poor or not meeting the standard if their first impression was negative. Or, the opposite, everything the employee does is great and they always deliver outstanding results. Other bias enter into the mind of the manager during the day-to-day interactions that end up influencing the performance rating of an individual at year end.

Biases affect a manager during performance management reviews, as well as any group calibration event within the process. If the manager feels an employee is lazy or inefficient, then the manager may seek out information or stories from others that confirm their bias about the employee. Additionally, a potential career-defining opinion may come from the leader's leader. In a traditional organization, if the boss' boss thinks the employee is a high performer, then that opinion will bias the manager's view on the employee's work. In a few cases, I have seen promotions given to employees after a global leader made a causal remark about how much they liked a certain employee. People were promoted to higher grades, given more responsible roles, and fast tracked by the management team in these cases, when, if an objective look at their performance was done, the level of impact and contribution fell short of this level of reward. In one case after the employee received a promotion from one band to another, the employee used the promotion as a way to land better role in a competitor company. Regardless, if the employee in question was performing at the peak of performance, the opinion of a manager's manager and manager's peers will influence the ranking given to an employee. This leads employees at all levels, to self-promote themselves and appease levels of leaders during the performance management cycle. In the end, it corrupts the intent behind what the performance management system is designed to provide to the organization.

Some leaders embrace this system of using the boss' opinion as the guiding factor for an employee's ranking. Other leaders perfect their skills at building up their employees' contribution many times by minimizing the contribution of others outside their span of control. After all, the performance management appraisal is one of the bigger hooks that a manager has to keep his subordinates loyal and build respect. If a manager can manipulate the appraisals to favor his team's performance, then many believe this will generate more loyalty within his team to the leader. In the end, this creates a toxic culture of favoritism and self-importance. In this scenario, the managers reinforce the traditional principle that they have control and power over the employees within the business unit. Performance management is used as a leverage over employees to obtain their loyalty through favors toward their pay and career development. Have you worked for a manager who demanded a higher level of attention and respect at the cost of a good or favorable performance evaluation? Some would say it is an easy tradeoff, but the impact that this practice has on the company's culture will derail collaboration, creativity, innovation, and performance. In practice, the ranking system for performance management is too subjective and clouded with mistrust. Employees and managers alike know this, and yet it still is the process adopted by most organizations.

How the performance management system instills purpose and a sense of performing at a higher level are the focus of change for a better performance management system. Another focus area is to prevent the gaming of performance management by employees and managers alike. It may be a little comical, but in a few organizations I have studied, employees seek a more favorable ranking through self-promotion during the months prior to the performance management cycle. If your company's budget works on the annual calendar of Jan–Dec, then the yearly performance management cycle ends in mid-December. As a result, the few months leading up to the cycle, anxious employees start their own propaganda machine to influence their year-end rating. Why not get as much face time with your boss during this period as you possibly can if it will give you a better chance at a higher rating? After all, your manager is busy and their memory will go only so far back when they are deciding this ranking. On the other side of this process's coin, the manager has their bias on the employee's performance. This bias may be shaped by the manager's peers and their boss more than the work or contribution the employee had over the year. The game that ensues is one where the employee attempts to gain favor and managers trying to fend off being influenced by employee's actions to win favor. Round and round this goes for 2 months. As mentioned, in the end, the manager's responsibility is to fit everyone into a ranking that meets their budget. This practice tends to give the manager's an edge in shaping which box an employee will fit into at the end of the year. From the employee's side of the equation, a little self-promotion prior to the actual recording of the ranking can only help, or at least make them feel like they gave it their best shot to influence the year-end ranking.

Let me share an example with you. In one company I've researched, the annual performance process came up as a topic for discussion in the weekly leadership team meeting. The discussion started with the HR Manager reminding the leadership team that there was no budget for anyone to be an exceptional performer or promoted for the year. The HR Manager reminded the leadership team that we need to keep our rankings fixed to the amount of money we budgeted for raises and promotions at the start of the year. All the leadership team agreed, and pledged to work within these constraints. For the company, there was a work-around for the leadership team on merit increases. If they had someone leave the department during the year, they were able to justify a higher increment or bonus payout based on their budget pool. Additionally, if a new employee joined the company within the last 3 months of the budget year, they were excluded from a merit increase or bonus payout. This left a little extra in each department's budget pool to give higher increments to a few employees. In discussions with the employees at this company, many didn't view the performance management process to be focused on talent development or performance appraising. The way it was practiced didn't encourage employees to work for a higher purpose, or strive to achieve something better. As practiced, it ensured long-service employees with stable employment (rarely were people rated low due to performance) and employees with 3–8 years realized they didn't need to outshine others to keep their job. The incentive to be innovative, risk-taking, and raising the bar for performance, was absent from the culture of this company in part due to its principles on performance management. In this case, performance management lacked a sense of authenticity, and as practiced only reinforced the conservative mindset and behaviors of a traditional organization.

Another example of experiencing a shocking view on performance management came from my time coaching a team in a country that was part of the former Soviet Union. At one meeting we started to discuss improving the performance management system by shifting it from a year-end ranking process to a more continuous, egalitarian, and objective process. In the discussion, the proposal to change was to remove the fear of being unfairly evaluated by a line manager. The basic idea was all employees are given the same ranking at the start of the year, and then throughout the year, their leader would coach them on growth and development opportunities through routine coaching sessions, and performance management vis a vis the 90-day planning cycle. The assumption was that this process would lead to higher-performing individuals, teams, and the organization since the fear of being rated poorly at the end of the year was absent. In the discussion, one leader, the head of human resources, had an objection to this approach. The HR manager reminded the team of the country's history. For this person, having a system where all were seen as equal, and merit was distributed equally within teams, seemed close to how the country operated under communist rule. As the objection was debated, statements like, "in the former soviet republic, everyone received the same performance rating, salary, food, shelter, etc … we don't want to go back to this!" As you can see, performance management can have deep roots into the culture of the organization, and at times, society itself.

Performance management does have an element of confidentiality to it. After all, there are personal actions or decisions that happen within the life cycle of the system. However, it only takes a year or two before new employees know how the performance management system is practiced. When employees learn what is considered valuable to the owners of the system (the managers) then their pace of work, rhythm of innovation, and motivation falls to the level of doing what the system provides for them. Being ranked as "meets, exceeds, or needs improvement" or a "3, 2, or 1" will impact the level of work that the employee will perform and their passion to take on new challenges. If being conservative, resistance to change, and slow to innovate are descriptors that strongly influenced a good ranking, then people will behave and make decisions that reflect these characteristics. This is the culture of the business. There are even times when employees feel that they don't fit into the culture because they see themselves performing to a different set of principles. However, knowing that their reward and recognition are impacted by their manager's bias, the amount of money in a budget pool, and at times a forced ranking model, their motivation is minimized to perform at a higher level. Knowing that performance management has this impact on the culture of the organization is a foundation of Breakthrough Agile.

Documenting the gaps in a ranking type of performance management system helps to create the case for change for this business process. In time, bias from managers can turn into systematic policies for the process. My introduction to this occurred when I was working at an organization that had a standing rule practiced by the management team. This unwritten rule was that "a new employee cannot receive an exceptional rating" in their first year of employment. Managers rationalized this rule by assuming the employee was trying to please their boss to get through a probationary period, and to make a good impression. Then, when the pressure is off, the new employee's performance level will drop to the norm of the team. (The question I found myself asking was, is this a self-fulfilling statement?) How can we evaluate if their performance falls because they were gaming the system in year 1, or that they realized after a year that going the extra mile or bringing innovation to their work doesn't get acknowledged or recognized? In most cases when there is an external hire, it is generally because the talent doesn't exist internally. So it seems to follow that when the new employee joins with a higher level skill set, that they should be doing something others can't in the organization, and if it is impactful and generates value, get rewarded for it. Wouldn't performing exceptionally be the right recognition for this employee? However, through this company's subjective performance management process, an employee's actions in the first year of employment were downplayed in terms of impact and contribution. The following year, this deadened their motivation to keep performing at the higher level.

The example where I saw this practice applied was in a medical device company with a strong paternalistic/maternalistic culture that embraced seniority and loyalty to individual leaders. In this case, a newly hired lab manager had implemented a number of continuous improvement ideas within the lab, and improved its efficiency to levels never reached before by the lab. Some of the improvements that were implemented included a U-shaped testing cell, daily meetings at a performance board, and a more streamlined approach to reviewing and approving test reports for releasing products. The manager eliminated the inefficiencies in the lab and had it running as part of the product flow versus a barrier in the plant. However, when it came time to rate this manager on their performance, the unwritten rule above applied. Since it was their first year in the organization, then their ranking would be a "meets." The logic was let's see how the manager does in year 2. It was a shock to me, as the managers were blinded to the fact that the employee's innovative motivation would be impacted by this ranking. Although the managers could rationalize the "meets" ranking, they didn't see the execution of this rule would send a message to the employee and entire organization about innovation and transformation. The message reinforced the current culture of the company via its performance management system. The message here was "we don't trust those that we don't know and that work harder than others." For this company, their mental model on new employees and maybe all employees were that if someone was working too hard, or performing too good, then maybe we don't trust them. They must be hiding something, or have a secret agenda. In today's business world, we have developed some peculiar mental models around performance management systems.

Across the world, people are constantly part of some type of performance management system. From an early age and as we grow into adults, we are groomed to accept an appraisal system that quantifies are skills and abilities. It is a feature of every culture on the planet. In most cultures, it starts with young toddlers entering pre-school and then extends into primary and secondary schools. Within this context, students will take a battery of tests that are designed to judge a student's potential for greater success within the education system. Students with higher scores are streamed into better school programs or institutions. The tests are designed to indicate the potential of an individual by how they retain information and apply a certain level of logic at a particular age and maturity. The tests also are used as a predictor of what the student can do in the future. Based on these evaluations, the person is put into the organizational grind of either higher education, time in military or private employment. Each of which has an embedded type of performance management system that will shape the experience of the individual and their mental models on life.

It starts with a grading system (A–F) to percentiles (LSAT, GRE's, etc.), to rankings based on Myers-Briggs, StrengthsFinder, even other features like physical fitness, charisma, intelligence, or communication skills. Everyone has taken part in some type of performance management system. As we continue to work under this system of rankings, we work to the level that will keep us secure and stable in the current environment. Reflect back on your own experience:

- How has a good or bad ranking impacted your performance at work?
- Did a bad ranking make you work harder, or instill in you a motivation to do just enough?
- Did a good ranking give you a sense that you had done the best work possible?
- Did a particular ranking help you make a decision to stay or leave a company?
- With this in mind, then think about how the culture of the organization was shaped by those that got promoted, or received a greater pay package at the end of the year?
- Did these people support innovation or experimentation?

■ Or did they grab more control over events and guide decisions that would strengthen their story to retain a higher ranking in the coming year?
■ Did a higher ranking reinforce certain behaviors in you or others that reflected more conservative and risk-averse actions?

The reward system reflects the current mindset of leaders within the organization. In traditional organization's, this is one of the leader's main control levers over their team. Who do they feel has the personality to fit into the higher level spots in the hierarchy. This is entrenched within the culture, and a transformation journey will expose this system's weakness at rewarding people for delivering value to the organization. When the gaps between the systems original intent and the way it is practiced become transparent, then people are in disbelief. Usually, the gaps are rationalized by statements like: "It is the best we have for now and we need to work with it."

Breakthrough Agile will shine a light on this process. Leaders need to take a serious stand on improving performance management, and making it more reflective of how teams are performing versus an individual's personality. In a transformation there shouldn't be unwritten rules about how people are evaluated or ranked. Additionally, the idea of a forced ranking system minimizes the work the team accomplishes during the review period. An individual's performance needs tied to the bigger picture of the transformation and reflect the value of changing the organization's culture. In Breakthrough Agile, the shift is away from individual achievement and focuses more on how the team performed. What was the accomplishment of the team, and the individual's contribution to helping others succeed? Think about it, "how can one member of a team exceed expectations when the entire team performed poorly?" Or, how can a team have 10% of its personnel needing improvement, yet have a reputation that it delivered on its targets for the year? That is an output of today's performance management system. For a performance management system to be successful, how team members supported others to succeed, and the overall success of the team, needs to be the focus of the ranking or grading of individuals. How individuals worked as part of a team and how the team created value for the organization is the starting point for the individual's evaluation. Performance Management needs to break away from the ranking systems or forced ranking systems that dominate today's way of working. Before reviewing Breakthrough Agile's approach, let's take a look at some different performance management approaches used today.

The landscape of performance management applications and how it is applied is very broad. From large to small, from non-profit to profit, from

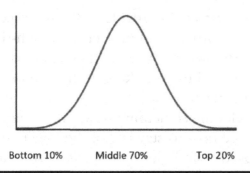

Figure 8.1 Typical bell-shaped curve for "Rank and Yank" performance management system.

governmental to commercial, they all have people that are performing some type of activity or work in them. With the exception of a sole proprietorship, such as a lawyer or doctor with their own practice, most organizations rely upon some type of performance management system to give employees an indication of their value and contribution to the organization. A quick review of these systems reveals a few common features. One feature is that most have a ranking feature to them. The most common used ranking system that has been termed the "Rank and Yank" approach. This approach was adopted by many businesses during the 1980–2010s. "Rank and Yank" was popularized by GE's practice and its stoical adherence to a bell-shaped curve with rankings. GE practiced the 20/70/10 approach to ranking the annual performance of employees in relation to their personal objectives and goals. In the Rank and Yank method, employees were either ranked in the top 20%, middle 70%, or low-performing 10% (Figure 8.1).

In theory, the system was designed to create competitiveness within GE. However, as practiced, it created a pool of employees that were vulnerable to discharge seemingly based on performance when financial pressure to reduce costs became a mandate. The poor ranking that this pool of employees received was subject to the arbitrariness of managers' bias, the external economic pressures, and types of assignments they undertook. In an attempt to reward high performers and trimming the organization of non-performers, the system actually culled innovation, and promoted employees to maintain the status quo. Employees would avoid risky assignments such as attempting to innovate current processes and challenge the status quo. Over time as the "Rank and Yank" process became more of a cultural norm at GE, innovation and experimentation suffered. Employees would spend more time focused on bragging about superficial accomplishments to their boss or review committee, than spending time looking forward at what new and innovative products or services their organization could provide to the customer. In this culture, the idea of taking on a turn-around project, or a high-risk assignment was avoided at all costs by employees as they realized that taking on tougher assignments risked their ranking at the end of the year. A plum assignment in the organization meant a person didn't have challenges with growing or developing something new, only maintaining the status quo and politicking the boss to stay out of the lower 10% range. In GE the organization moved from innovation for tomorrow to protecting their current market, and the products that were making them successful at the time. The lack of customer centricity and innovation eventually impacted the profitability and future competitiveness of GE. From this brief description one can easily see how the performance management and culture are strongly linked, and that it can highly impact the business in terms of value and growth.

In the early years as GE broadcasted its adoption and limited success with the "Rank and Yank" approach, other organizations saw the forced ranking as a way to cut cost through the lens of trimming low performers. Employee salaries being one of the higher cost line items on a budget, organizations with a cultural principle of cost reduction realized that this system was compatible with its culture. Cost-cutting and efficiency principles now entered an area that affected the livelihood and standard of living of their employees. With this intent, the level of fear of being laid-off created a toxic work culture within the organization. Who would take on a risky assignment or look to make an innovative change with products or processes knowing that if the results were not stellar, then it would lead to your departure from the company? One bad yearly review and your career was in jeopardy. These cultural principles associated with the 'rank and yank' pressured managers to make judgment decisions on employees' future. It gave them tremendous power and control over their employees. The loss of talent and fear within the organization was masked by a tagline that the company was competitive, when actually, it was nothing more than managers protecting their careers by a systematic way to lower costs. As the culture at GE and other organizations become more toxic and siloed, people began to realize that this crude linear ranking of employees had more negative impact than positive. The goal of being more competitive was lost in a game of survival at the end of the year. As one could predict, the pendulum swung back toward a more human approach to performance management. Unfortunately, the next model based itself on the "Rank and Yank" method.

The matrix model emerged around 2008–2010 within organizations. Similar to the rank and yank model, the matrix model rated a person from 1 to 3 within two dimensions instead of one. Now an employee could be seen as a high contributor based on their contribution and impact, but how they achieved their results was evaluated. Managers relied upon cross-department feedback from people who worked with the employee throughout the year. Typical questions that were used for the feedback were: How did they work on a team? What was their attitude during team meetings? What are their strengths? What are their development areas? What were the contributions of the employee? In theory, a person who exceeded their goals, but was not a team player, would have a ranking that displayed the extremes, that is, 1–3 or 3–1. This two-dimensional rating allowed for employees who didn't have a good year to still be ranked within the middle of the organization based on how they showed up on the team and worked with others. The matrix model gave manager's more space and discretion to make an evaluation, and led to a more robust appraisal of the employee. You could still end up with someone in the lower quantile of the matrix, but it needed more justification by the manager, and feedback from peers. As with the prior system, how much a manager could award monetary increases in salary and bonus was determined by the budget pool. Managers were still required to meet a budget limit for merit and bonus. This meant that someone outstanding for the year, who deserved a high ranking was rewarded for their work, at the sacrifice of another team member who performed well, or possibly a low performer. Or, some managers would give a higher merit increase and lower bonus as a way to reward outstanding performance. The influence of managerial subjectivity and favoritism easily finds its way into the matrix model as it did with the rank and yank. Here is a sample of how a matrix performance management model looks.

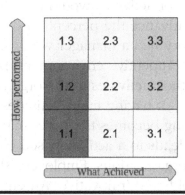

Figure 8.2 Generic ranking matrix.

The color coding of the table indicated the appraisal from the manager. "Red" indicated a developmental process needed to be started for the employee. "Yellow" didn't carry many adverse actions however those that were at the "yellow" extremes (Ranking that included a 1) were usually put on a development program and would become the following year's "red" candidates. These were also the individuals that ended up with less than full merit increases as others compensation increased. Those individuals with the "2" ratings or higher, or those individuals ranked in the "Green" portion of the table had been appraised as meeting their objectives for the current year and their behavior was in alignment with the culture of the organization. One particular feature of any ranking system is that it renews itself annually. This led to a repetitive cycle of employees reliving the fear of being ranked low and feeling the powerlessness over their evaluation by their manager. To manage these emotions, employees found ways to keep themselves in favorable opinion with their boss, and to find enough work to keep them busy. The matrix model can be correlated to how companies began to embrace an activity-based culture as a way to measure performance. It didn't necessarily matter if your activities added value either internally or externally, but as long as the activities filled up an 8-hour day, then you felt safe when your performance was evaluated. In the activity-based culture employees avoid the appearance of being under-utilized that could lead to a potentially low ranking.

For those that had a favorable rating, their reaction would be different. Individuals who made it through an annual appraisal process without any adverse action felt the pressure to keep themselves out of the lower section of the table in the following year. Here the "gaming" of the system would renew. To keep safe, employees would accept less challenging projects or assignments, and spend more time marketing themselves to their boss and their boss' peers. Minor activities would blossom into game-changing results by a manager to advance the perception of high performance. Employee's in this category had a manager who had a halo bias on their performance. In a competitive environment, pressure intensifies for employees to showcase their activities to the organization. Under the guise of meritocracy the feeling of having many activities completed to guarantee a "safe" performance rating becomes the performance management way of working. This mentality leads to a activity-based culture over an outcome based culture for many organizations. Employees shifted away from experimenting, being bold, and innovative. An employee can complete more work tasks when the solution is known and the complexity is low, and this fills the "ledger" for performance management. In the activity-based culture, doing more equated to being in more meetings, joining a team without a specific role, spending your day on a personal pet project, etc. However, the more complex and unknown assignments or tasks that need research and investigation are given little attention by employees. These projects or assignments ended up being legacy initiatives on the PMO portfolio. Since most challenging assignments include not knowing the solution, the element of experimentation and failure surface as a potential outcome. These assignments generally take more than a year to complete in a traditional organization, and can consume much of the employee's energy and time. Experimentation, trying something new or different, taking a risk on an assignment is an antithesis to the activity-based culture.

The ranking model rewarded those who are conservative and working in their comfort zone. Both employees and managers reinforce the ranking model as being effective; in a sense, it has made them who they are in the company today. In the face of changing to something new, or giving higher recognition to employees that work differently creates a sense of fear or anxiety for many. The task of leading a transformation or being a key change agent in a transformation is complex and unknown. Employees who take on this challenge show the courage and foresight to bring the organization to a higher level of performance. If one believes in the saying that employees are the most valuable assets of the company, and they are the ones that will bring us to the next level, then wouldn't it be wise to create the ecosystem that will support the work at achieving the next higher level. To me, maintaining the status quo means delivering the same results as in the past, while the competition is moving ahead. As you can deduce, how the performance management system is practiced in a transformation will impact the motivation of early leaders and champions of the journey. If these early champions are marginalized in terms of impact, then the impact of the transformation will also be minimized by the culture.

As all of these emotions and fears get mixed together, the end game is people avoid taking on assignments that have risk or possibly viewed negatively by line managers or senior leaders. The principle of learning from failure is missing from the culture that practices a ranking system of performance management. In this type of culture, the underlining fear is that a failure will pigeonhole someone's career or future growth. Reactive managers will continually relive another manager's or team's failure during the calibration step to validate a low rating. This helps the leader justify their opinion of who is outstanding and who meets the requirements of the organization. Although a little less brutal than the "Rank and Yank" method the negative impact of the "matrix" approach leads to a deadening of innovation, risk-taking, and treating each other with respect

As part of the study on performance appraisals, I reflected back on my military career and how they managed performance appraisals in the United States Army. In the 1990s, the military had a system to prevent soldiers from "resting and vesting." The military's principle for career development was either you are "moving up or moving out." What this meant, is that a commissioned officer would reach a promotion window and could stay there for 1–2 years. At higher ranks the window for the grade may increase to 4 years since fewer positions are available at colonel or above ranks. Each year, when the officer was up for promotion to the next higher rank, their application for promotion was submitted. If they failed to achieve the next level rank after two attempts, then the officer was subtly exited from service. The idea that a soldier could obtain a certain level rank, and stay there until they hit their retirement service level of 20 years didn't apply to active duty officers. The system was established to foster a certain selectivity for higher-ranking officers to meet military personnel budgetary limits. Promotion boards would meet and review stacks of applications for the next level. There were always open positions in the budget, and the process for the review board was to pick the best out of the stack of applications to fill those roles. Imagine the benefit if you as an applicant went to the same school as a board member, or worked in the same unit as the board member. As long as one did move up, then the career journey continued. This system was stressful for officers who were in the higher ranks of the military as the number of open budgeted spaces were always outnumbered by candidates to fill them. The selectivity of who moved up at times became more subjective as almost all candidates had stellar and high rankings in the evaluations. With so many candidates, the military used an OER, Officer Evaluation Report, to help decide who moves up.

The OER was a qualitative ranking of an officer's performance compared to peers as perceived by their commanders and the unit's senior military officer. The document was a single page with a front and back that had subsections for both the individual and their commanding officer to complete. At the bottom of page 2, there was a section for the senior leader (boss' boss) to rank and comment on the potential of the office being evaluated. This senior ranking was the deciding indicator for a review board

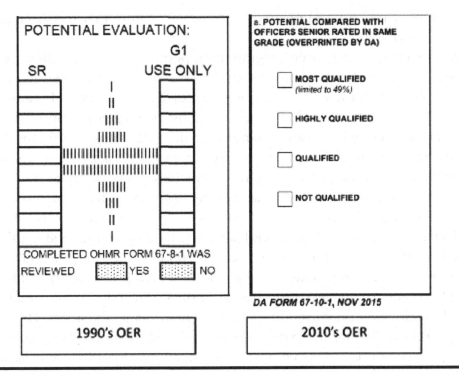

Figure 8.3   Generic military senior rater's ranking box.

when it met. At times it was the determining factor in future promotions and positions within the military. In my military career any ranking less than top box would seal the person's career for future promotion at a higher level. Meaning, when they hit that certain grade, O–3 or O–4, they would not be promoted due to the "2" block that a senior leader gave them 12 years earlier. In the military, it was either a top block or start planning for a new career. Figure 8.3 shows what the senior rater's box looked like in the 1990s and now today. My assumption today is that anything less than the top block is still career-limiting for an officer.

Whether in a military branch, a multinational organization like GE, or a small local enterprise, employees eventually realize that the performance management system is an uneven playing field filled with exceptions and personal bias. Within a short time, an employee's drive for innovation or risk-taking normalizes to what others are doing. This creates a culture of maintaining the status quo and protecting the current patterns of work for the individual to benefit from receiving an adequate performance rating. The implications for an individual is to maintain the status quo, and don't do anything stupid, e.g., take a risk and make a mistake. This becomes the culture of the organization. In the end, the performance management process fosters an activity based culture that resists change and transformation.

As this cycle of employee programming perpetuates itself, ranking leads employees to developing non-value-adding behaviors. Behaviors such as gaining favor with their direct manager, highlighting their contributions at the expense of others, holding grudges against peers that perform better, and dramatizing their actions, regardless of their significance in innovation or adding value are experience by everyone. In many cases, these behaviors are reflective of a hierarchical organization where social status of one's role is valued in terms of influence and creating opinions. A leader can pre-define for others the opinion of an employee based on whether they like or dislike an employee. If a senior leader wants to raise someone up, then they have the organization power and position to make it happen. Likewise, a senior leader can pigeonhole and block the development of an employee on a lower-level manager's team based on their perception of the employee. One last comment on current performance management systems. The people responsible for the system know the limitations of it. They know that managers favor one employee over another, at times for arbitrary reasons. Everyone knows that the system is compromised by the budget process regarding wages and salaries for the given year. It would seem the group to lead the charge on a new approach or system would be those that deal with the limitations of it and hear the complaints. However, in a culture that is resistant to change, changing something as pivotal as the performance management system is too challenging.

Performance management and decision making are likely the two business processes that shape the organization's culture more than the other three cultural business processes. As a company launches its transformational journey addressing these two at the start is a priority. When employees understand how their performance is measured using the new ways of working, will greatly increase the shift in mindsets and behaviors toward the Agile organization. If the ranking system is still in place, then leaders need to recognize the performance of an individual in both the transformation and routine daily work of the organization. Clear communication across the organization needs to reiterate that being an enabler to the transformation is viewed as impactful to the short and long-term success of the business.

As the transformation journey gains momentum, evidence that the performance management system has been re-designed to encourage transformation activities needs showcased. Promotions, new assignments, and introducing new ways of working like the Scrum and the 90-day planning cycle are evidence of this change. This ensures all employees know the transformation is being taken seriously by those who shape opinions and guide the organization. Employees need to see that the system is creating a culture where people are rewarded for being innovative, taking risks, learning from mistakes, and being bold. A new performance management system needs implemented that limits the focus on traditional behaviors and encourages employees to relearn new behaviors that align with the company's future principles. As this seems obvious to the reader, in reality it is difficult to accomplish. At the start of most transformations, usually performance management is left untouched as part of the change management program. Generally, at the end of the transformation's first year, the question arises as to how to recognize those who exceeded in building transformational efforts. The answer to this question is that it is left up to the individual's manager. In some companies, they might start a dual performance management process. Managers and leaders can choose between following the ranking system as designed, or practice an Agile version of it.

The human resource function and others make efforts to change the performance management system when starting a transformation. Knowing that the current system has flaws and isn't practiced as objectively as needed drives this effort to change it. However, this also creates a challenge, as people see this as a process that has inherent traps to improvement. In an effort to make the process more objective and data based, some may even question if it is possible to eliminate the subjectivity that is inherent in the process because it is driven by people. It might even be debated that the subjectivity of a leader is important to the process. After all, isn't this leader the role model of values and behaviors for the organization? Didn't the leader get to where they are at, by being one that made things happen in the organization? Wouldn't the leader know what good looks like in an employee? Maybe and then, maybe not. The move toward changing the performance management system is strong in an Agile organization. How to couple the rapid iteration and rhythm of work of an Agile organization with an annual performance score. The two main outcomes of performance management do not go away in an Agile organization. We still want to grow and develop talent to sustain the business in the future, and recognize performance over the past time period. So, asking ourselves what does this look like, and how to do it are key questions. One aspect of an Agile approach may require a continuous performance management dialogue throughout the year. Leaders and team members discuss performance in 1–1 discussions 20–30 times a year. As this is practiced, the amount of time managers and individuals spend on writing individual goals and year-end summary reduces or is eliminated, since issues, gaps, and success are discussed throughout the year. If there is a legal requirement for a summary performance, then a brief statement can be adopted and written by the team's coach. With this hybrid approach, employees get feedback from their leader continuously, and are coached to self-correct and strengthen their weaknesses during the year. In the hybrid approach, there might be a ranking at the end of the year but the ranking shouldn't be a surprise for the employee due to the ongoing discussions throughout the year.

If the organization is bold enough to change its performance management system at the start of the transformation then all employees need to be included in the process. It not only applies to individual contributors, but to senior leaders: Leader of leaders, who are the opinion makers on performance. These individuals can create opportunities for others to succeed, as well as prevent people from growing and developing careers. Everyone's performance management appraisal needs to be tied to the principles of Breakthrough Agile. A robust performance management system creates a sense of ownership and accountability for creating value. When the senior leadership cadre is omitted from the new processes, along with other higher-level employees, then there is a high risk that people will see the transformation as another "flavor of the month" activity. There is an abundance of articles on why transformation activities succeed and fail. In most of these articles, the top reason given is the lack of senior leader involvement or support. Digging deeper into this cause, one can deduce that these senior leaders aren't being appraised on their impact and contribution of changing the culture of the organization, or leading the transformation! In the perspective of ownership and accountability, the question that needs asked is how are these leaders evaluated in terms of performance as it relates to the organization's transformation? Usually, it is absent from their annual performance appraisals. In transformations where senior leaders are excluded, they continue to be appraised on the business-as-usual KPIs. Transformation activities are sidelined, or delegated to direct reports, as attention and focus on delivering the short-term results for the business supersedes transformational outcomes. This influences the way direct reports behave and respond to the transformation efforts. The transformation champions are marginalized and their work minimized to avoid the conflict of having to reward these people highly in performance management appraisals. The end result is people continue to work as before because they see those that maintain the status quo are being rewarded and recognized by the senior leadership. This sends a message to everyone that career prospects aren't link to the transformation activities. The early adopters lose motivation, and start to see that performance recognition and career advancement still reflects how things were done in the past. Ironically, senior leaders say they are 100% on board with leading the change, but then they are evaluated on a completely different set of goals.

In fairness, the ranking system does have features that should be continued in Agile organization. Rising star employees should be given more challenging and complex assignments. Employees who are squeaking by on performance need to have the light shown on them and their performance addressed. However, if the current ranking system of performance management is not changed, it practice will undermine the momentum of the transformation and hinder its impact on the organization.

An Agile organization needs a different performance management system. The "Rank and Yank" or "move up or out" approach will subdue the creativeness and innovation of employees. Breakthrough Agile requires a more holistic, and continual feedback loop mechanism as an approach to performance management. Peers and those who are directly impacted by the employee's contribution need to be polled when generating a statement on a person's impact to the organization. When it comes to growth and development, the employee is the self-author of their journey. Leaders need to allow bandwidth and support employees as they identify areas within the business that they want to learn more about. Breakthrough Agile performance management is redefined from a merit and bonus system, to one that creates an ecosystem of feedback and learning. Moving from an annual event to a continuous series of feedback loops with peers, and coaching sessions between the employee and their team's coach, replacing the annual performance management cycle. Employees are responsible for designing their own development path with input from their team's coach. Both of these features define the performance management approach used in Breakthrough Agile. The employee's leader changes in this new ecosystem. The role now provides performance guidance and development support vis-a-vis coaching and feedback. In Breakthrough Agile, employees no longer fear being capriciously judged by one person on their performance, or a committee of senior leaders. The link between how people behave within an organization and the way they are evaluated so strongly influences the culture of any organization, that more people around the employee need included in an individuals evaluation. The pitfalls of not changing the performance management system during the transformation are numerous and we have discussed some of them here. Let's take a closer look at Breakthrough Agile's principles for performance management.

- Team first, individual second
- Peer feedback drives high performance
- Level playing field each cycle. Avoid confirmation and halo bias
- Team objectives are clear, focused, and challenging

Team First, Individual Second

In Breakthrough Agile and most Agile organization's the focus is on team results. In the new performance management system this is the foundation of the evaluation. How did the employee's team perform, what was the contribution of the team on the overall success of the business, and what was the impact of the team on the customer and other stakeholders is the measure of performance. Viewing performance from the point of view of a team, includes most people within the organization. Teams of individual contributors spanning a large geographic region, to more specific and discreet job focused teams. Of course it is easier in production, sales, or human resource teams; teams with process or discreet activities that can easily be seen and quantified. Collective ownership and team impact is half of how the system should work. Within a function or business unit there might be multiple teams with hundreds or thousands of employees. Or it could be a team with a small number of team members. Regardless of the size of the team, the measured performance for the individual is based on how well the team performed and made an impact. Supporting this feature of the system, objective and key results (OKRs) will provide realistic outcomes that the team focused on achieving for the year. Teams should self-asses themselves against the OKRs that they set for themselves. Within the team, feedback loops between team members provide the structure to give team members opportunities to become better. Teams can establish a series of reviews and retrospectives on a weekly, monthly or quarterly frequency. As part of the system, teams need to start identifying what achieving an outcome looks like versus completing a series of activities. Impacting the customer or stakeholder by the team shows exceptional performance over activities. A simple peer evaluation form can assist a team in evaluating themselves and the contribution of each other. Leader's with accountability for the team's success serve as coaches and mentors as they journey through this process. Like a scrum master for a sprint, the leader is actively engaged in keeping the team aligned to the performance management process. The leader also provides insights into the team's performance and the work completed within the given cycle (weekly, monthly or quarterly) One priority for the leader is to keep the team focused on delivering value for the organization. Within the new way of working, activities can overshadow what is important.

In today's business world, the tendency is to be "activity" based when impact and contribution are discussed. Activity-based results are a byproduct of the ranking performance management system. In organizations where conservatism, maintaining the status quo, avoiding risk and innovation dominate the behaviors of its employees, then the measure of an employee's impact is the number of activities they complete. This reflects that "more is a better" mindset for individuals. In this culture, individual accomplishment supersedes the success of the team. For examples, employees will want to join as many meetings as possible. Creating a plan that never is acted on is seen as a success. There are countless examples of activities that are performed that don't add value to the customer or organization. By following this approach, an individual can retell their story of attending meetings, writing proposals, reliving conversations, and being in the loop on all decisions as a measure of their success for the year. The fear of missing out on meetings where decisions are made, or not being seen by a senior leader in a meeting, creeps into the minds and behaviors of employees thinking how this might affect their performance ranking at the end of the year. Just being in the room, and being seen by others, defines the impact of the employee in a traditional organization. For some, it is easier for them to quantify their impact, because their routine tasks and assignments are easily identifiable. They can measure their contribution in terms of the number of meetings attended, notebooks full of notes, or invoices processed, reports read/approved, products built, reports completed/submitted, etc. This approach highlights the achievements of individuals over the team.

In Breakthrough Agile, high performance is measured by teams that exceed their customers' needs through effective teamwork. High performance is a byproduct of clear objectives and measures of success, or OKRs. This is how an effective OKR system focuses' the performance evaluation on the outcomes achieved and true value to the customer. A team that is able to change the lead-time of a product or service that impacts the customer to buy more should have considerable more recognition in the performance management system, than an individual that attended multiple high-level manager's meeting and gave a presentation or two during that time. OKRs will enable the team to clearly identify the what and how of their team's contribution at the time of a performance evaluation.

The individual component is present in the Agile performance management discussion as well. Individuals working on team's need to understand how they impacted the performance of other team members. An individual's behaviors and actions during the past review cycle is a part of the performance management process. Through a team retrospective, individuals will be given feedback on how their actions affected others on the team. Was the individual an anchor to slow down progress? Did they support others in their assignments? Did an individual do what they said they were going to do? Did they meet deadlines on time? Did they offer feedback to others, or take risks with their ideas? All of these questions illustrate how performance management is conducted within a Breakthrough Agile organization.

Peer Feedback Drives High Performance

Growth and development of an individual is a key feature of the new performance management system and it leads to achieving breakthrough results. Adults are strongly influenced by how others view their actions and behaviors at work. Being accepted and complimented on the quality of one's work by a peer will easily motivate and keep an employee focused. Feeling as if one's efforts are inconsequential, and unimportant to the bigger picture of the organization works contrary to the intent of high performance. Through peer feedback during the team retrospective, an employee is able to self-correct their behavior and how it impacts the results of the team. The principle that everyone is required to give and receive feedback from their colleagues regardless of their social level in the organization is a foundation for performance management within an Agile Organization. Establishing an active feedback system within the performance management system requires all individuals to have the capability to both give and receive feedback. Surprisingly, many people do not give constructive feedback to help another person grow and develop. This is a skill that needs attention by an Agile organization. When this skill is lacking, feedback is often criticism and judgmental. People may be told that they are not a good listener, or don't speak up often enough. Or it might be more around completion of assignments. Feedback may come across as suggesting the person is lazy or doesn't pay attention to details. These are what I would call half feedback statements. What needs to happen next, is the feedback giver should explain how that makes them feel. For instance, if someone is giving feedback to a peer about a presentation that contained errors, the feedback may follow this pattern: "I wanted to talk to you about the presentation you gave yesterday. I noticed in the presentation that you had a few misspelled words, and some of the data was incorrect. As a team member, I felt embarrassed that this presentation represented the work of our team. I am worried that others in the meeting will think this is the standard for all of our work." At this point, the receiver of the feedback should be self-reflecting on the statement. Following a simple framework of feedback will shift the culture toward being more high performance and trusting. Criticism, as a type of "feedback" permeates the business world today. It is especially prevalent in a hierarchical organization. Leaders or managers provide feedback by criticizing the work of their direct reports, or direct reports of other managers. When practiced in this context, there is often this sense that a leader is adding value by providing this type of "feedback" to an individual. When leaders don't know how to coach, or develop their team, criticism fills the gap. In practice, criticism results in disempowering employees, and reinforcing the hierarchical decision-making principle that decisions are made by the higher-ups, and individuals are there to follow orders and do the work.

Another element of a broken feedback system is when an individual feels that only their manager or leader can provide them feedback. It has developed over time, that feedback is the job responsibility of the manager, and that horizontal or bottom-up feedback isn't significant or important. Does a leader need to listen to the feedback of his team? Whose mindset is more important to align with as a leader? The people that he has control over in terms of pay and performance, or the person that has control over their own compensation? Knowing this presence of power and control over an individual by a leader, is present when a subordinate is asked to give their manager or leader feedback. How could what they say about their boss influence their performance ranking or development opportunities? The risk that a person's boss may take a subordinate's feedback critically, and reveal the leader's insecurities, strongly influences what a team member will say to their line manager. Again, the risk of falling out of favor with the boss, the person who controls the individual's career prospects, annual salary increments, and development from a "feedback" statement, is too great a leap of faith for employees. Being honest and authentic then shows up with different degrees, based on who is giver and receiver of the feedback.

One could say giving only positive feedback is the respectful thing to do, however, that is contrary to what a good feedback system is designed to do.

An Agile feedback system linked to performance management ignores hierarchy, positional authority, and drives fear of retaliation out of the organization. Since most organizations still adhere to a traditional ranking system, the system reinforces the conservative behaviors among leaders and pleasing behaviors of employees around feedback. Feedback highlights how great a leader wants to be, and limits performance for employees. For the feedback system to be effective, and perform as designed, the organization needs to develop people's skill at giving and receiving feedback.

All individuals need to be able to receive feedback, and internalize it from any individual regardless of their social status within the organization. This would include senior leaders taking feedback from individuals who report to them. Internalizing feedback means that a person listens to understand, acknowledges that they heard and understood the feedback, and takes time to reflect on how the details of the feedback can reshape their mental models and behaviors. After the self-reflection, the individual self-corrects themselves and modifies their behavior that triggered the feedback. Without an effective feedback/performance management system to support the performance management system the transformation will slowly come to a halt.

As with receiving feedback, individuals throughout the organization need to know how to give constructive feedback. This will enable the feedback system to stay above petty personal likes and dislikes, and allow individuals to help each other grow and develop. In giving feedback, an individual needs to be clear on a specific event, what happened at that time, and how it impacted them. They need to be able to state how they were affected on a personal level both emotionally and physically. The number of cases that would support the feedback system as a part of performance management is overwhelming. In numerous meetings that I have sat through, hearing a senior leader strike down an idea from a team member with a toxic attack leads to all others in the room recalibrating what risks they want to take. In these situations, the innovative spirit and air gets sucked out of the room by the toxic attack. This culling effect on others, results in individuals not speaking up or sharing ideas that are bold and outside the team's comfort zone. In the end, this behavior creates a culture that condones toxic attacks by anyone in the company. The lack of skill in delivering feedback leads to a culture that maintains the status quo, and follows the ideas or suggestions of those that can deliver the sharpest toxic attacks. The concept that everyone can contribute is pushed to the shadows, and the organization lacks in creating innovative and disruptive solutions to make it better in the future.

Level Playing Field Each Cycle, Avoid Confirmation and Halo Bias

Employees need to understand that at the start of each performance management cycle the playing field is level, or re-leveled. All employees start the new cycle knowing that the new cycle starts without baggage from the year before, both good and bad. They need reassurance that the system is free of bias, both positive and negative. This ecosystem is regenerated at the start of each performance management cycle. Team members, leaders, and others are influential in creating an atmosphere that allows individuals to show up as their whole selves. This puts the weight of accountability back on the employee, and gives everyone an equal chance of contributing their best to the organization's outcomes. Employees need to feel the freedom of fear from previous events and that these results do not carry over into the current cycle. Likewise for star performers. Each year starts new, and they cannot rest on the previous year's success. The principle of learning from failure or experimenting needs to be exemplified in the next cycle. Each cycle of performance management incorporates the newly gained knowledge from the past cycles, for employees to become higher performing. This will positively impact the outcomes and goals for the organization. Also, the organization needs to communicate to all employees that resting and vesting on past accomplishments doesn't guarantee favorable performance evaluations going forward.

One tactic to meet the intent of Breakthrough Agile, is to start the cycle by assuring all employees that they will have a satisfactory performance evaluation at the start of the new cycle. By eliminating this pressure or stress, employees are able to be more innovative, and work without the fear of disapproval for taking risks. Employees can show up in full force, to apply their talents and experience to the customer needs in the coming year. This isn't a free ride for employees. They are still coached on their impact and contribution. Their performance needs to meet the expectation for the role and level for which were hired for by the organization. Falling short of this triggers an intervention by the individual's coach (leader). At times, employees dread and fear the performance management process because a manager may come across as arbitrary and capricious when it comes time to rank employees. Additionally, employees rated poorly the prior year may internalize their value to the team and regress into aberrant or anti-social behavior. While employees who were rated exceptional will perceive themselves to have a higher status/value within the team or organization.

In Breakthrough Agile, the outcomes and experiences of the past do not influence the successive year(s) performance evaluation. Assuring employees that their performance for the next cycle has already been set at the acceptable level creates this safe work environment for employees to recharge and strive for higher performance in the coming year.

As team's practice the new performance management system, those employees who are seen with the "halo" due to being selected for high-profile projects or activities, need to be integrated back into the team. In multiple experiences, as a team gets formed for special assignments or ad hoc projects, the leaders of the organization pick the same individuals over and over again. This form of "cherry picking" or "developmental" streaming creates barriers for growth and development across the team. In most cases, one or two people from the same team are chosen as team members for these type of special assignments. It can also lead to others feeling as if the organization doesn't provide opportunities to showcase their skills and talents to a broader group. In Breakthrough Agile, as new opportunities arise, the team needs to decide who takes on what assignments, and every person on the team should be allowed to take on higher risk and higher profile assignments during the year. This can be managed by a simple rotation process for ad hoc or special assignment meetings. This self-management feature within the team prevents the manager from cherry-picking the same employees year after year for key assignments or projects that most likely will lead to a higher performance rating.

As an employee feels safe within the current environment and senses the assurance that taking risks and being innovative will not jeopardize their career and compensation, then natural competitiveness emerges to perform at a higher level occurs. Employees start to work for a higher purpose other than trying to achieve a good performance appraisal. Adopting a level playing field with performance ratings in essence gives employees the permission to take risks. As organizations practice this approach to performance management, naturally high performance and low performance will surface throughout the review cycle. These cases are addressed by the team through the feedback system, and the 90-day planning cycle reviews. Team leaders are engaged in this OKR review for the team. In that dialogue, team members should discuss individual performance. Personal accountability shines in these discussions, or the lack of accountability draws the attention of the team and team leader. Employees who are showing higher performance and demonstrating exceptional contribution, are highlighted by the team, and at the appropriate time, the team should decide who gets an exceptional or needs improvement appraisal. At the end of the performance review cycle, the system then resets and everyone is then brought back to satisfactory for the next cycle.

Team Objectives Are Clear, Focused, and Challenging

As the transformation into a Breakthrough Agile organization is underway, how teams perform is key to achieving the both the business and transformation results. Everyone is responsible for creating the culture of Breakthrough Agile. Performance management is a system that greatly influences the culture and is influential to getting things done. For the principles on performance management to be effective, a team's objectives need to be clear, focused, and challenging. All of the cultural business processes need to follow the principles as outlined in Breakthrough Agile. Utilizing Agile systems such as OKRs, Scrum, or daily stand-ups supports the level of transparency of work that is needed for teams to manage their own performance. By having a robust process to manage work such as OKRs or Kanban, everyone on the team knows what the others are doing. When new work enters into the team's space, the team's decision-making principles come into play. Conflicts and prioritization will affect how work is assigned and completed. With such a high level of transparency, it is much easier for team members to support, provide feedback, and collaborate with their peers on helping the team succeed.

However, real confusion arises at this touchpoint within a team. Agile leaders and coaches are influential at this crux, by communicating clearly that daily and routine accountabilities are as important as strategic and high-risk projects. These daily team accountabilities are defined through documents such as job scope, job description or job classification. Having documentation that defines the product or service that the team provides the needed transparency for team members to perform. In Agile organizations these are usually found in organization units such as squads, chapters, value streams, agile release trains, work product teams, to name a few. Through these team units, the strategic and routine actions are completed. At times, the purpose of the team might reflect the daily accountabilities of the team. Individuals need to know that a majority of their annual performance is based on how they meet and achieve these routine responsibilities. In one coaching session I had, a manager questioned me about the dilemma with an organization-wide OKR and how individuals on a team should interpret this with an Agile mindset.

The organization-wide OKR was written to focus the organization on being the number 1 vendor for a particular product across the country. One of the key results for this OKR was to increase sales revenue. The dilemma for the manager was that his sales team had this same accountability in their job description. The manager wanted to know if the organization-wide OKR, with its measures of success (KRs) was now the OKR of the sales team. His question focused on how do OKRs make goals clearer when they appear to restate someone's routine scope of work? A deeper discussion on OKRs occurred with the manager on how his team can align overall with the OKRs key result on more sales, but also align horizontally with the marketing team on supporting the OKRs overall direction. In summary, the sales team still has its responsibilities to generate more sales for the organization, but there is also a subset of the manager's team that is working on this particular product line, to achieve the OKR of being the number one vendor in the country. The smaller focused team, for example a work product team, needs to spend more time brainstorming, and thinking of out of the box solutions to increasing the sales of the particular product line. This is an example of how to differentiate the routine tasks from the strategic/OKR goals. By following the OKR process, the sales work product team identifies new actions it would take to support the market penetration of the newly launched product in certain regions of the country. The marketing work product team aligns horizontally with the sales work product team by increasing their communications of the new product in these same regions. This horizontal alignment of both work product teams supports the organizational OKR of being the top vendor. From a performance management perspective, the each function has to decide how to support the organizational OKR. With a few team members supporting the OKR, the remaining team members still had the accountability of working their channels for sales growth. The added focus on sales provided by the OKR only increased the enthusiasm and passion for the sales team to perform at a higher level. Having a strong OKR system provides teams with the clarity needed to know what is success and how it is measured, and provides team members with the psychological safety of knowing what is important for the team, organization, and company. Team members can identify how their work contributes to the overall success of the organization.

Summary and Key Takeaways

Performance management is a critical factor in defining a company's culture. How people act, think, behave, and perform reflect the process that the organization chooses for its appraisal process for employees. The purpose of Performance Management and its inclusion as part of Breakthrough Agile's principles indicate that a more holistic and team-based approach will change the culture of an organization to be more competitive, higher performing, and inclusive for its employees. By applying a feedback system, 90-day planning cycles, and clear team OKRs, employees are able to determine how they are performing at any time during the appraisal cycle. This clarity and ownership of work will support teams in managing their own performance evaluations.

Performance Management Sensing Guide				
Different Roles in the process	Experiencing	Seeing	Hearing	Anti-Pattern
Team Member / Individual	Stability in performance evaluations, Clarity of tasks and assignments, more individual drive to innovate and take risks. Strong sense of belonging and acceptance. Less team politics and posturing by team members. More requests from others for feedback	High degree of respect between team members. Less influencing through positional authority. More decisions being made by team members instead of leaders. Team members receiving feedback and taking feedback sincerely and being thankful.	Phrases that reflect positive reinforcement for experimenting and taking risks. Less talk about how completion of certain tasks will affect a person's merit increase or bonus. Constructive feedback from others on ideas and solutions instead of personal attacks.	Team members are included in meetings but excluded from discussion topics. Some employees have additional privileges because they are seen as high performers by rating groups. Company seniority(yrs with company) plays a part in work assignments and development opportunities
Manager/Front Line Leader	Decisions being made at contributor level. Team performance is owned by the team. Accountability for work is owned by the team. Team members give feedback to the manager on their performance and how they show up.	Team members having deep discussion on work and tasks. Team members helping other team members grow through constructive feedback. Teams functioning where everyone shows up giving their best.	People admitting they don't know the answer. Team members asking each other for help without fear of being perceived as unskilled or untalented. Team members recognizing their peers for high quality work.	Members of the team win debates by stating that they are the voice of the manager. Eg. This is what the boss wants. Team members avoid taking responsibility for their assignments or tasks. Feedback is given arbitrarily and usually is glowing in praise of another person.

Chapter 9

Leadership

The possibility that we may fail in the struggle ought not to deter us from the support of a cause which we believe to be just. It shall never deter me.

Abraham Lincoln, Eternal Fidelity to the Cause of Liberty

By design, I am ending this book with a chapter on leadership. Leadership is embedded in all of the five cultural business processes of Breakthrough Agile. As many know, this topic dominates business writing today and alone fills the shelves of major bookstores. Leadership is also a topic that has an eternal element to it. One could say since the start of civilization there have been leaders, and analysis on what makes a good leader. Leaders trigger a behavioral response in people. I remember as a military leader walking into a room of soldiers and experiencing the conversation stopping, people readjusting their posture, and being conscious of my movements. In today's business world, this impulse continues. People are curious about leaders. Whether in business, government, education, or any other organization, leaders will draw people's attention to uncover how they act and behave. Throughout history, influential business leaders reach the status of public figures. America with its early industrial tycoons like John D. Rockerfeller, JP Morgan, and Henry Ford, to the kings and queens in Europe and Asia. Today it's Elon Musk, Mark Zuckerberg, Richard Branson, Jack Ma, Jeff Bezos, and Bill Gates who are all in the public eye. We are drawn to their lifestyle and want to know more about them. From a business perspective, people are curious as to how the work, make decisions, strategize, get things done, and select people to lead their companies. This fascination makes its way into mainstream media for all of us to read and vicariously

 DOI: 10.4324/9781003335702-9

relate to their personalities with concluding observations about what made the individuals who they are today.

I am a student of leadership and interested in what makes a good leader. As a graduate student over 30 years ago, I remember a professor of organizational psychologist reminding us of one thing. As future business leaders, his guidance to us was, "if you can find a way to motivate people, then the business world will beat a path to your door." At the time, the intent of this message seemed a little simple to the students in the room. But after a lengthy career, I still reflect back on this saying, and ask myself, if this the key to what makes great leadership. Being able to motivate a person or team to perform? And as you start to investigate leadership and motivation, it becomes clear that there are good and bad tactics for anyone in the role. that go off into good and bad tactics. However, the question seems timeless, "What motivates people to perform better?"

In today's VUCA world, motivation is a key concern with the next generation of workers. In this context, the psychological complexity of finding what motivates people is continuously getting deeper and broader. In today's corporate world, leadership development conversations are pivoting to a newer perspective: What is the leader's impact and contribution on their team? To me this is implying an evolution to the idea that leaders need to know how to motivate others. Motivation implies the carrot or stick philosophy to leadership. The impact and contribution mindset asks how does the leader show up and through their own skills, makes a difference for the team and organization. Throughout Breakthrough Agile, one main premise is that motivated and engaged employees will be happier and more productive. Leaders create this environment and nurture its sustainability toward higher performance. In a Breakthrough Agile organization, this is the role of the leader, the builders of the environment. Today, we talk about psychological safety as a key element in motivating employees to excel at work. An environment where employees feel safe to raise ideas, objections, and pursue innovative solutions that deliver value to the customer and organization increases the value created by the organization. This Agile environment is characterized as being free of fear from being ridiculed or retaliated against by leaders or peers for diverse opinions or challenging the status quo. As employees develop the capacity to challenge the status quo and the opinions of others with the aim to change the direction of an action or decision, then they are more engaged with the vision and strategic focus of the company. Breakthrough Agile create more passionate employees who care about the results they deliver. As a people leader, I advocated and practiced this type of leadership as a Lean and Servant Leader for many years. As a leader, the reward can be great.

Leading people is a very rewarding experience. I have people today, that I led on teams years ago, who still refer to me as their leader. Watching people earn promotions, and take on greater responsibilities is an output of this type of leadership. Giving your team development opportunities to learn and grow allowed team members to explore new areas of the business. This learning environment allowed them to grow in their careers through work activities, upskilling, and networking. The future impact they had on the business is still occurring because of this talent development. As a word of caution, some team members didn't quite understand the approach or see the structure of how this new leadership approach works. As a Servant or Agile leader, employees also need to learn how the leader will show up, the new leadership behaviors, and how they impact by coaching within the team. This change for some employees will generate fear and distrust. For instance, an employee who has always asked what to do who now works in an Agile organization, will feel insecure at the beginning. There is a change for team members as the leader changes their behaviors, and this is a journey for them to learn. This transition needs to be navigated with the support of strong coaching. This will be uncomfortable for everyone as it begins to happen, both leader and team members. Navigating the transition is where internal coaches can step in to support the organization as it moves forward in the transformation.

Be prepared for the extremes during the transformation journey. In my research, I had team members that went to the extreme in terms of being empowered. In this case, I saw team members assuming ownership/responsibility for activities and processes across the organization that they lacked the experience and capabilities to perform diligently. These team members had ambitious needs to demonstrate that they could work at a higher level without understanding the bigger picture at the time. Working in an Agile organization has structure, roles, governance processes, and ways of interacting with others. It isn't a chaotic, anything goes organization. After coaching startup self-managed teams, and seeing this overzealous pattern recur, it became apparent that the 5 cultural business processes need to be defined prior to the transformation. Newly empowered teams needed to understand what is a decision making methodology, before taking on the responsibility to make their own decisions. In one case, a team member on a self-managed team said they now make all decisions without consulting anyone on their team or within their network. When the team and its

members are left alone to figure it out without guidance, then the result
might be surprising and a little off-target. This is where the role of the new
leader and internal coaches in the Agile organization can coach and guide
the team through the transition toward being a self-managed team.

Leading the transition is the space the leader needs to step into during
the transformation. Coaching not only the why and what of the change but
also the transition: How the new systems are to work in the new model.
The leader needs to understand what good should look like, and then
guide their teams in this direction. As team members now grapple within
themselves to understand how the new culture operates and what makes it
more effective than the old, the leader is there with them, experiencing the
same ups and downs, and providing a reassuring guiding hand to keep the
employee, team and organization on the path to breakthrough results.

The leadership role in Breakthrough Agile changes how leaders lead. It
requires them to step away from traditional ways of working, and embrace
a new mindset and set of behaviors based on the platform's principles. As
the transition occurs, employees may forget that the leader still has business
needs while guiding the organization or team toward a new future. This is
work that needs to be done by teams throughout the organization. During
this transition, different team dynamics will emerge. At times, team ends
up with too much of a "me" versus a "we" mentality. Since we talk about
empowerment and giving individuals more control over their work, team
members lose focus on how their work contributes to the bigger picture
of the team. Team and individual activities may not align with the strategic
outcomes set by the organization's senior leaders. This lack of alignment
creates a gap in how resources are allocated. Team members who want
to work on projects that don't deliver value for the customer, become
misaligned with the purpose of the transformation. In these cases, team
members start to use the language of the transformation as a weapon to
resist coaching or feedback on their activities. The classic example that
resonates with me personally is the Andon cord on an assembly line or
machining operation in a Lean organization. The intent of the Andon is to
give the employee the control and power to stop production when a defect
is found. The Lean principle that guides this thought is that no employee
will pass a defective part to the next operation. The Andon was a signal,
usually electronic that the employee would trigger to stop the operation to
allow time to investigate the quality defect. However, the rule gets abused.
The Andon gets activated when someone needs to use the toilet, or take a break.
The rule is abused through personal retaliatory schemes over work issues.

The list goes on. In a more administrative scenario, an employee may decide not to attend a team meetings because they were told only to attend meetings where they add value. In this case, the team member doesn't attend, or attends at a distance, since they don't have anything to say, or want to express their opinion. I saw this in a daily standup, where all the team members gathered around their Kanban board to discuss the in-process work: All except one team member. This person stayed at their desk, away from the board, and at times, glaringly looked at the team as if they were interrupting them with the standup's conversation. As you can imagine, the team leader had to work with this individual privately and spend extra time coaching them through the transformation transition. During the time when this behavior was ongoing, the team sensed the conflict, and would at times limit their creativeness and discussions during the standup meeting to appease the non-committed team member.

Agile leaders need to relearn new skills and behaviors. Vulnerability, influence without authority, risk-taking, humbleness, and letting go of control as they transition into the Breakthrough Agile culture. Leaders need to be transparent with their teams and acknowledge that they are working on changing their behaviors. Success in the transition is gaining the team's support. Feedback from the team on how the leader is showing up day to day is evidence of this support. Teams will help the leader develop into a better person. Leaders asking for this support will sound completely opposite to what a traditional leader should be saying. Another behavior the leader needs to develop is their story-telling skills. Especially, when motivating their team or others to take risks. Stories that contain details about challenging the status quo, or questioning routine business practices, will inspire others to embrace the transformation. Leaders need to provide their own reason for "why" they support the transformation. Leaders need to display a sense of passion for the new way of working, and hopefully, leaders have one or more stories about the drawbacks of working in a traditional organization, and how changing to an Agile organization will benefit the company. There might be a common communication on the "why" from a high level, but to truly win the hearts and minds of people, leaders need to relate the transformation to something person to them. A story that comes from their heart.

A personal "why" usually comes from an experience. Stories I find the most inspiring are true stories that happened to the leader. These specific stories left a permanent doubt in the leader's mind about the current ways of working, and prompted them to ask what is a better way to work. One leader that captured this story from the heart, retold the story any chance they had to help inspire others to change. The story was about the company's budgeting process. The first time I heard the story, I felt the spirit to be bold and to take risks, as it was that powerful. This leader told everyone that this is personal "why" for championing the transformation. The story was linked back to the company's transformation and helped define why change was so important. In the story, the leader heard the constant feedback from the organization over the budget process. Its intent didn't resonate to value for many of the leaders, and people found it hard to justify the time and resources spent on it annually. So this leader took action. Leveraging their current innovative mindset, a high-level task force (team) was chartered to develop a better process. In the following months, the team was formed, allocation of time to complete the project was calculated to the hour, project lead, and steering committee identified, and an entire communication plan launched about the effort. After the first few months of work, in the first steering committee review, the team presented a solution that was little more than a revision of the current budget process that included a few pre-formed templates for information. The output of this high profile team confused the leader who was beginning to think like an Agile leader at this time. Why didn't the team take a bolder approach? What are the barriers preventing the team to be more creative? So, they sent the team back to the war room, with further direction to be more bold and innovative. A second time at the steering committee, still similar results. The leader was clearly frustrated now, and started to ask the team members questions about their process, and creative approach. What was revealed is that the team was following the direction, "fix the problem with the current budget process." The leader then realized that the wrong question was being asked. Instead of problem-solving the current process, the leader posed these question to the team, "can the organization stop doing the process? What would it take to maintain fiscal responsibility and stop the budget process we use today?" From that point on, the billion-dollar organization found its way into eliminating the annual process, and saving the hundreds of hours of work by countless people. Financial accountability and responsibility is a part of the day-to-day work at the organization; however, it is more fluid and event based. Flexing of resources, budgeting specific actions, and more frequent reviews of spend were activities that were adopted. To me, this is a great example of a leader who was immensely successful, confident, and directive, giving up their current leadership style to embrace an agile leadership role.

The Agile leader will listen more than they speak, ask curious and open-ended questions, and have the ability to control their emotions in times when conflicts arise concerning business outcomes or the transformation. The Agile leader has to rally the support from their team through storytelling, and linking the team's work to the vision. Additionally, the leader's team is ambassadors for the transition. They need to be able to manage the space between the change and the outcome; learning and growing in this transition space and broadly communicating what the organization is doing clearly and profoundly to others is part of the new leaders role. It can easily happen that as an Agile leader you are a minority on your leadership team. If this is the case, then how you are perceived by your peers and line leaders becomes distorted. When the team you are leading, doesn't assume the ambassador role or embraces the organization's "why" for change, then a misaligned impression of your leadership style emerges. To your peers, as an Agile leader you may seem indecisive or weak. Traditional leaders will see the Agile leader as a person who has a lack of control or direction over their team. In a traditional work environment, experimentation and failure don't align with the organization's principle of perfect, right first time, or controlling the output of a communication or project. As the Agile leader, you might be feeling uncomfortable within the organization if the transformation isn't supported broadly by other leaders.

Generally, the scenario occurs less frequently today than 10–15 years ago. Today, the general agreement is that leadership is evolving and how leaders led in the past needs to evolve to achieve higher performance. Leading by coercion or fear, or some other lever of control through the manipulation of information, leads to more collateral costs for the organization. Distrust, low performance, turnover, and other undesirable outputs are common. Leaders today are seeking a way forward and most are eager to experiment with a version of leadership that has a less micro-managing and controlling feel to it. It is a balance for leaders. How to maintain control yet empower others (give control away) is an example of the duality that leaders are faced with as they evolve into Agile leaders. As leaders learn new skills and behaviors, they will inevitably run into the perplexing area of dualities. Dualities are those paradoxes that influence decisions and actions due to the external forces present. Here are some examples of dualities the leader may face.

- Task focused versus relationship building
- Big picture versus small picture (focus on best for organization or team/department)

- Cost control versus investment in people
- Positional authority versus equality across teams
- Standardization versus flexibility
- Efficiency versus experimentation
- Profit margin versus purpose

Take any one of the principles of Breakthrough Agile, and leaders will have to navigate through a duality associated with it. Plan for the long term and execute on the short term. Single decision making on an inclusive and engaged team. This list will grow and influence actions. This is a strength of the principle-based approach to transformation. Leaders start with what they know, which are these dualities. By sensing them in their day to day work, like making a decision, the leader grows to understand what good looks like. Knowing this will allow them to coach others on what is a good system, what is needed to change from the old to the new. At this point, then the culture starts to change. If leaders adopt the Agile principle, then they will continue to reinforce the cultural change that is occurring. Now, leaders need the skill to balance two opposite forces, both of which benefit the business, to produce an outcome that will deliver value to the customer.

My intent is to keep this chapter short. Throughout this book, I discuss how leaders will show up in a Breakthrough Agile organization. Opening up a more in-depth discussion on Leadership may be the subject of a future book. As a final word, leaders in the new organization need to show that they are changing. The sensing element for me when I coach leaders is to see and hear the leader(s) performing differently. The leader's team should be experiencing a different type of leadership. For a legacy or brownfield organization how the current leadership shows up, will determine the extent to which the organization transforms itself, or keeps to the same principles of the old organization. One key measure of a successful transformation is to sense the number of leaders who adopt the Agile leadership approach. It is a positive correlation to the depth and breadth of your transformation.

Index

Note: *Italicized* page numbers refer to figures.

Printed in the United States
by Baker & Taylor Publisher Services